D1798214

The Catholic Church and Soviet Russia, 1917–1939

This book, based on extensive research including in the Russian and Vatican archives, charts the development of relations between the Catholic Church and the Soviet Union from the Bolshevik Revolution of 1917 to the death of Pope Pius XI in 1939. It provides background information on the animosity between the Orthodox and Catholic churches and moves towards reconciliation between them, discusses Soviet initiatives to eradicate religion in the Soviet Union and spread atheist international communism throughout the world, and explores the Catholic Church's attempts to survive in the face of persecution within the Soviet Union and extend itself. Throughout the book reveals much new detail on the complex interaction between these two opposing bodies and their respective ideologies.

Dennis J. Dunn is a Professor of History and Director of the Center for International Studies at Texas State University, San Marcos, Texas, USA.

Routledge Religion, Society and Government in Eastern Europe and the Former Soviet States

Series Editor

Lucian Leustean is Reader in Politics and International Relations at Aston University, Birmingham, United Kingdom.

This series seeks to publish high-quality monographs and edited volumes on religion, society, and government in Eastern Europe and the former Soviet states by focusing primarily on three main themes: the history of churches and religions (including, but not exclusively, Christianity, Islam, Judaism, and Buddhism) in relation to governing structures, social groupings, and political power; the impact of intellectual ideas on religious structures and values; and the role of religions and faith-based communities in fostering national identities from the nineteenth century until today.

The series aims to advance the latest research on these themes by exploring the multi-facets of religious mobilisation at local, national, and supranational levels. It particularly welcomes studies which offer an interdisciplinary approach by drawing on the fields of history, politics, international relations, religious studies, theology, law, sociology, and anthropology.

1 **The Russian Orthodox Church and Human Rights**
Kristina Stoeckl

2 **The Russian Orthodox Church, 1917–1948**
From decline to resurrection
Daniela Kalandjieva

3 **Monasticism in Eastern Europe and the Former Soviet Republics**
Edited by Ines A. Murzaku

4 **The Catholic Church and Soviet Russia, 1917–1939**
Dennis J. Dunn

The Catholic Church and Soviet Russia, 1917–1939

Dennis J. Dunn

Routledge
Taylor & Francis Group

LONDON AND NEW YORK

First published 2017
by Routledge
2 Park Square, Milton Park, Abingdon, Oxon OX14 4RN

and by Routledge
711 Third Avenue, New York, NY 10017

Routledge is an imprint of the Taylor & Francis Group, an informa business

British Library Cataloguing in Publication Data
A catalogue record for this book is available from the British Library

Library of Congress Cataloging in Publication Data
A catalog record for this book has been requested

ISBN: 978-1-138-21943-4 (hbk)
ISBN: 978-1-315-40886-6 (ebk)

Typeset in Times New Roman
by Apex CoVantage, LLC

Printed and bound by CPI Group (UK) Ltd, Croydon, CR0 4YY

Contents

Acknowledgments

My first book, titled *The Catholic Church and the Soviet Government, 1939–1949*, had the good fortune of being described in a review in *The Times Literary Supplement* by Rev. Canon Michael Bourdeaux, founder of the Keston Institute in Oxford, as "a fully documented, objective and clearly major work . . . which makes a substantial contribution to the subject." Sabrina Ramet, coeditor of Cambridge University's *Politics and Religion*, hailed my second work, called *Détente and Papal–Communist Relations, 1962–1978*, "a breakthrough in the field." Gregory Freeze praised my third effort, *The Catholic Church and Russia: Popes, Patriarchs, Tsars and Commissars*, in *Church History* as a work that "will become the standard account of the political history of Catholicism in Russia." The present volume covers the history of the Catholic Church in Soviet Russia and the relationship between the Vatican and the Soviet regime between 1917 and 1939. It tries to add new detail to the story of the Church's experience in Soviet Russia in the interwar years and to put the relationship into the broad context of international relations and world history.

It is with great pleasure that I acknowledge my intellectual debt to a group of Russian and Eastern European scholars who have helped influence my views on history, including Oliver Radkey of the University of Texas at Austin, Bohdan Bociurkiw of Carleton University, Michael Pap and George Prpic of John Carroll University, and Alfred Levin and Alfred Skerpan of Kent State University. I also thank my colleagues and students in the Department of History at Texas State University and the many librarians and research assistants who helped me pull together the sources to write this work. A special note of gratitude goes to the archivists at the Vatican's Secret or Private Archive who helped me locate records pertinent to this story. Chad Petroski and Alex Trussell helped translate some of the correspondence of Bishop Eugene Neveu that I found in the Vatican archives for the 1934–36 period. Maksat Abamov helped me find some documents in the archives in Moscow. I dedicate this book to my wife, Margaret, and my daughters, Denise and Meg, who have been a constant source of inspiration and motivation to me. I am responsible for any errors that appear in this work.

Dennis J. Dunn
San Marcos, Texas

Cast of characters

Battista della Chiesa, Giacomo Paolo Giovanni (1854–1922): elected Pope Benedict XV in 1914; set up a separate department for Eastern Catholic affairs and relations with the Orthodox world that was called the Sacred Congregation for the Eastern Church.

Braun, Léopold, AA (1903–1964): American priest sent to Moscow as chaplain of the American Embassy in 1934 and became pastor of St. Louis des Français Church in 1936 when Bishop Neveu departed the USSR; Braun left the USSR at the end of 1945.

Gasparri, Pietro Cardinal (1852–1934): papal secretary of state for Pope Benedict XV and Pope Pius XI until 7 February 1930.

Giobbe, Filippo (1874–1970), second in command of the Pro Russia Commission under Bishop Michel d'Herbigny and then acting head after d'Herbigny's departure in 1933.

d'Herbigny, Michel, SJ (1880–1957): confidant of Pope Pius XI and appointed the Pro Russia Commission's general consultant in 1925 and then its head in 1930; ordained a bishop in 1925 and secretly named bishops and apostolic administrators when visiting the USSR in 1926.

Hitler, Adolph (1889–1945): Chancellor of Germany from 1933 to 1945 and Führer of Nazi Germany from 1934 to 1945.

Maglione, Luigi (1877–1944): archbishop and apostolic nuncio to Switzerland, 1920, nuncio to France, 1926; cardinal, 1935; secretary of state, 1939–44.

Molotov, Vyacheslav (1890–1986): chairman of Council of People's Commissars, 1930–41; Soviet foreign minister, 1939–49 and 1953–56; Stalin's confidante.

Montini, Giovanni Battista (1897–1978): attaché at Polish nunciature, 1923; pro-secretary of state for extraordinary affairs, 1952; archbishop of Milan, 1954; cardinal, 1958; elected Pope Paul VI, 1963.

Mussolini, Benito (1883–1945): leader of the National Fascist Party and prime minister of Italy from 1922 until his fall in 1943.

Neveu, Pie Eugène Joseph (1877–1946), AA: ordained priest in 1905 in a branch of the Assumptionist religious order dedicated to ministering to Slavic Christianity; pastor of Makeyevka in southern Russia (Ukraine), 1907; ordained bishop and named apostolic administrator and pastor of

St. Louis des Français Church in Moscow by Bishop Michel d'Herbigny in 1926; chief reporter of the condition of the Catholic Church in USSR until he departed for medical care to France in 1936.

Orsenigo, Cesare (1873–1946): apostolic nuncio to Holland, 1922; nuncio to Hungary, 1925; nuncio to Germany, 1930–45.

Pacelli, Eugenio (1876–1958): appointed apostolic nuncio to Germany, 1920–29; secretary of state, 1930–39; elected Pope Pius XII in 1939.

Ratti, Achille (1857–1939): apostolic visitor and then nuncio to Poland and Lithuania, 1918–19; cardinal archbishop of Milan, 1921; elected Pope Pius XI, 1922–39; established the pontifical Pro Russia Commission, 1922.

Roncalli, Angelo Giuseppe (1881–1963): bishop and apostolic visitor to Bulgaria, 1925; apostolic delegate in Greece and Turkey, 1935; apostolic nuncio to France, 1944; cardinal and patriarch of Venice, 1953; elected Pope John XXIII, 1958–63.

Roosevelt, Franklin Delano (1882–1945): president of the United States from 1933 until 1945 and leader of the Western allies opposed to the Axis Powers during World War II.

Stalin, Joseph (1878–1953): Soviet leader and committed communist who was determined to push international revolution in order to overturn the Western world order and to create a communist society in the Soviet Union by eliminating through violence and force private property, religion, and any opposition to his goals.

Tardini, Domenico, Cardinal (1888–1961): undersecretary of the Sacred Congregation for Extraordinary Ecclesiastical Affairs, 1929; took over control of Pro Russia from d'Herbigny in 1934; cardinal and secretary of state, 1958.

Abbreviations

AAS   *Acta Apostolicae Sedis* (*Acts of the Holy See*; Vatican publication that records official acts of the Holy See).

AES   L'Archivio della Sacra Congregazione degli Affari Ecclesiastici Straor-dinari, Pontificia Commissione, Pro Russia, Archivio Segreto Vaticano (Archives of the Sacred Congregation for Extraordinary Ecclesiastical Affairs, Pro Russia Commission, Vatican Secret Archives).

GARF   Gosudarstennyi arkiv Rossiiskoi Federatsii (State Archive of the Russian Federation), Moscow.

RGASPI   Rossiiskii gosudarstvennyi arkiv sotsial'no-politcheskoi istorii (Russian State Archive of Social and Political History), Moscow.

Introduction

This is a book about the relationship between the Catholic Church and Russia from the advent of the Soviet era to the death of Pope Pius XI in 1939. It is based on archival material in both the Russian and Vatican archives and on secondary sources. The Vatican archives covering between 1917 and February 1939, when Pope Pius XI died, are open, and the Vatican has published select materials from its archives between 1939 and the end of World War II in a multivolume compendium called *Acts et documents du Saint Siege relatives guerre Mondale*. In addition, the archives of the Assumptionist priests, who were assigned to Moscow's one Catholic Church, St. Louis des Français, are open for the Soviet period. The Russian archives that are available and that relate to the Catholic Church are sparse and eclectic, but sufficient enough, when used with secondary sources, to sketch the story between 1917 and 1939. Other primary sources that throw light on Soviet–Catholic relations include the lives of Catholics in Soviet Russia that the Martyrology Commission published in 2000, which was edited by Father Bronislaw Czaplicki and Irina Osipova, translated by Geraldine Kelly, and made available as *Book of Remembrance: Biography of Catholic Clergy and Laity in the Soviet Union (USSR) from 1918 to 1953*, University of Notre Dame at https:// biographies.library.nd.edu/catalog.

The story of Catholic–Soviet relations from 1917 to 1939 is worth recounting because it provides insight into human nature, borderland politics, international relations, ideology, the role of religion in establishing order in the individual and society, a comparative perspective on two different cultures that interacted with one another in Eastern Europe and around the world, and the place and vitality of religion in individuals, Russia, and the world. It also gives insight into one of history's major themes, namely the expansion of Western values around the globe and the attempt by a small group of radical left ideologues called the Communist Party to halt that advance.

The history of the relationship between the Catholic Church and Soviet Russia is somewhat complicated because the Catholic Church was a world religion and not a sovereign political state, like Soviet Russia, but was led by the pope, who was both a spiritual leader and a political sovereign who ruled in an independent city-state called Vatican City, which was located in the heart of Rome, the capital city of Italy, yet another separate, sovereign nation. In addition, Soviet Russia was more than a state. It was a sovereign empire that housed more than 100 different nationality groups. It was also the self-proclaimed leader of an international revolutionary ideology and movement that sought to eradicate all religions, including the Catholic Church, and to overthrow capitalist governments and the Western value system that was the basis for global order and to replace them with the communist worldview and communist regimes that answered to the Kremlin. As a major source and support of Western values and Western civilization, the Catholic Church was, directly or indirectly, a target of the Soviet government and its international revolution. The story of Catholic–Soviet relations thus has an international and domestic aspect, and for the period studied here the Soviet government wielded the initiative, and the Catholic Church and Vatican were largely in the position of reacting to Soviet policies. Of course, the Catholic Church as a missionary faith was always attempting to convert the Russians, but, aside from the realm of prayer and faith, it had to work within the Soviet government's policy parameters. It was never an independent force in the Soviet Union.

Domestically in Soviet Russia, the story of Catholic–Soviet relations is one of persecution. The Catholic Church had a small, structured presence in the Soviet Union because some Soviet citizens were Catholic, belonging to at least three Rites, including the Eastern Rite (mainly Ukrainians, Belorussians, and some Russians) and sometimes called the Uniate Rite; the Latin Catholic Rite that included Catholics who were Russian, Polish, Lithuanian, Belorussian, Ukrainian, Latvian, German, and even Italian; and the Armenian Catholic Rite, which was quite minute. Soviet Catholics were located overwhelmingly in the western borderlands of the Soviet state.

Internationally, the narrative of Catholic–Soviet relations is one of competition. The Catholic Church had many followers around the globe, was the largest Christian faith in the world, and had a potent political influence in some countries. It was also a main originator and supporter of Western civilization, of Western values, and of the Western-dominated global order. The Soviet government aimed to replace that order and value system with communism. Its strategy to reach that goal was to promote revolution by exacerbating crises and organizing communist parties in countries around the world that answered to it. Because of their beliefs and with minimal direction but much encouragement from the Vatican, Catholics of various stripes, including politicians, writers, and ordinary believers, competed with, opposed, and blocked the expansion of communism. The communists, for their part, while they disliked and disparaged the Church and persecuted it in the Soviet Union, were not focused internationally on attacking the Catholic Church. Their target was the Western global order that the Catholic Church had championed for more than a millennium. The communists looked at life through the prism of economics. They held religion to be a consequence of economic exploitation – exploiters used it to keep the people ignorant and confused about their exploited condition. They believed that if they overthrew capitalism and private property and replaced it with communism and communal or nationalized ownership of property, then exploitation would no longer exist and, therefore, religion would collapse because its purpose was gone. For the communists then, the central focus of activity had to be the international revolution, not parrying with the Catholic Church. In Soviet Russia, the Church would be pummeled to expedite the growth of communism in a country not yet fully industrialized, but in the industrialized world of capitalism, religious persecution was beside the point and, in some countries, counterproductive, although the international communist movement generally was inimical to the Catholic Church.

The Catholic Church did not look at life from that view. It did not believe that economics was the foundation of Western society and values. It recognized that the economic system of the West had aspects that produced imperialism and wealth disparity and it condemned consistently the excesses of capitalism, but believed that those anomalies could be resolved within the existing economic order through collective bargaining, market forces, laws, and taxing policy that could turn individual greed and self-profit into policies and programs that promoted human life and dignity and, very important, benefited the community and advanced the common good. Its view of life focused on God, the value and nobility of the human being who had a physical and spiritual dimension, natural law, and the journey of salvation, from birth to death, which was guided by faith, grace, the sacramental Church, and the teachings of Jesus Christ.

An additional factor that has to be considered in a study of Catholic–Soviet relations was that Soviet Russia, although officially an atheistic regime committed to eradicating all religion from its lands and eventually from the world, was the home of the largest and most significant Orthodox Church in the world, namely the Russian Orthodox Church. It also ruled over other large national Orthodox Churches, including the Belorussian Orthodox Church, the Georgian Orthodox Church, the Armenian Apostolic Church, and the very large Ukrainian Orthodox Church, one branch of which was affiliated with the Russian Orthodox Church and another of which lined up with the Orthodox patriarch of Constantinople.

The existence of an impressive and influential Russian Orthodox Church added a new and volatile aspect to Catholic–Soviet relations because the Russian Orthodox Church had historically viewed the Catholic Church as a rival that was heretical and encroaching on its ministry in Eurasia. The animosity was useful for the Soviet government in its campaign against the Catholic Church. But it was also complicated because the Soviet regime aimed to destroy the Orthodox Church.

Chapter 1 provides a brief overview of the differences between the Catholic and Orthodox traditions, which partly explain the animosity between the Catholic and Orthodox Churches, but also suggest ways in which the two traditions might resolve their conflicts and move toward a partnership. This chapter also covers the history of the Russian, Ukrainian, and Belorussian peoples as they emerged and as they came to grips with the value systems that Catholic and Orthodox cultures encouraged or endorsed.

Chapter 2 provides a brief overview of Catholic–Russian relations from the time of the emergence of the Muscovite state in the fifteenth century through the rise of the Russian Empire in the eighteenth century to the fall of the Russian Empire in 1917. It notes the importance of what ultimately became four revolutions in

Russia in the first three decades of the twentieth century, two of them taking place in this period – the 1905 and the February 1917 Revolutions – each one profoundly affecting the Catholic Church. Chapters 3 and 4 cover the history of the Bolshevik Revolution in October 1917, the creation of Soviet Russia, and relations between the Soviet government and the Catholic Church from 1917 to 1924, including Catholic efforts to reach out to the Kremlin and the Soviet people and Soviet policies to destroy the Catholic Church in the USSR, to expand the communist revolution around the globe, and to replace the Western value system that the Catholic Church supported with the communist value system.

Chapter 5 covers Vatican initiatives to counter Soviet efforts to undermine the Catholic Church and religion generally in the Soviet Union from the mid-1920s to 1930. It highlights the so-called Albertyn experiment and Bishop Michel d'Herbigny's Mission. Chapter 6 looks at the Fourth Revolution, namely Soviet collectivization and its impact on the Soviet people and the Catholic Church from 1928 to 1933, including reports from the Vatican archives on the utter horror of collectivization. Chapter 7 covers the period between 1933 to 1934, including the international reaction to communism, the Soviet government's attempt to corral that reaction, particularly Nazism and Japanese imperialism, to advance its international agenda, and the Soviet government's abiding and unabated determination to create domestically a society without private property or religion, including the eradication of the Catholic Church. Chapter 8 focuses on the period from 1935 to 1939, when Pope Pius XI died. Chapter 9 offers a brief conclusion.

The style of transcribing Russian words used here follows the Library of Congress system. If the name or phrase was already well known in English, for example, Rurik or Alexander, I used it. For the names of clergy and places, I deferred to the version at https://biographies.library.nd.edu/catalog unless widely accepted versions of names of cities and towns already existed in English, for example, Kiev instead of Kyiv and Lviv instead of L'viv. Dates for events in Russia before 1918 follow the Julian calendar; the Gregorian calendar is referred to, to date events taking place thereafter.

1 Background

Christianity: Early history of the Orthodox and Catholic traditions

Starting in the first century CE, Christianity grew to constitute perhaps by the fourth century 10 percent of the population of the Roman Empire. In 313 CE, the emperors Constantine, who was the senior emperor who resided in Constantinople, the capital of the eastern half of the Roman Empire and also called the "second Rome," and Licentius, the junior co-emperor who managed the western side of the Empire, issued the Edict of Nantes, which gave toleration to Christianity. In 380, Emperor Theodosius made Christianity the state religion of the Roman Empire. Christianity was a missionary faith that sought to spread and unite the world in universal fellowship. It was the first world religion. Of course, there were much older religions than Christianity, including Judaism, Hinduism, Buddhism, Zoroastrianism, and many others, but none of them except Buddhism, was a world religion and none, including Buddhism, sought to unite the entire world in a belief system of universal fellowship.

Once Christianity was granted toleration and then the status of state religion, it was important to define clearly what Christians believed. The emperors called together the bishops of the Christian Church to produce a summary of the key doctrines of Christianity, and the result was the famous Nicene Creed, which all Christians, in both East and West, accepted.[1] Those who did not adhere to the Nicene Creed were declared heretics and they and other dissenters and pagans were then discriminated against and persecuted. Agreement on beliefs did not mean uniformity in the sacraments and liturgy that celebrated those beliefs. Different traditions called rites developed, usually reflecting the diversity of national cultures. The two major ones were the Latin and Byzantine Rites.

The structure of the Church was also confirmed. At the apex of the Church were the five patriarchal bishops – Rome, Constantinople, Jerusalem, Antioch, and Alexandria. Among these, the pope, the bishop of Rome, claimed primacy, which the other patriarchs disputed, but generally acquiesced in. The pope's position was supported by the scriptural passage found in Matt. 16:18–19: "Tu es Petrus, et super hanc petram aedificabo Ecclesiam meam" ("You are Peter, and upon this rock I will build my Church"). It was also reinforced by the fact that

Rome was the first capital of the Roman Empire, the hallowed tradition that Sts. Peter and Paul were buried in Rome, Peter was Jesus' most important apostle and the first bishop of Rome, the Roman pontiff's decisiveness in matters of faith and morals, and the pope's willingness to invest his resources in people and activities that boosted his authority. The early emperors were not enthralled with the notion of a top religious leader outside of their control, but they generally were willing to tolerate the pope provided he supported their policies.

In the fifth century a turn of events led to the beginning of two separate Christian churches. In 476 the Western emperor was removed by Germans, who then installed a series of German kings. They were mainly Arian Christians who did not hold to the Nicene Creed. The pope asked for help against these heretics from the Eastern emperor in Constantinople. The eastern half of the Roman Empire did not fall to Germans or any other invader. It was strong and powerful and had resources and wealth based on its mining concessions and control of sea and land trade in the eastern Mediterranean, where numerous trade routes crisscrossed. It wanted to assist the Westerners, but found itself involved in a series of wars with the Persian Empire to its east. In the sixth century the Easterners finally defeated the Persians, and, under Emperor Justinian (r. 527–65 CE), conquered and reestablished imperial authority in Italy, Spain, and North Africa. Justinian also brought to the newly reconquered lands the *Corpus Juris Civilis*, the vast compendium of Roman law that his government had put together. It was an incredibly valuable work – one of the most transforming developments in the history of the ancient world. At the core of the *Corpus* was natural law – the commonsense principles that made human interaction productive, knowable, and orderly and that human reason found in experience. The Christian Church embraced the natural law and concluded that it was both a product and reflection of the divine creator. It was God's law. The pope, in particular, endorsed and valued natural law.

Although the help from the East was most appreciated, it did not last beyond the reign of Justinian. Persia revived and attacked the Eastern Roman Empire again. The new Emperor Heraclitus (r. 610–41) stripped the West of its Roman armies, except for some provinces in southern Italy and Sicily, to use them against the Persians. He decisively defeated the Persians at the Battle of Nineveh in 627, but he and his successors now focused on consolidating Roman power in the East rather than launching another campaign to reestablish Roman authority in the West. This decision led to the emergence of the Byzantine Empire, which was dominated by Greeks and largely consisted of the former eastern half of the Roman Empire.[2]

The Christian Church within the Byzantine Empire became known as the Byzantine or Greek Orthodox (right or correct beliefs) Church or, more simply, the Orthodox Church. The Christian Church in the West was eventually called the Roman Catholic (meaning universal) Church or, more simply, the Catholic Church. The Churches officially split in 1054, thus formally inaugurating the Orthodox and Catholic Churches.[3] Both Churches had the same Nicene Creed. They also had similar but varying rituals, liturgies, and customs. Such variations were largely accidental and not substantive and included such things as differences about the shape of a monk's tonsure, kneeling and standing in church, blessing oneself with two or three fingers, baptism by immersion or aspersion, austere versus moderate monastic rules, the role of icons and statues as prayer aids, married or celibate clergy, and the use of leavened or unleavened bread in the sacrament of Communion.[4]

Some differences were more significant and included such things as the pope's jurisdiction. The Catholics thought that the pope was the supreme Christian leader whereas the Orthodox were perhaps willing to concede that he was the first among equals but that an ecumenical council of bishops was superior to the pope. Another issue was a disagreement over the nature of the Trinity. The Catholic Church added the so-called *filioque* clause to the Nicene Creed in the ninth century in order to clarify the relationship among the Father, Son, and Holy Spirit. The Orthodox Church rejected the clause. It was not sacrosanct for Catholics. In 2004 Pope John Paul II and Patriarch Bartholomew of Constantinople recited the Nicene Creed together without the *filioque* phrase. Even though the Christian Churches split, many Christians in the East continued to accept the pope as their leader while practicing the Orthodox liturgy or their own traditional liturgy. The Catholic Church accommodated these differences by creating rites, an effort that today has reached, by some counts, some twenty-two rites.

Although Catholic and Orthodox believers shared the same faith, they existed within political cultures that favored and pushed different values, which the religions helped cultivate.[5] Because Christianity focused on spiritual matters, it could generally accept any political order, including autocracy, constitutional monarchy, aristocracy, democracy, and other political configurations. Orthodoxy existed and evolved in the world of the Byzantine Empire and of that empire's main successors, Muscovy and the Russian Empire. There it endorsed autocracy and absolutism; subordination of religion to the state, a tradition called caesaropapism or symphonia; public as opposed to private property; community over individual rights; elites or oligarchs who were state servants; central or federal authority as opposed to local and city-town rights; fixed truth that promoted a type of theological mysticism over reason and new insights; and a certain messianism that had the Byzantine and Muscovite-Russian Empires as the vehicles for bringing truth to the world.

In the West, the value system was different. There, with the Western Empire in shambles, the pope took on the role of both political and religious leader. Over the course of some five centuries he and the Western Christian bishops, monks, and ruling German elites helped build a new order called Christendom or Western civilization. Its values consisted of constitutionalism and democratic government, separation of church and state, the rule of law based on the natural law, private property, individualism in the service of the community, autonomous bodies, free towns and cities and the principle of subsidiarity, compatibility of faith and reason with the idea that faith evolved, and the importance of the evolution of knowledge, which included the founding of universities and the scientific method. Although the pope and the Catholic Church did not always endorse these values when they first emerged, they did eventually approve of them and they were in any event the product of Christianity (including its Judaic roots) working within the environment of a collapsed Roman world in the West, German tradition, and Greco-Roman culture.

In the course of the centuries that rounded out the first millennium and into the first centuries of the second millennium, both the Orthodox and Catholic Churches sought to expand their faiths and respective value systems. Both were world religions with universal fellowship as their mission. Catholic missionaries converted the people who eventually became known as Irish, English, French, Spanish, Portuguese, Italians, Germans, Austrians, and Scandinavians, including the Danes, Norwegians, and Swedes. In the eighth, ninth, and tenth centuries they also moved into Eastern Europe and converted the West Slavs, including the Poles, Czechs, and Slovaks, and part of the South Slavs, including the Croats, Slovenes, and some Bosnian-Herzegovinians. In the fourteenth century they converted the Lithuanians. The converts to Catholicism also adopted the Latin alphabet in order to write their spoken languages. In the fifteenth and sixteenth centuries Catholic missionaries devised one of what would become a group of new Eastern Rites that allowed Orthodox believers to accept the pope as their spiritual leader but practice Orthodox liturgy and traditions, including using the Cyrillic alphabet and having married priests. The first Eastern Rite was initially intended for the Greeks in the Byzantine Empire who were under siege by Muslims and thus was often called the Byzantine Rite. National variations of this Rite eventually found followers in Bulgaria, Hungary, Romania, and especially in Ukraine and Belorussia, where it often had a national moniker such as the Ukrainian or Greek Rite Catholic Church to distinguish it from Latin Rite Catholics who resided in, say, Poland's Ukrainian regions.

Orthodox missionaries converted the Georgians, Armenians, Albanians, and the people of Dacia who eventually were known as the Romanians. They also moved into Slavic regions of Eastern Europe and the Balkan Peninsula and converted most of the South Slavs, including the Serbs, Montenegrins, most Bosnian-Herzegovinians, the Slavicized Bulgarians and Macedonians, and the East Slavs or Rus peoples, who eventually became known as the Ukrainians, Belorussians, and Russians.[6] The Slavs who converted to Orthodoxy adopted the Cyrillic alphabet, which was devised by St. Cyril and based on Greek, to give written form to their spoken language. The Orthodox Church tended to evolve national Orthodox churches that had autonomy but accepted the patriarch of Constantinople as a nominal leader.

World history was deeply affected by the fact that a world religion split into two traditions and then evolved in two separate societies based on different values. It meant that Western and Eastern Christian societies often ended up being global rivals and opponents. The Byzantine and Russian Empires were motivated to expand not only Orthodoxy, but also Byzantine and Russian values around the globe. The Western states were similarly driven to spread Catholicism and Western values around the world. There were attempts at unity and of alliance when one of them was threatened by enemies, often from the world of Islam, which was a third world religion that also sought universal fellowship and supported the expansion of the values of Islamic societies, but such partnerships were expedient and often self-serving. The crusades, for example, which were an effort by the West to help the Orthodox in the face of a threat from the Muslim Seljuk Turks who had devastated the Byzantine army at the Battle of Manzikert in 1071, ended up straining relations between the Orthodox and Catholic regions. When the Russians supported a Ukrainian revolt against the Poles in 1654, they ended up occupying part of Ukraine and destabilizing Catholic Poland. In short, Catholic and Orthodox cultures had different approaches to organizing society. They competed, along with the Muslims, to determine the value system upon which universal fellowship or its end product, globalization or world interdependency, would evolve. The power that each of their societies could generate and project would be critical in deciding which political order would prevail as a basis for global order and integration.

East Slavs: Ukrainian, Belorussian, and Russian national identities

The early history of the East Slavic or Rus peoples is vague. The origin of the name "Rus" is uncertain, but many scholars now think that it is derived from the Finnish word *ruotsi*, which means "rower" or "Sweden," a reference perhaps to the Scandinavian invaders who rowed their boats into the rivers flowing into the Gulf of Finland and Eastern Baltic Sea, like the Neva and Volkhov Rivers, and through portage to the other great rivers, like the Dnieper, the Volga, and their tributaries, that flowed south to the Black and Caspian Seas.[7] The Rus were not related to the Teutonic Scandinavians, but instead were the eastern branch, geographically speaking, of a large group of people who spoke a Slavic tongue and were divided into three parts based on their position relative to the Carpathian Mountains, that huge serpentine chain of mountains that veers north from the Alps and the Danube River basin. The Slavs west of the Carpathians were called West Slavs, and they lived on the plains and along the rivers that flowed into the Baltic Sea; the South Slavs resided mainly on the Balkan Peninsula, south of the Carpathians and the Danube River basin; and the East Slavs occupied the slopes and plains along the rivers extending east of the Carpathian Mountains to the Ural Mountains, which marked the end of Europe and the beginning of Asia.

The first organized state among the East Slavs was called Kievan Rus. It was set up sometime in the ninth century by Scandinavians, as mentioned, who wanted to control the people and the trade on the plains and rivers – the Dnieper, Dniester, Don, and Volga – that stretched between the Baltic and Black Seas. Eventually the East Slavs absorbed the Scandinavian conquerors and transformed Kievan Rus into a strong state with its capital at Kiev on the Dnieper that was based on agriculture, fishing, hunting, and trade with the Byzantine Empire, the Baltic Sea region, Persia, and the West. In 988 Prince Vladimir, the Grand Prince of Kievan Rus, accepted Orthodox Christianity and imposed it as the state religion upon the East Slavs. According to the *Primary Chronicle*, which is the best source for the early history of Kievan Rus, he and his main supporters were impressed with the Greek Orthodox Church's liturgy and rituals, beautiful icons, and awe-inspiring church architecture.[8] They were also impacted by the military and economic power of the Byzantine Empire, which in the tenth century was one of the world's most powerful states. It took a few centuries for Christianity to be absorbed by the general population, who mingled with it some of their pre-Christian customs and beliefs, but Christianity eventually permeated the lives of the people.[9] Orthodoxy, as many scholars have noted, gave the East Slavs their religion, alphabet, architecture, morality, and worldview.[10] Inevitably, the clerical leaders of Kievan Rus' Orthodox Church were Greeks and answered to the patriarch of Constantinople, including the highest official who resided in Kiev and was known as the metropolitan of Kievan Rus. The Greeks used the Cyrillic alphabet to develop Church Slavonic, which was a written form of the Slavic tongue developed to celebrate the Orthodox liturgy.

The acceptance of Orthodox Christianity from the Byzantine Empire did not mean that the East Slavs rejected the Western Christian tradition or trade and political relations with the various peoples and kingdoms that constituted Western civilization. In fact, at the time of the East Slavs' conversion, the world of Christianity was still unified, and Kievan Rus had trade relations with Scandinavia, Poland, and the Kingdom of Bohemia. Even after the Great Schism of 1054, which formalized the emergence of the separate Orthodox and Catholic Churches, Kievan Rus persisted with relations with the Catholic West and eventually developed dynastic ties through marriage with many of the ruling dynasties of Europe.[11] The fourth crusade in 1204 led to some strain, but by then Kievan Rus was already destabilized by endemic civil war over leadership succession and by constant harassment from tribal marauders and nomads from Asia who entered the western side of the Eurasian Plain through the famous Ural Gap between the Ural Mountains and the Caspian Sea.

Catastrophe struck in 1237–40 when the Mongols came through the Ural Gap and conquered and occupied Kievan Rus. They made Kievan Rus the most western satellite of the Mongol Empire, which they called the Golden Horde, with its capital at Sarai near where the Volga River flows into the Caspian Sea. They cut the East Slavs off from the Byzantine Empire and the West and set up a political order that relied on force, visceral violence, and fear to effect self-deprecating and abject obedience.[12] It was a model of government that buttressed Byzantine absolutism but added the element of violent, overwhelming, and arbitrary force as a political strategy to maintain order and preempt rivals. This form of absolutism was different than Byzantine absolutism and the kind of absolutism that evolved in some countries of Western Europe, for example, the absolutism of the French Bourbon kings such as Louis XIV. Absolutism in Constantinople and in the West was restrained and checked by law and powerful institutions, and, in the case of the West, was a form of government the people desired in order to control feudal aristocrats. Mongol-Byzantine absolutism demanded complete obedience in mind and soul and the acceptance of the monarch as an omniscient representative of God who ruled without restraint and engaged in gratuitous violence as a tool to instill fear and surrender among his subjects. It was a brutal, sweeping authoritarianism that had a lasting impact on those East Slavs who resided deep in the eastern part of the Golden Horde and eventually emerged as the Muscovite Russians.[13]

In 1252 the Mongols converted to Islam, but showed no interest in attempting to change the religion of the East Slavs. They were content to rule over the East Slavs, collect taxes and recruits for their armies, and allow the East Slavs to continue to adhere to Orthodox Christianity. In fact, they exempted the clergy and the Church from taxes and showed respect to the religious leader, the metropolitan of Kiev, thus giving to Orthodoxy a role in protecting the East Slavs' political and ethnic identity, especially among the East Slavs who were geographically in the heart of the Golden Horde and close to Asia's borderland with Europe, the Russians. When the Russians eventually made their move to free themselves from Mongol control, it was the Orthodox Church that inspired and motivated them with that mystical messianism mentioned earlier – a sense of being a unique and special people, chosen by God to protect and promulgate the Orthodox Christian faith and value system in the face of rivals and enemies, particularly Catholics and Muslims. Russian religious philosopher Nikolai Berdyaev called it in 1915 Russia's "divinely chosen and God-bearing nature."[14]

There was one part of the former state of Kievan Rus that the Mongols treated differently than the other East Slavic regions, and that was Novgorod. It was located in the marshlands of the far northwest, about ninety miles from the Baltic Sea. Because Novgorod offered to abide by Mongol dictates before the Mongol armies reached it and because of its difficult terrain, the Mongols agreed to allow Novgorod to remain an autonomous region under its prince, Alexander Nevsky, on the condition that Nevsky acknowledge the Mongol ruler, called the Grand Khan, as his suzerain and deliver annually to the Mongols Novgorod's quota of taxes and soldiers. Nevsky and his successors did not disappoint the Mongols and, as a result, continued to enjoy a modicum of independence.

The existence of an autonomous Novgorod under Mongol suzerainty was an anomaly and an irresistible attraction for the Western Christians who resided on the western border of the Golden Horde. In 1240 the Swedes probed Novgorod's defense, but Alexander Nevsky's army stopped them. Two years later the Teutonic Knights, from bases on the eastern shore of the Baltic Sea, tried their hand against Nevsky and were repulsed. The stout defense discouraged the West from further military and political forays against Novgorod, but not from economic and cultural overtures, which Novgorod reciprocated. The West soon developed commercial relations with Novgorod the Great, as the region came to be called, and made the town of Novgorod the most eastern terminus of the Hanseatic League, a maritime trading association of mainly German city-states that stretched from the eastern Baltic Sea to Lisbon on the Atlantic seaboard. Sometime in the late thirteenth or early fourteenth century a Catholic church was set up in Novgorod to accommodate the spiritual needs of Western traders. Novgorod the Great flourished under this system of Western trade and Mongol benign neglect and eventually expanded commercial operations into the Arctic region and northern Siberia in the fourteenth century. Its ties to the West were strong and clearly included the adoption of some variation of Western economic values and institutions.

The Mongols ruled the rest of the East Slavic peoples with an iron hand. How-ever, they found it convenient to have one of the East Slavic princes be their chief tax collector with the title of Grand Prince with enough power to coerce, if necessary, the annual payment of taxes and manpower levies. Alexander Nevsky of Novgorod initially had the title, but with his death it soon passed to the prince of the Vladimir-Suzhdal-Moscow region, who moved his residence to Moscow, which was a main town on the Moscow River that was part of the Volga-Oka river system in the eastern part of the Golden Horde. The Moscow Grand Princes held onto the title and became the permanent chief tax collector of the Mongols. They used their position to expand their writ, with the approval of the Mongols, and build a mini-state called Muscovy in the bosom of the Golden Horde. In 1325, Metropolitan Peter of Kiev, who was a Greek, also decided to move to Moscow, which brought prestige to the Moscow prince and increased his influence with the East Slavs and the Mongols. Of course, other ecclesiastical leaders – bishops and abbots – continued to live in Kiev, Novgorod, and the many other East Slavic towns of the Golden Horde. In fact, the patriarch of Constantinople eventually named another metropolitan in Kiev. And there were other political centers, most notably Novgorod the Great, which with its powerful commercial class stood in sharp contrast to the protean Muscovite state with its Byzantine-Mongol model of the strong hand.

The birth of distinct nationalities among the East Slavs took place during the period of the Mongol overlordship, and surprisingly the midwife was the West and the Catholic Church. Separate ethnic identities among the East Slavs started in the second half of the fourteenth century when the Lithuanians, a fierce tribe wedged between the Golden Horde and the Baltic Sea and increasingly attracted to the Catholic culture of Poland, decided to challenge the Golden Horde. The Lithuanians pushed into the western side of the Golden Horde below Novgorod. The Mongols were surprised, but knew that they could not allow this incursion to go unanswered because it struck at the core of their power, namely the intimi-dating belief that they would level with unrelenting and unmerciful violence any challenge to their authority. In 1362 the Mongol army met the Lithuanian forces on a tributary of the Southern Bug River in what was called the Battle of the Blue Waters. The Lithuanians pummeled the Mongols and then went on to conquer the entire western side of the Golden Horde.

After defeating the Mongols, the Lithuanians joined in a dynastic union with the Poles when their ruler Jagiello (r. 1377–1434) married Queen Jadwiga of Poland, converted to Catholicism, and initiated a new dynasty that came to pre-side over a vast state called Poland-Lithuania that stretched between the Baltic and Black Seas.[15] The East Slavs who slipped under Polish-Lithuanian rule were treated as second-class citizens, but they were exposed to Western culture and val-ues, to such concepts as schools, universities, political pluralism, representative government, the rule of law, elected monarchs, and vigorous intellectual debate. Of particular importance was the University of Cracow, later called Jagiellonian University, which was founded in 1364 and where Copernicus was educated. This "Romanization" or Westernization of the East Slavs was the central catalyst in the birth of the Ukrainian and Belorussian nationalities. It separated them from the East Slavs who remained under Mongol control and became by default yet a third and by far the largest nationality and ethnic group among the East Slavs, namely the Russians.

The Russians did not experience Romanization and the pivotal events that were then or were soon to be evolving in the West, including the Renaissance, the age of discovery, constitutionalism, parliamentary government, the intellectual revolution, the scientific revolution, and the early tremors of the Protestant Reformation and Catholic Counter-Reformation. Instead, the Russians were influenced largely by the Mongols, who continued to rely on force, ruthlessness, and a caste-like social order based on fixed, revealed truth, either Islam for the Muslims or Orthodoxy for the Russians. Most of the population was serfs who worked the land to support the Russian boyar class and princes and the Mongol overlords. The Mongolization of Russian culture stood in sharp contrast to the Westernization of Ukraine and Belorussia. Among the Russians, Novgorod the Great developed some aspects of Romanization, particularly in the economic sphere, but it, like all other East Slavic regions under Mongol control, was increasingly being subjected to rule of the Muscovite Russians and, thus, to Mongolization. The Muscovite Russians developed a profound distrust and hatred of the Westerners and Catholics, who, they believed, were fracturing the East Slavic peoples, were perhaps complicit in the Mongol conquest and continued occupation of the land of the East Slavs, and were, at least, taking advantage of the East Slavs' plight.[16] For the Russians the differences between Ukrainians, Belorussians, and Russians were artificial, and they did their best to blur them and to maintain that all of the East Slavs were one people, namely Russians, and that Kiev was a Russian city where Russian Orthodoxy started – claims Ukrainians found preposterous.[17]

The Muscovite Russians were undoubtedly ambivalent over the Lithuanian victory at the Battle of Blue Waters. On one hand, they were certainly pleased to learn that the Mongols were not invincible, but, on the other hand, they had to be upset and suspicious over the expansion of Catholic influence among Ukrainians and Belorussians whom they believed should be under Russian Orthodox control. In 1380 Muscovite Grand Prince Dmitri Donskoi engaged a Mongol army at the Battle of Kolikovo Field near the Don River, hence Dmitri's name "Donskoi" (of the Don). The Russian Orthodox Church played a major role in rallying the Russians on behalf of Dmitri, and he defeated the Mongols. However, the victory was more of a premonition of change than a watershed. In 1382 the Mongols stormed Moscow, burned the Kremlin (the walled fortress in the center of the city) to the ground, and reestablished their suzerainty and annual quotas of taxes and manpower over the Russians. The Mongols, though, were clearly in decline. By the end of the fourteenth century they had also largely merged with the numerous Turkish tribes, often called Tartars, spread across Central Asia, the lands around the Caspian Sea, the Caucasus, the Volga basin, and the Crimean Peninsula.

In the fifteenth century the Westernization of the East Slavs under Polish-Lithuanian rule strengthened when the Vatican created a new Rite called the Eastern Catholic Rite. The Eastern Rite was approved in 1439 at the famous Council of Florence, which took place against the Ottoman Turks' siege of Constantinople and the Byzantine Empire, when the patriarch of Constantinople, with the approval of the Byzantine emperor, agreed to unite with the Catholic Church and to accept the pope as the spiritual leader of Orthodox Christians. The Orthodox Church continued with its own liturgy and traditions, so the only essential change for Orthodox Christians was that the pope was now their leader. The Metropolitan of the Muscovite Orthodox Church, Isidore, who was a Greek, endorsed the union and after the Council made his way east to promulgate the news. He publicized the union in the Orthodox lands of Poland-Lithuania, which led some Orthodox there to accept the pope and become Ukrainian or Belorussian Catholics or Uniate Catholics, that is, in "union" with the pope. Although the union idea soon floundered because the pope lost sympathy with it after Constantinople fell in 1454, many Orthodox Christians within the Poland–Lithuania borders found some merit in closer association with Western ideas and institutions, a development that helped to reinforce the emergence of the Ukrainian and Belorussian nationalities.

At the time of the Council of Florence, the ruler of Muscovy, still under Mongol control, was Grand Prince Basil II (r. 1425–62). The Golden Horde by then had split into the khanates of Kazan, Astrakhan, and Crimea, and the Ottoman Turks had established control over the Crimea and its Tartars. With the Mongol disintegration, Basil and the burgeoning state of Muscovy achieved autonomy but continued to pay tribute to both the khans of Astrakhan and Crimea. Basil had allowed Isidore, the Greek metropolitan of the Muscovite Orthodox Church, to attend the Council of Florence, but warned him not to bring back to Muscovy anything new.[18] When Isidore returned to Muscovy with news of the union, Basil rejected it and jailed Metropolitan Isidore, who eventually escaped to Poland-Lithuania.[19] In his place Basil appointed a Russian monk by the name of Jonas, which signaled Muscovite Russia's intent to name its own clerical leaders and to gain autonomy from the Greeks. When Constantinople fell in 1453, Jonas blamed the defeat on the patriarch's agreement to accept the pope as the leader of Orthodox Christians. In 1458 he concluded: "For as long as Constantinople had adhered to the true faith, she had resisted all invasions but, once having betrayed it and united herself with the Latins, she fell under the infidel's yoke."[20]

Notes

1 For information on early Christianity, the basic source is Eusebius [290s?] 1989. Also quite useful are H. W. Crocker 2001; Dawson [1959] 1981; MacCulloch 2010.

2 For background on the Byzantine Empire, see Mango 2002; Norwich 1997; Ostrogorsky [1969] 1986; Runciman 1965.

3 For comparative studies of Orthodoxy and Catholicism, see Dvornik 1966; Meyendorff 1992; Nichols 1992; Runciman 1977.

4 Dunn 2004, p. 29.

5 It is important to note that Christianity was based on Judaism and saw itself as the fulfillment of the Jewish faith and that the Christian tradition was really a Judeo-Christian legacy.

6 For background, see Vlasto 1970, pp. 274–75. On the expansion of Orthodox civilization into Eastern Europe, see Obolensky 2000.
7 Bremer [2007] 2013, p. 8.
8 Cross and Sherbowitz-Wetzor 2012, pp. 110–14.
9 Bremer [2007] 2013, pp. 9–10.
10 Billington 1970, pp. 4–13; Pares 1962, pp. 5–7.
11 Billington 1970, p. 4; Dunn 2004, p. 4; Obolensky [1953] 1970, p. 24.
12 D'Encausse 1993; also see Truscott 1997, pp. 16–17.
13 G.P. Fedotov 1946, p. 26, argued that even the Byzantine legacy had totalitarian aspects.
14 Fagan 2013, p. 1. Also see www.berdyaev.com/berdiaev/berd_lib/1915_007.html (accessed 1 April 2016).
15 Davies 1982, 1, pp. 115–58. Also see Halecki 1952.
16 Bremer [2007] 2013, p. 14.
17 Bremer [2007] 2013, p. 2.
18 On the Council of Florence, see Gill [1959] 2011, and Halecki 1968.
19 Cherniavsky 1955, pp. 347–59.
20 Cross 1948, p. 88; Miliukov [1942] 1972, p. 15.

References

Berdiaev, Nikolai, www.berdyaev.com/berdiaev/berd_lib/1915_007.html (accessed 1 April 2016).

Billington, James H. 1970, *The Icon and the Axe: An Interpretive History of Russian Culture*, New York, Vintage Book.

Bremer, Thomas [2007] 2013, *Cross and Kremlin: A Brief History of the Orthodox Church in Russia*, Eric B. Gritsch (trans.), Grand Rapids, MI: Eerdmans.

Cherniavsky, Michael 1955, "The Reception of the Council of Florence in Moscow," *Church History* 24, pp. 347–59.

Crocker, H. W., III. 2001, *Triumph: The Power and the Glory of the Catholic Church*, New York: Primama Publishing, Forum.

Cross, Samuel H. 1948, *Slavic Civilization Through the Ages*, Leonid I. Strakhovsky (ed.), Cambridge, MA: Harvard University Press.

Cross, Samuel H. and Sherbowitz-Wetzor, Olgerd P. (eds. and trans.) 2012, *The Russian Primary Chronicle*, Cambridge, MA: Medieval Academy of America.

Davies, Norman 1982, *God's Playground: A History of Poland*, 2 vols., New York: Columbia University Press.

Dawson, Christopher [1959] 1981, *Christianity in East & West*, John J. Mulloy (ed.), La Salle, IL: Sherwood Sugden.

D'Encausse, Hélène 1993, *The Russian Syndrome: One Thousand Years of Political Murder*, Caroline Higgitt (trans.), Adam Ulam (foreword), London: Holmes & Meier.

Dunn, Dennis J. 2004, *The Catholic Church and Russia: Popes, Patriarchs, Tsars and Commissars*, Aldershot, UK: Ashgate.

Dvornik, Francis 1966, *Byzantium and the Roman Primacy*, Edwin A. Quain (trans.), New York: Fordham University Press.

Eusebius [290s?] 1989, *History of the Church from Christ to Constantine*, G. A. Williamson (trans.), Andrew Louth (rev. and ed.), New York: Penguin Books.

Fagan, Geraldine 2013, *Believing in Russia: Religious Policy After Communism*, New York: Routledge.

Fedotov, G. P. 1946, *The Russian Religious Mind*, Vol. 1, Cambridge, MA: Harvard University Press.

Gill, Joseph [1959] 2011, *The Council of Florence*, Cambridge: Cambridge University Press.

Halecki, Oscar 1952, *Borderlands of Western Civilization: A History of East Central Europe*, New York: Ronald Press.

Halecki, Oscar 1968, *From Florence to Brest (1439–1596)*, 2nd ed., Hamden, CT: Archon Books.

MacCulloch, Diarmaid 2010, *Christianity: The First Three Thousand Years*, New York: Viking.

Mango, Cyril (ed.) 2002. *The Oxford History of Byzantium*, New York: Oxford University Press.

Meyendorff, John 1992, *Rome, Constantinople, Moscow: Historical and Theological Studies*, Crestwood, NY: St. Vladimir's Seminary Press.

Miliukov, Paul [1942] 1972, *Outlines of Russian Culture*, 3 parts, part 1: *Religion and the Church in Russia*, Michael Karpovich (ed.), Valentine Ughet and Eleanor Davis (trans.), New York: A. S. Barnes and Company, Perpetua Book.

Nichols, Aidan OP 1992, *Rome and the Eastern Churches: A Study in Schism*, Edinburgh: T & T Clark.

Norwich, John Julius 1997, *A Short History of Byzantium*, New York: Knopf.

Obolensky, Dmitri [1953] 1970, "Russia's Byzantine Heritage," in *The Structure of Russian History: Interpretive Essays*, Michael Cherniavsky (ed.), New York: Random House, pp. 3–28.

Obolensky, Dmitri 2000, *The Byzantine Commonwealth: Eastern Europe, 500–1453*, London: Phoenix Press.

Ostrogorsky, George [1969] 1986, *History of the Byzantine State*, New Brunswick, NJ: Rutgers University Press.

Pares, Bernard 1962, *Russia: Between Reform and Revolution: Foundation of Russian History and Character*, New York: Schocken Books.

Runciman, Steven 1965, *The Fall of Constantinople 1453*, Cambridge: Cambridge University Press.

Runciman, Steven 1977, *The Byzantine Theocracy*, Cambridge: Cambridge University Press.

Truscott, Peter 1997, *Russia First Breaking with the West*, London: I. B. Tauris.

Vlasto, A. P. 1970, *The Entry of the Slavs Into Christendom: An Introduction to the Medieval History of the Slavs*, Cambridge: Cambridge University Press.

2 Muscovy, the Russian Empire, and the Catholic Church

Ivan the Great to Peter II, 1462–1762

Ivan III or the Great (r. 1462–1505), Basil's successor, continued with the policy of not only separating Muscovite Russia from Greek control, but also of having Russia replace the Greeks, who were now under Muslim control, as the God-ordained leaders of Orthodox Christianity, leaders who would put the pope in his place and reclaim the Orthodox peoples and lands of Poland-Lithuania. The first order of business was to subject other Russian princes to Muscovite control. The major rival was Novgorod the Great. Ivan attacked Novgorod in 1471 and then again in 1478 when he took firm control and purged the Western-leaning elite and closed Novgorod's one Catholic Church. Ivan also subjected other Russian principalities to his authority and became known as the "gatherer of the Russian lands."

In 1472 Ivan took another step to support Muscovy's claim to be the successor of the Byzantine Empire. He married the niece of the last Byzantine emperor, Zoe Paleologue, who was a ward of the pope. Ivan prevailed upon Zoe to abandon the Byzantine Catholic Rite in favor of Russian Orthodoxy when she arrived in Moscow, a return to Orthodoxy that she marked by changing her name to Sophia. The pope approved of the marriage in the hope that the gesture would lead to an alliance between Ivan and various Western states against the Ottoman Turks, who were threatening the Holy Roman Empire in Eastern Europe. Ivan rejected the idea of an alliance because the Turks and their satellite, the khanate of the Crimea, were too strong and were being helpful by distracting the Europeans from interfering in Russian affairs. However, Ivan was impressed with the learned envoys the pope had sent to accompany Zoe to Muscovy and immediately employed Rodolfo ("Aristotle") Fioraventi, the brilliant Renaissance architect from Bologna, to build Assumption Cathedral inside the Kremlin and to teach a group of Muscovites Western building techniques. In a real sense, Muscovite Russia now opened a door to the West that continued into modern times, but the Russians were not excited about Western values. They wanted Western weapons, science, and technology in order to make Muscovy powerful and capable of defeating the Westerners and the Muslims. The Muscovites were seemingly unaware or unwilling to acknowledge that Western power was the result of Western values.

In 1480 Ivan made another decisive move to assert Muscovite Russia's claim to be the successor of the Byzantine Empire when his army faced off against the remnants of the Mongols at the Ugra River. The Mongols retreated, marking the formal end of the Mongol yoke and the start of an independent Muscovite Russia, which was supported by serf labor and aristocratic military and government service. Ivan then adopted the Byzantine Empire's double-headed eagle as Muscovy's coat of arms and proclaimed in 1489 to Nicholas Poppel, an ambassador from Holy Roman emperor Frederick III, who offered to make Ivan a king, that he was "invested with power by God" and did "not need investiture by anyone else." In 1491, the new Russian metropolitan, Zosima, declared that Ivan was the "new Constantine of the new Constantinople."[1] In 1505 during the reign of Ivan's son, Basil III (r. 1505–33), the monk Philotheus called Moscow the Third Rome, implying that it had succeeded the capitals of both the western (Rome in Italy) and eastern (Constantinople or Second Rome) parts of the former Roman Empire.[2]

Ivan the Terrible or IV (r. 1533–84), the first Russian ruler to be called *tsar* (a Russian rendering of *caesar*), expanded Muscovite Russia's territory and power and transformed Muscovy into a multinational and multi-religious empire. By the mid-1550s he annexed two of the three remnants of the Golden Horde, the khanates of Kazan and Astrakhan. Russian soldiers, explorers, and missionaries then began the conquest of Siberia, which carried on into the eighteenth century and brought more Muslims, Buddhists, and multiple minority faiths under Russian rule.

Ivan thought about attacking the third remnant of the Golden Horde, the khanate of Crimea, but it was a satellite of the powerful Ottoman Empire. Instead, Ivan decided to attack the small western state of Livonia on the Baltic Sea. He wanted access to the Baltic in order to increase trade, obtain Western technology and weapons, and establish a beachhead against Poland-Lithuania and Sweden. He also thought that Livonia, which was part Protestant and part Catholic, was small, divided, and vulnerable. In 1558 he attacked this small country.

Livonia immediately appealed to Poland-Lithuania for help. The Swedes also decided to intervene against Ivan. Stephen Báthory, the newly elected Hungarian king of Poland-Lithuania, was a brilliant general and he eventually routed the Russians and invaded Muscovy. Facing disaster and likely partition, Ivan appealed to Pope Gregory XIII (r. 1572–85), the inventor of the Gregorian calendar, to intercede and stop the Catholic forces. It was a curious demarche on Ivan's part. It indicated that he thought the pope, unlike the Orthodox metropolitan and patriarch, was an independent authority who had real influence and could sway powerful Catholic rulers even though the pope had no army.

As it turned out, the pope did have some clout with Catholic rulers, particularly in the profoundly Catholic lands of Poland and Lithuania and particularly with the very devout Stephen Báthory. Pope Gregory sent the Jesuit Antonio Possevino to Báthory to plead with him to sign an armistice with Ivan. Possevino held out the possibility that Ivan might be persuaded to join an alliance against the Turks and might be open to some sort of union between the Russian Orthodox Church and the Catholic Church. Báthory accommodated the pope and signed in 1582 the Armistice of Yam Zapol'ski. According to its terms, Ivan relinquished all claims to Livonia and agreed to work on an alliance against the Ottoman Turks.[3] Once free of Báthory, Ivan refused to consider either an alliance against the Turks or any rapprochement with the Catholic Church. For the Poles, it was an object lesson in the art of dealing with the Russians.

With Ivan's death in 1584, a period of turmoil ensued because there was no clear successor. Ivan's one living son, Theodore I, was infertile and mentally impaired, and when he died, Boris Godunov (r. 1598–1605), a Tartar advisor of Ivan and Theodore, tried to establish his own dynasty. The Muscovite elite rebuffed him. One major accomplishment was his ability to persuade Patriarch Jeremias II of Constantinople to name a Russian patriarch in 1589 during a visit to Moscow. Godunov and the Russians wanted this office to solidify Muscovite Russia's claim to be the successor of the Byzantine emperor and to balance the pope's prestige as the only Christian patriarch not under Muslim control. In addition, they wanted it to impress the Orthodox in Ukraine and Belorussia and sway them against joining an Eastern Catholic Rite that the pope and the Jesuits were in the process of reviving in the late sixteenth century.

After losing perhaps as many as one-third of the Catholics in Europe to Protestantism, the pope saw a way to recoup the loss by revisiting the issue of union with the Orthodox Christians in Poland-Lithuania. He and the Jesuits resurrected the Eastern Catholic Rite that had been fashioned at the Council of Florence with an agreement called the Union of Brest in 1596.[4] With the support of the pope and the Jesuits, this rite grew and took firm root in Ukraine and Belorussia and expanded in time to Romania, Bulgaria, Hungary, and render as Transcarpathia. The Jesuits soon opened up schools and colleges throughout Belorussia and parts of Ukraine. In 1661 they set up the University of Lviv, which had actually existed as a Jesuit college since 1608. According to a Polish report, the city of Kiev alone had twenty Catholic churches.[5] The Orthodox who did not join the Eastern Rite were also influenced by the Western pursuits in education and science, and they began to open their own schools modeled on the curriculum of the Jesuits. The peripatetic Orthodox metropolitan of Kiev, Peter Mogila (r. 1633–47), founded the famous Kiev Academy in 1632. He also persuaded the Polish king to allow the Orthodox Church to use the Ukrainian language in its schools and churches. Romanization of Orthodoxy in Ukraine and Belorussia accelerated throughout the seventeenth century and helped firm up the evolving national identities of the Ukrainian and Belorussian peoples.[6]

With Godunov's death in 1605, Muscovite Russia went through a tumultuous period called the Time of Troubles. Peasants revolted against serfdom, Cossacks rebelled against military service, and pretenders to the throne abounded. Poland-Lithuania and Sweden both decided to take advantage of Muscovy's weakness and occupied parts of Russian territory. The Poles advanced to Moscow and occupied the Kremlin in 1610. The Russians eventually rallied, elected Michael Romanov as the new tsar, and forced the Poles and Swedes to retreat. In time, a ceasefire was signed between the Romanov government and the Poles and Swedes. For the Russians, the Poles and the Catholic Church, particularly the Eastern Catholic Rite, were archenemies who had to be curtailed and, if possible, destroyed. According to Adam Olearius, a member of a trade mission from Holstein-Gottorp who traveled to Muscovite Russia in 1633 and 1636, the Russians harbored an "ancient hatred and seemingly inborn hostility to the Papists."[7] They also detested Protestants, but they found them more acceptable because their religion, unlike Catholicism, was so different from Orthodoxy that they concluded Russians would not be attracted to it. In addition, the Protestants were generally anti-Catholic, at least some of them, and that was viewed as a redeeming quality.

In 1645 Alexis (r. 1645–72), Michael's son, became tsar and he saw an opportunity to take advantage of Poland-Lithuania. The Poles had developed a number of weaknesses and vulnerabilities over time, but none more draining than the so-called liberum veto, which allowed any member of parliament to explode the diet. Foreign governments, including the Russians, Swedes, French, and Austrians simply had to bribe a member of parliament to thwart the ability of the Polish government to rule. Another vulnerability was the multinational character of the state and its discrimination against non-Poles, particularly Jews and Orthodox Ukrainians and Belorussians. In 1653 a rebellion broke out among Orthodox Christians who wanted to be treated equally and to be able to obtain justice in Polish courts and to have representation in the sejm. It was led by one Bogdan Khmelnitsky, a Zaporozhe Cossack leader. In 1654 Tsar Alexis declared war on Poland, and the Poles went down to defeat. The Russians, Swedes, Crimean Tartars, and Cossacks fought against the Poles and one another. In the Armistice of Andrusovo in 1667, Muscovite Russia annexed the left bank of Ukraine (Ukraine east of the Dnieper River) and they grabbed Kiev on the right bank and later gave the Poles some minor territory in compensation. In 1686 the Russians and Poles signed an agreement called the Eternal Peace that ratified these border changes.

The annexation of Kiev and the left bank of Ukraine was a seminal event for the Muscovite Russians. Suddenly they were exposed to Ukrainian learning, which had developed as a result of Ukraine's contact with the West. This immediately led to a schism in the Russian Orthodox Church. Some leaders, including Tsar Alexis and Patriarch Nikon, wanted to reform the Russian Orthodox Church in light of Ukrainian insights. Others, like the so-called Old Believers, said no change was possible – the faith received over the ages could not be altered. Tsar Alexis won out in the end but removed Nikon because he showed interest in the Western idea of separation of church and state.[8]

Tsar Alexis also increased Muscovite Russia's effort to obtain Western weapons, science, and technology. He set up a foreign or German village (the Russian word for foreign and German is the same) called *nemetskia sloboda* near Moscow, where he recruited Protestant and Catholic scientists and engineers to modernize the Russian armed forces and to instruct selected Russians to learn Western techniques. In the village, Protestants could have both churches and ministers, but Catholics were permitted neither.

Tsar Alexis's son, Peter I or the Great (r. 1682–1725), eventually became a regular visitor to the foreign village where he learned about shipbuilding, military strategy and weapons, Western bureaucracies, political and military organization, and political philosophies. He also renamed Muscovy the Russian Empire in recognition of the vast lands and many non-Russian peoples and non-Orthodox believers over whom the Russians ruled and he moved the capital westward from Moscow to St. Petersburg on the Gulf of Finland. He eventually launched a series of wars that immersed Russia into Europe's balance of power scheme, including a long, drawn war with Sweden that saw Russian arms victorious and enabled Russia to emerge as the dominant power in the eastern Baltic and to interfere almost at will in the internal affairs of Poland-Lithuania.

Peter also commissioned Dane Vitus Bering to explore the Artic and Pacific waters off the coast of Kamchatka, where Bering claimed Alaska and the Aleutian Islands for Russia. Peter supported Russian Orthodoxy but decided to replace the patriarch with an agency called the Holy Synod, which was made up of clergy, and over the Holy Synod he placed a lay official called the Ober Procurator of the Holy Synod, who reported directly to the tsar. He was not sympathetic to the Catholic Church, but he admired its learned clergy and debated with Jesuits on the merits of unifying the Orthodox and Catholic Churches when he visited the Sorbonne.[9] His half-sister, Sophia, who had ruled as regent during his minority, had allowed some Jesuits into the German village and Peter, too, eventually permitted them and the Franciscans into the Russian Empire. Although Peter expelled the Jesuits in 1719, his engagement with them and the West more generally irritated the Russian Orthodox establishment. In the nineteenth century such Russian nationalist groups as the Slavophiles and such intellectuals as Fyodor Dostoevsky condemned Peter's Westernizing trends and called him the "anti-Christ."[10]

Peter's immediate successors, most notably his daughter Elizabeth (r. 1740–62), carried on with his policies of expansion and of discriminating against Catholics and interfering in Polish affairs. They also persisted with the policy of importing Western weapons and technology and some Western institutions. In 1756 Elizabeth founded the University of Moscow, the first university in the Russian Orthodox Empire. When she died in 1762 power was turned over to her pro-Prussian nephew, Peter II, who was married to a German, Sophie Augusta Friedericka von Anhalt-Zerbst-Dornburg, who had learned Russian and converted from Lutheranism to Russian Orthodoxy. With the acquiescence and involvement of the Russian elite, including Church officials, she arranged to have Peter assassinated and to assume the Russian throne, taking the name of Catherine II, later proclaimed Catherine the Great.

Catherine the Great to Alexander III, 1762–1894

Catherine the Great (r. 1762–96) added to the size of the empire by taking territories from Turkey and, particularly, from Poland as a result of joining the Prussians and Austrians in the Partitions of Poland. The Russians annexed the eastern side of Poland that included Belorussia, Lithuania, and part of Ukraine and held as many as 1.6 million Roman Catholics and 2.5 million Eastern Rite Catholics and their dioceses. They placed the Roman Catholic Church under a government office called the College of Justice of Livonia, Estonia and Finland where it was prohibited from communicating with the Vatican and where all clerical appointments and assignments had to be approved. They restructured the Church by creating the first Catholic archdiocese in Russia, the archdiocese of Mogilev, with a seminary, a cathedral (St. Catherine's), and a residence for an archbishop in St. Petersburg. Mogilev was the world's largest Catholic archdiocese in terms of space with jurisdiction over land that stretched from the Baltic Sea to the Pacific Ocean. As for the Eastern Catholic Church, the Russian intention was to destroy it. By the end of Catherine's reign, the Russians had forced more than 1 million Eastern Rite Catholics to convert to Russian Orthodoxy.[11] They also imposed the Russian system of serfdom, absolutism, and bureaucratic centralization on the Poles, Ukrainians, and Belorussians, which was a demoralizing shock.[12]

Catherine did allow the Jesuits to exist and thrive in Russia because she recognized them as highly educated individuals who could elevate the education of Russians, particularly the nobility on which the government depended for service in the government and the military. There was another reason Catherine liked the Jesuits, and it was the more important factor in allowing them to thrive in the Russian Empire. The pope disbanded the Jesuits in 1783 in a weak moment when France and Spain pressured him because they resented Jesuit criticism of their colonial policies.[13] The Russian tsarina was delighted to be able to thwart the pope by undermining the papal decree abolishing the Jesuits. She also encouraged with promises of land grants and personal and religious freedom some 25,000 German Catholic and Protestant farmers, called Volga Germans, to settle and cultivate the Crimea and the land north of the Black Sea that she had conquered in a series of wars with Turkey. She knew Western farmers would make the land productive. Undoubtedly Russian farmers would have also produced bountiful crops if they had been given freedom and land, but the Russian government was committed to serfdom, which gave it control over the peasantry at the cost of low productivity, inefficient labor, and despondent and resentful farmers who formed the vast majority of the population of the Russian Empire.

Under Paul I (r. 1796–1801), Alexander I (r. 1801–25), and Nicholas I (r. 1825–55), the Russian Empire continued to expand with new acquisitions in Central Asia, the Caucasus, East Europe, and the Baltic Sea region. The Russian Empire was so huge and encompassed so many different nationalities and religions that the ruling Russian Orthodox were no longer the majority of the population and faced growing demands for national independence and religious freedom. The Russians responded during the reign of Nicholas I with a policy called "Autocracy, Nationality, and Orthodoxy," which was a reassertion of Russian absolutism supported by a humongous police force and an attempt to force all subjects to use the Russian language and convert to Russian Orthodoxy in the hope that such policies would produce the cultural cement that would bind together the empire's many disparate groups. The policy largely stirred resentment, opposition, and revolutionary movements.

During the first half of the nineteenth century, the Russian–Catholic relationship remained strained, although there were instances of amity. Paul encouraged the Jesuits, enlarged the number of Latin Catholic dioceses, and allowed the surviving Eastern Catholic Church to organize three dioceses (Minsk, Lutsk, and

Polotsk). During the early campaign against Napoleon, the Catholic Knights of Malta also elected him their grandmaster. However, he did not reverse Catherine's forced merger of the Eastern Catholics with the Orthodox Church, opposed naming a metropolitan for the Eastern Rite Catholics, and reached out to Napoleon, who was on the warpath against the Catholic Church. His assassination in 1801 ended a baffling period for Catholic–Russian relations.

His son, Alexander I, thought the Catholic Church might be an ally against the revolutionary ideas coming out of the French Revolution and the Napoleonic Wars and, accordingly, he was initially tolerant of Catholics in the Russian Empire, established diplomatic ties with the Vatican, and befriended the Jesuits. However, after the Congress of Vienna in 1815, which rearranged borders after Napoleon's defeat, the Russians annexed most of the Polish heartland. As a result, the number of Catholics in the Russian Empire increased enormously. Although the Russians maintained the façade of recognizing Poland as somehow different than other national and religious lands subject to Russian rule by calling it the Kingdom of Poland or sometimes Congress Poland, they ruled Poland with an iron fist, imposed their system and values on the Poles, and discriminated against Catholics. It was not surprising that the Poles resented and rejected the Russian jackboot. In response, Alexander broke diplomatic ties with the Vatican, expelled the Jesuits from Russia in 1820, and put an end to a trend that saw a number of Russian nobility and their children, who were educated by the Jesuits, convert to Catholicism.[14]

Nicholas I, the brother of Alexander, went further. He decided in 1839 to force the entire Eastern Catholic Church, except for the tiny Chëlm diocese in Congress Poland, to abandon its tie to the pope and to merge with the Orthodox Church, a brutal blow that lost more than 1.5 million Catholics to the Catholic Church and produced an alienated, underground opposition.[15] Fortunately, the Austrians, who controlled Galicia and its key city of Lviv and render as Transcarpathia, supported the Eastern Catholic Rite or, as they called it since 1774, the Greek Catholic Church. As a result, the Greek Catholic Church flourished under Austrian rule and numbered more than 3 million believers, overwhelmingly Ukrainian, by the end of the nineteenth century. An additional 470,000 Greek Catholics lived in render as Transcarpathia.[16]

Nicholas also went after the huge number of Latin Rite Catholics in Poland. After the Poles rebelled against Russian rule in 1830–31, Nicholas responded by arresting clergy, closing Catholic schools, and relocating a sizeable number of Poles and Lithuanians to Siberia where Catholics suddenly emerged as a significant minority. He also tried to control the Catholics by involving the pope as an ally. He visited Pope Gregory XVI in Rome in 1845, signed a concordat with the Vatican in 1847, and allowed some vacant episcopal sees to be filled and some new Catholic churches to be built, including St. Louis des Français and St. Peter and Paul in Moscow and Notre Dame in St. Petersburg. These churches were intended to serve foreigners, mainly French, Poles, Germans, Lithuanians, and Italians, who lived in the Russian Empire.

The concordat allowed the Church to restructure its dioceses to reflect the political changes that had occurred since the end of the Napoleonic wars and the

Congress of Vienna. Administratively, the Catholic Church was now divided into two main parts: Congress Poland and the Russian Empire. Congress Poland had the archdiocese of Warsaw and the dioceses of Kielce, Lublin, Podolia, Plock, Sandomir, Sejny and Augustowo, and Wladislaw. Russia had the archdiocese of Mogilev and the smaller dioceses of Minsk (Belorussia), Lutsk (Volhynia), Zhytomyr (Volhynia), Kamenets-Podol'skiy (Podolia), Samogitia (Lithuania), Kherson, and Vilna (Lithuania and part of Belorussia). In 1852, the new, huge diocese of Tiraspol replaced Kherson and its jurisdiction stretched across southern Russia. Catholics in the south lived mainly in Odessa and Saratov near the Caucasus, where a seminary was located, and included the Volga German Catholics whom Catherine the Great had brought into Russia.

Unfortunately for Nicholas, neither Pope Gregory nor his successor, Pope Pius IX (r. 1846–78), were inclined to undercut the Catholics in the Russian empire. Pius IX certainly joined Nicholas in opposition to a number of Western political movements and ideologies, particularly nationalism, liberalism, and socialism, but he complained bitterly about Russian repression of the Catholic Church and of the Poles. Nicholas dismissed publicity about intolerance as the propaganda of Polish émigrés.[17]

Nicholas wanted to level the Catholic Church and to promote Russian Orthodoxy as the unifying element in a multinational and multi-religious empire. Intolerance, however, was not working out.[18] The Poles continued to be bitter foes of the Russians, who usually responded with more repression, a cycle that destabilized the empire. A number of Russian intellectuals advocated a different approach to Catholicism. Mikhail Lunin thought it was the key to Russia's modernization and argued that the West, which the Russians were attempting to emulate, was the result of the Catholic faith and Western values. Peter Chaadayev, a leader of a group of Russian intellectuals called the Westerners, suggested that the Catholic Church was the midwife of freedom and creativity in Europe and might perform the same role in Russia. Nicholas censored his work and declared him a "madman."[19] The tsar died in 1855 after the Russian Empire suffered a defeat during the Crimean War, fought in part to improve the Russian Orthodox Church's control of Christian sites in the Holy Land in the Ottoman Empire.

Under Alexander II (r. 1855–81), the Catholic–Russian relationship remained conflicted. The Poles rebelled again in 1863–64, and Alexander answered with repression and more exiles to Siberia.[20] He also abandoned the concordat with the Vatican. In 1866 he forced the small Eastern Rite Catholic diocese of Chëlm in Congress Poland to merge with the Orthodox Church and he suppressed the Latin Rite dioceses of Podlachia in Poland and of Minsk and Kamieniec-Podolski in Russia.[21] The Holy See refused to recognize these suppressions, so the dioceses existed canonically but had no bishops. To the consternation of the Russians, the Poles won international sympathy and support while the Russians garnered nothing but scorn and opprobrium for their policy of oppression and persecution.[22]

On the other hand, Russia started to embrace some Western values. It set up elected assemblies in the countryside called *zemstvas*, which became the foundation for the growth of a liberal political party called the Constitutional Democrats or Kadets early in the next century, initiated some judicial reforms, including trial by jury, and took the step of beginning the emancipation of the serfs, which was massively complicated because the government did not establish a practical way for the peasants to own land and decided that the peasants had to remain in communes until they paid the government the expense of reimbursing the landed nobility for the loss of their serfs, euphemistically called "redemption payments." In addition, Russian intellectuals like Vladimir Soloviev (1853–1900), who some called Russia's John Newman, urged dialogue and reconciliation of the two major Christian religions, particularly in the face of such growing anti-Christian ideologies as nihilism, anarchism, communism, racism, and social Darwinism. Alexei Khomiakov, one of the leaders of a Pan-Orthodox movement called Slavophilism, urged continued repression and lamented, revealingly, that if freedom of conscience became law in Russia the upper and educated classes would all convert to Catholicism.[23]

For the popes, the interest in Western values and in Catholicism among some Russians intensified Rome's long-felt desire for reunion with the Orthodox Church in the latter half of the nineteenth century and led to a major push called the Church Union movement. It peaked in the first three decades of the twentieth century under the papacies of Popes Benedict XV and Pius XI.[24]

Under Alexander III (r. 1881–94), the son of Alexander II, the Russian government reversed policy and curbed Western influences, except for burgeoning industrialization, and persisted in seeing Catholics as an enemy. Fyodor Dostoevsky painted Catholics and Poles as the archenemy of the Russians.[25] Konstantin Pobedonostsev, the Ober-Procurator of the Holy Synod and the key advisor to both Alexander III and his son, Nicholas II, declared that every Catholic was a foe of Russia and a tool of the Vatican.[26] However, Alexander reestablished diplomatic relations with the Vatican and allowed some vacant bishoprics to be filled in the hope that a more normal relationship would help stem Polish resistance and a growing Russian revolutionary movement that found not only Poles and Lithuanians, but also Jews, Georgians, Ukrainians, Belorussians, Latvians, and Russians organizing to end serfdom, absolutism, imperialism, and religious persecution.

Nicholas II and the Provisional Government, 1894–1917

Under Nicholas II (r. 1894–1917), who was unprepared to rule and who faced a set of bewildering challenges, Catholic–Russian relations continued to be strained, but then suddenly in 1905 they took a dramatic turn for the better. The 1905 Revolution, the first of what turned out to be four revolutions in the first three decades of the twentieth century, occurred. In the wake of the disastrous Russo–Japanese War and Bloody Sunday, this massive popular revolution almost succeeded in bringing down the autocratic state. To break the back of the revolution Nicholas issued a decree of religious toleration in April and his famous manifesto in October, which promised a duma (parliament), elections, political parties, and protection for civil and human rights. The concessions split the revolutionaries and gave the government a temporary lease on life. The length of that lease depended on

Nicholas's ability to understand and successfully embrace two critical lessons from the 1905 Revolution. It was clear that the vast majority of the population, the peasants who had stuck with the "Elect of God" absolute monarchy through centuries of neglect and abuse, were revolutionary-minded, open to another form of government, and desirous of an array of Western values, including, above all, landownership and private property. In order to win back the peasants by giving them a stake in the existing system, the government had to address the burning issue of land reform. Second, war was a lethal danger to the regime and had to be avoided at all costs. The domestic issues confronting Nicholas, everything from industrialization to land reform to minority nationalism to religious freedom, were so vast, divisive, and delicate that they could be addressed, if at all, only with brilliant and focused leadership. Another war would open Pandora's box.

The government grasped the first lesson. Under Nicholas's prime minister, Peter Stolypin, it immediately started on the issues of land reform by eliminating economically untenable small strips of farmland and then establishing a peasant land bank to make low-interest loans to peasants in order to purchase land. It was a positive move and continued even though Stolypin was assassinated in 1911. Other reforms were also enacted, many of them stemming from the promises the government made in 1905. The government published a constitution called the fundamental law that transformed the autocratic monarchy into a constitutional monarchy and organized elections for the duma. The government did its best to qualify the concessions it had made in 1905 by limiting the right to vote to large landowners, damaging the duma by orchestrating protests and agents to disrupt its proceedings, and increasing the size of the police force to control or divide labor unions, minority nationalities, religious groups, political parties, and revolutionaries of sundry stripes. The period between 1905 and 1914 was chaotic and unsettling, but change was afoot and the possibilities were encouraging. Russia was moving, ever so incrementally, toward the Western value system.

The Catholic Church was ambivalent about Nicholas's religious policy. On one hand, it was pleased with the religious freedom law. It organized a political party called the Catholic Constitutional Party to solidify the promise of religious freedom and to push for separation of church and state. It also improved its organization, and by 1914 it had, excluding Congress Poland, 1,158 parishes, 1,491 churches, 1,358 chapels, 2,194 priests, and some 5 million believers.[27] With Congress Poland included, the number of Catholics in the Russian Empire in 1914 was close to 13 million, which constituted probably just more than 9 percent of the total population. The Church also published the first edition of a journal and newspaper and planned to organize a Russian Catholic Church with a unique Rite similar to the Ukrainian (Greek) Catholic Church. The pope asked Metropolitan Andrei Sheptytsky of Lviv (1865–1944) to help set up and find native Russian priests to organize and lead the new Russian Catholic Church. Sheptytsky was a dynamic Pole who had become Ukrainianized and was the leader of the Ukrainian Greek Catholics in nearby Austrian-controlled Galicia.

On the other hand, the Russians refused to grant toleration to the Eastern Rite Catholics who had been suppressed by Catherine the Great, Nicholas I, and

Alexander II, and were quite disturbed when some 233,000 of them still decided to return to the Catholic Church, albeit to the Latin Rite.[28] They also rejected the idea of a Russian version of the Eastern Rite, which frustrated Sheptytsky's plans. They were not happy over Catholic publications and decried the Catholic Constitutional Party. Increasingly, Nicholas listened to an uneducated monk by the name of Rasputin, curbed the duma, neglected land reform, or repressed dissent.

More ominously, the Russian government engaged in provocative intervention in the Balkans and, with French encouragement, turned increasingly hostile and belligerent to Austria-Hungary and its ally, Germany. Nicholas II failed to absorb the second lesson of the 1905 Revolution and, in doing so, opened the door to World War I. Instead of avoiding war at all costs, he embraced it as a distraction from reform. When the Russian army invaded Austrian Galicia, he jailed Sheptytsky and sent in "trainloads" of Orthodox clergy in order to prepare for the forced unification of the Ukrainian Greek Catholic Church with the Russian Orthodox Church.[29] He also suppressed the Catholic political party, Catholic newspapers and periodicals, and the embryonic Russian Catholic Church. When it turned out that the Russian army, though brave, could not win a victory against the Germans because of a shortage of weapons and supplies, inadequate logistics, poor leadership, and untrained and unarmed soldiers, Nicholas, who was notoriously indecisive, left the capital, Petrograd, renamed because St. Petersburg sounded too German, and went to the front where he proved that he was as incompetent a general as he was a monarch. By 1916 and early 1917 most Russians desperately wanted out of the war. No one was in charge in Petrograd. Soldiers left the front and went home to their villages. Food shortages cropped up everywhere, including the capital, where food riots broke out in early 1917. The Russian Empire was hemorrhaging.

In February 1917 the Second Revolution took place when Nicholas abdicated. This was a popular revolution in response to incompetence, arbitrary rule, brutal authoritarianism, and a failure to reform and Westernize. The people wanted out of the war and they wanted land. In place of the tsar a temporary regime drawn from the state duma called the Provisional Government took power. It announced that it would wield power only until such time as elections could be held and a more representative government could be installed. In the meantime, it reversed some of Nicholas' repressive measures and restored some basic freedoms. It was especially intent on religious freedom and toleration. It placed parochial schools under the Ministry of Education and it promulgated the Law on Freedom of Conscience, which effectively curtailed Russian Orthodoxy's place of primacy. The Russian Orthodox hierarchy was not pleased, but the Provisional Government allowed the Church to fill the office of patriarch that had been vacant since 1701. Patriarch Tikhon was elected in October 1917, a few days before the Bolshevik coup.[30]

As far as the Catholic Church was concerned, the Provisional Government established diplomatic relations with the Vatican and named A. I. Lysakovsky as its ambassador. It released Sheptytsky from prison and allowed him to convene an assembly or *sobor* of Russian Catholic priests in Petrograd, including Fathers Leonid Fedorov, Alexis Zerchanninov, and eventually Vladimir Abrikosov (1880–1966). Fr. Abrikosov was notable because he and his wife, Anna Ivanovna

Abrikosova (1882–1936), who took the religious name of Mother Catherine, began to build a Dominican order that belonged to the Byzantine Rite in Moscow that included nuns and third order laypersons. They also established a new parish called the Nativity of the Blessed Virgin Mary. Mother Catherine was particularly effective in attracting competent women (Poles, Russians, and even one Jewish convert) to become members of her Dominican convent.[31]

The *sobor*, which Sheptytsky had called, elected Fr. Leonid Fedorov as the exarch or leader of the new Russian Catholic Church. At the same time the government permitted the Latin Catholics to reorganize.[32] Their leaders named Bishop Eduard der Ropp of Vilnius as the archbishop of Mogilev and Bishop Jan Cieplak as his co-adjutor. Der Ropp and Cieplak immediately started authorizing the establishment of new churches and parishes throughout the Russian territory, from Petrograd to Moscow to Vladivostok. On 11 May 1917, Pope Benedict XV (r. 1894–1922) established the Congregation for Eastern Churches that had as its main task the coordination of a missionary effort in the Christian East. Pope Benedict sensed that the future of the Catholic Church in Russia was bright. He and Catholic leaders in Russia were optimistic and hoped that the Provisional Government could hold on to power.

Unfortunately, the Provisional Government proved almost as incompetent and ineffective as Nicholas II. First, it refused for months to set a date for an election, which compromised its credibility. Second, it postponed addressing the burning need for land reform, which alienated the peasantry. Third, it was not popular and did little to consolidate its authority and legitimacy or counter competition from assemblies called *soviets* that claimed to represent workers, soldiers, and peasants – the vast majority of the population. Finally, and most important, it not only failed to understand that the people wanted to get out of the war, but also, incredibly, concluded that Nicholas lost power, not because he pursued war, but because he pursued war incompetently. The Provisional Government decided that it should push the war more vigorously, even to the point of ordering the broken and defeated Russian army to launch a new offensive in the summer of 1917, which turned out to be a disaster. The Provisional Government was also naïve in terms of its political opponents. It believed that the monarchists or some general from the aristocratic fighting class would try to overthrow it. It discounted threats from the radical left, from the Bolshevik or Communist Party of Lenin, which was increasing its standing in the *soviets*.[33]

The communists were Marxists who opposed private property. They believed in an economic law called historical materialism, which claimed that life – all relationships, indeed history itself – was defined by economic class exploitation where one class expropriated the labor of a subject class, causing hardship, suffering, and conflict. The nature of the exploitation was shrouded by such extraneous things or superstructures as religion, nationalism, and patriotism, which the exploiting class wielded to keep the exploited class confused and distracted from its unjust condition. Such distractions would collapse as history moved forward and the true relationship of conflict between classes became apparent.

This law was as certain and automatic as the law of gravity. It engaged when conditions were ripe, which meant when a given society reached the point where the exploited overwhelmingly outnumbered the exploiters and moved to improve their condition. In medieval times, the middle class arose and took power from the landed nobility. It set up a system of private property and enterprise called capitalism that featured the creation of industries in some countries in the West. In industrialized countries, the peasants, who had worked the manors of the feudal nobility, improved their standard of living and evolved into a new economic class called the working class or *proletariat*. By the end of the nineteenth century the working class was the majority in the industrialized states of Germany, the United Kingdom, the United States, and elsewhere, and its dominant position foreshadowed the coming transformation or revolution where the working class, led by its leaders called socialists and eventually communists, would replace the capitalist class and establish a socialist society, that is, a society without private property. When that occurred, exploitation would end and dead skin like religion or nationalism would flake off and fall by the wayside. The Western value system would be toppled. Ironically, Marxism originated in the West where, while providing some insight on economic history, it was largely rejected because it was the antithesis of the Western value system. It was embraced in Russia for precisely that reason.

But the communists were not only Marxist socialists. They were also Leninists or Leninist-Stalinists. They represented an activist firebrand element of socialism that called for immediate revolutionary action because, they claimed, economic conditions were ripe for revolution everywhere around the globe. Lenin, the leader of the communist movement, argued that Marx had died (d. 1883) before capitalism gave birth to imperialism, which by the end of the nineteenth century had allowed the capitalist powers to appropriate the labor and raw materials of virtually every country and region of the world, thus creating a capitalist global order. According to Lenin, this development opened an opportunity for socialists to try to take power through any means available in undeveloped regions of the world like Russia, China, and India. In fact, it was easier to organize revolutions there than in the capitalist countries because the capitalists had fewer police and armies in their colonies than in their home countries. Revolution in undeveloped countries could be the spark, according to Lenin, that would precipitate the world revolution, that is, the worldwide movement toward socialism. Lenin changed the geographic and social focus of Marxism – from West to East and from workers to peasants.[34] He and his fellow communists demanded action. Conditions for revolution, according to Lenin, were already ripe.

Lenin's position on religion flowed from his belief that communists had to advance international revolution and take power. He believed that religion should be broadly attacked as part of the effort to push class warfare and revolution, but that the antireligious campaign was secondary to taking power and pushing revolution. It had to be dynamic and opportunistic. In a tract that helped crystalize communist policy on religion, he wrote:

> A Marxist must be a materialist, i.e., an enemy of religion. But he must be a *dialectical* materialist, i.e., one who organizes the struggle against religion not on abstract, detached, purely theoretical grounds . . . but concretely, on the basis of the *currently* proceeding class struggle, a struggle which is

educating the masses more and better than anything else. A Marxist ought to be able to judge the concrete situation as a whole; he must always be able to determine the boundary between anarchism and opportunism (this boundary is relative, mobile and ever-changing, but it exists); he must be not fall either into the abstract, verbal, and, in fact, empty "revolutionism" of the anarchist, or into the philistinism and opportunism of a petty-bourgeois or liberal *intel-ligent*, who is afraid of the struggle against religion, forgets about the task of his, reconciles himself with faith in god, and is guided not by the interests of the class struggle but by petty, meager little calculations: not to insult, not alienate or frighten away, (in line with) a wise rule: "live and let live," etc.[35]

Lenin and the communists thus were lethal opponents of the Catholic Church and of Western values, which the Church supported. They planned to annihilate the Catholic Church and every other religion, including the Russian Orthodox Church, and overturn the Western global order. Persecution of the Catholic Church would be geared to their political advantage and would have different domestic and international aspects, but the Catholic Church would be annihilated.

Notes

1 Cherniavsky [1953] 1970, p. 68; Strémooukhoff [1953] 1970, p. 113; Vernadsky 1968, p. 92. Also see Dunn 2004, p. 16 and Ostrowski 1998.
2 Miliukov [1942] 1972, p. 15; Strémooukhoff [1953] 1970, pp. 113–15. Also see Wolff 1959, pp. 291–311.
3 Dunn 2004, p. 17. Ivan left Possevino with no illusions about accepting the Florentine union. See Miliukov [1942] 1972, pp. 16–17.
4 Gudziak 1998, pp. 43–58.
5 L'Archivio della Sacra Congregazione degli Affari Ecclesiastici Straordinari, Pontificia Commissione, *Pro Russia*, scatola (box) 644 P.O., fascicolo (file) 29, Polish Embassy to the Holy See, Rome, 5 March 1934, fogli (sheet(s), 10r (2840/33) (henceforth cited as AES, *Pro Russia*, s., fasc., f.).
6 Ukrainian Orthodoxy showed the growth of Western influence in Russia in the seventeenth and eighteenth centuries. See Okenfuss 1995. Also see Hughes 1998, p. 300; Nolte 1969, pp. 113–14; Raeff 1994, pp. 286–87; and Treadgold 1973, pp. 58–62.
7 Olearius 1967, pp. 278–83.
8 Patriarch Nikon repeated the Catholic view that the church and state each operated in its own sphere but should a clash occur, then spiritual authority was supreme. He paid for his views by being removed as patriarch by Tsar Alexis. See Miliukov [1942] 1972, pp. 128–29, 136–37.
9 Dunn 2004, pp. 29–30.
10 See, for example, Frank 2002, p. 715.
11 Lencyk 1966, pp. 14–20; Zatko 1965, p. 8.
12 Davies 1982, 2: 84–86.
13 Inglot 1997, pp. 51–63. The Vatican reauthorized the Jesuits in 1814.
14 Dunn 2004, p. 44; Flynn 1970, pp. 249–65.
15 Konstantin Pobedonostsev, the Ober-Procurator of the Holy Synod under Alexander III and Nicholas II, believed the forced reunion was mishandled. See Curtiss 1940, p. 178. Also see Lencyk 1966, pp. 26, 32–89, 106.
16 Magocsi [1996] 2010, pp. 416, 419, 424, and 449.

17 Boudou 1923, 2: 3–4; Kelly 1986, p. 313.
18 Davies 1982, 2: 84.
19 Chaadayev 1969.
20 Catholics were sent to Siberia from as early as the reign of Ivan IV. Catherine II and the tsars in the nineteenth century were the main sponsors of forced resettlement of Catholics from the western provinces of the empire to Siberia. See Dunn 2004, pp. 15, 38, and 52.
21 There were other schemes afloat that aimed at forcing the Latin Rite bishops to join the Orthodox Church. See GARF, fund 109, opis. 2, dela. 712 (April 1866).
22 Boudou 1923, 2: 205–398, 448–86; Dunn 2004, pp. 57–58; Graham 1959, p. 68. Also see GARF, f. 109, op. 2, d. 482 (29 August 1864), d. 666 (28 February–10 March 1876).
23 Quoted in Palmieri 1907, p. 4.
24 On the challenges facing reunion, see Miliukov [1942] 1972, pp. 132–50. On the collapse of the Church Union movement, see Pettinaroli 2011, p. 83.
25 Davies 1982, 2: 92–93.
26 Byrnes 1968, p. 212.
27 Czaplicki 2000, p. 1.
28 Dunn 1977, p. 13; Zatko 1965, p. 25.
29 Paléologue 1923–25, pp. 213–14, Zugger 2001, pp. 96–97.
30 On the critical Moscow Council that elected Tikhon and created the conciliar institutions of the Russian Orthodox Church, see Destivelle 2015. Archbishop Evdokim, who came from North America to participate in the Council and who was unable to depart Soviet Russia after the Bolshevik Revolution, worked on an effort to find some basis of cooperation between the Russian Orthodox Church, the Anglican Church, and the Church of the Old Catholics. See GARF, f. 3431, op. 1, d. 645 (1/17 September 1918), l. 6.
31 Czaplicki and Osipova 2014, "Biography of Servant of God, Anna Ivanovna Abrikosova (Mother Catherine of Siena, OP)," at https://biographies.library.nd.edu/catalog/biography-0004, (accessed 2 April 2016); Dunn 2004, p. 65; also see Swift 1986, p. 30.
32 GARF, f. R1041, o. 1, d. 84 (1917), l. 28. There was some confusion about diocesan borders because of the burgeoning independence movements. See, for example, the bishop of Tiraspol's recommendation that reorganization wait until "normal order" prevails: GARF, f. R1041, op. 1, d. 84 (1917), l. 4.
33 Lenin changed the name of his party to the Communist Party in March 1918.
34 Adam Ulam in his dated but still valuable analysis of Lenin made this point. See Ulam 1974, pp. 28–29.
35 Lenin 1969, pp. 72–73.

References

Boudou, Adrien 1923, *Le Saint Siège et la Russe: Leurs Relations Diplomatiques au XIXe siècle*, 2 vols., Paris: Plon-Newrit et cie.

Byrnes, Robert F. 1968, *Pobedonostsev: His Life and Thoughts*, Bloomington: University of Indiana Press.

Chaadayev, Peter Yakovlevich 1969, *Peter Yakovlevich Chaadayev: Philosophical Letters & Apology of a Madman*, Mary-Barbara Zeldin (trans. and intro.), Knoxville: University of Tennessee Press.

Cherniavsky, Michael [1953] 1970, "Khan or Basileus: An Aspect of Russian Mediaeval Political Theory," in *The Structure of Russian History: Interpretive Essays*, Michael Cherniavsky (ed.), New York: Random House, pp. 65–79.

Curtiss, John S. 1940, *The Russian Church and the Soviet State, 1917–1950*, New York: Columbia University Press.

Czaplicki, Bronisław 2000, "A History of the Persecution," from *Kniga pomiati* 2000 Found at a History of the Persecutions: Catholic Church in Russia, pp. 1–42 (accessed 2 April 2016).

Czaplicki, Bronisław and Osipova, Irina 2014, *Book of Remembrance: Biography of Catholic Clergy and Laity in the Soviet Union (USSR) from 1918 to 1953*, Geraldine Kelly (trans.), and made available by University of Notre Dame at https://biographies.library. nd.edu/catalog/biography-0004 (accessed 2 April 2016).

Davies, Norman 1982, *God's Playground: A History of Poland*, 2 vols., New York: Columbia University Press.

Destivelle, Hyacinthe O. P. 2015, *The Moscow Council (1917–1918): The Creation of the Conciliar Institutions of the Russian Orthodox Church*, Metropolitan Hilarion (foreword), Michael Plekon and Vitaly Permiakov (eds.), Jerry Ryan (trans.), Notre Dame, IN: University of Notre Dame Press.

Dunn, Dennis J. 1977, *The Catholic Church and the Soviet Government, 1939–1949*, New York: *East European Quarterly* Series, distributed by Columbia University Press.

Dunn, Dennis J. 2004, *The Catholic Church and Russia: Popes, Patriarchs, Tsars and Commissars*, Aldershot, UK: Ashgate.

Flynn, James 1970, "The Role of the Jesuits in the Politics of Russian Education, 1801–1820, " *The Catholic Historical Review* 56, no. 2 (July): 249–65.

Frank, Joseph 2002, *Dostoevsky: The Mantle of the Prophet, 1871–1881*, Princeton, NJ: Princeton University Press.

GARF (Gosudarstennyi arkiv Rossiiskoi Federatsii) f. 109, f. 176, f. R1041, Moscow.

Graham, Robert A., SJ 1959, *Vatican Diplomacy: A Study of Church and State on the International Plane*, Princeton, NJ: Princeton University Press.

Gudziak, Borys A. 1998, *Crisis and Reform: The Kyivan Metropolitante, the Patriarchate of Constantinople, and the Genesis of the Union of Brest*, Cambridge, MA: Harvard University Press.

Hughes, Lindsey 1998, *Russia in the Age of Peter the Great*, New Haven, CT: Yale University Press.

Inglot, Mark, SJ 1997, *La Compagnia de Gesù nell Impero Russo (1772–1820) e la sua parte nella restaurazione general della Compania*, Rome: Editrice Pontificia Universita Gregoriana.

Kelly, J. N. D. 1986, *Oxford Dictionary of the Popes*, New York: Oxford University Press.

L'Archivio della Sacra Congregazione degli Affari Ecclesiastici Straordinari, Pontificia Commissione, *Pro Russia*, scatola (box), fascicolo (file), fogli (sheet(s)), Archivio Segreto Vaticano (cited as AES, *Pro Russia*, s., fasc., f.).

Lencyk, Wasyl 1966, *The Eastern Catholic Church and Czar Nicholas I*, Rome-New York: Ukrainian Catholic University Press.

Lenin, V. I. 1969, *V. I. Lenin ob ateizme, religiy i tserkvi*, Moscow: Misl.

Magocsi, Paul R. [1996] 2010, *A History of Ukraine: The Land and Its People*, Toronto: University of Toronto Press.

Miliukov, Paul [1942] 1972, *Outlines of Russian Culture*, 3 parts, part 1: *Religion and the Church in Russia*, Michael Karpovich (ed.), Valentine Ughet and Eleanor Davis (trans.), New York: A. S. Barnes and Company, Perpetua Book.

Nolte, Hans-Heinrich 1969, *Religiöse Toleranz in Russland, 1600*–1725, Göttingen: Musterschmidt-Verlag.

Okenfuss, Max J. 1995, *The Rise and Fall of Latin Humanism in Early-Modern Russia: Pagan Authors, Ukrainians, and the Resiliency of Muscovy*, Leiden: E. J. Brill.

Olearius, Adam 1967, *The Travels of Olearius in 17th-Century Russia*, Samuel H. Baron (ed. and trans.), Stanford, CA: Stanford University Press.

Ostrowski, Donald 1998, *Muscovy and the Mongols: Cross-Cultural Influences on the Steppe Frontier, 1304–1589*, Cambridge: Cambridge University Press.

Paléologue, Maurice 1923–25, *An Ambassador's Memoirs*, F. A. Holt (trans.), vol. 1 London: Hutchinson.

Palmieri, Aurelio 1907, "Catholic Ideas and Tendencies in Modern Russian Thought," *The New York Review* 3, no. 1 (July–August 1907): 3–23.

Pettinaroli, Laura 2011, "Afterword," in *The Holy See and the Holodomor: Documents from the Vatican Secret Archive on the Great Famine of 1932–1933 in Soviet Ukraine*, Athanasius D. McVay and Lubomyr Y. Luciuk (eds.), Toronto: University of Toronto, pp. 83–87.

Raeff, Marc 1994, *Political Ideas and Institutions in Imperial Russia*, Boulder, CO: Westview Press.

Strémooukhoff, Dimitri [1953] 1970, "Moscow the Third Rome: Sources of the Doctrine," in *The Structure of Russian History: Interpretive Essays*, Michael Cherniavsky (ed.), New York: Random House, pp. 108–25.

Swift, Mary Grace OSU 1986, "Moscow's Catherine of Sienna," *America*, 26 July 1986, p. 30.

Treadgold, Donald 1973, *The West in Russia and China, Vol. 1: Russia 1472–1917*, Cambridge: Cambridge University Press.

Ulam, Adam 1974, *Expansion and Coexistence: A History of Soviet Foreign Policy, 1917–1973*, New York: Praeger.

Vernadsky, George 1968, *A History of Russia*, New Haven, CT: Yale University Press.

Wolff, Robert Lee 1959, "The Three Romes: The Migration of an Ideology and the Making of an Autocrat," *Daedalus* 88, no. 2 (Spring): 291–311.

Zatko, James 1965, *Descent into Darkness: The Destruction of the Roman Catholic Church in Russia, 1917–1923*, Notre Dame, IN: University of Notre Dame Press.

Zugger, Rev. Christopher Lawrence 2001, *The Forgotten: Catholics of the Soviet Empire From Lenin Through Stalin*, Syracuse, NY: Syracuse University Press.

3 Soviet Russia and the Catholic Church, 1917–1921

Communist government and the Catholic Church, 1917–1920

Lenin made his appearance in Petrograd in April 1917, courtesy of the German military. The Germans wanted to bring the war to an end. In January 1917 they announced that they were going to engage in unrestricted submarine warfare on the open seas, that is, the German navy would sink any ship that approached England or France even if the ship belonged to a non-belligerent and neutral state. The United States objected to the policy, but the Germans went forward anyway. When they refused to back down, the United States declared war on Germany in April 1917. The Germans had anticipated the American entrance into the war and responded with Lenin.

Lenin, the leader of the Bolshevik Party, was living in self-imposed exile in Switzerland (a neutral country), where he was bankrolled and mothballed by the German government in the event that it might be able to use him someday to rattle the stability of the Romanov regime.[1] What appealed to the Germans about Lenin was that he was the only leader on the Russian political scene who favored an end of the war between Russia and Germany and who had a real chance to take power in Russia in the near anarchy enveloping Petrograd in the wake of Nicholas's abdication, the tone-deaf Provisional Government, and the emergence of popular peasant and workers' assemblies called *soviets* that, in effect, rivaled and curtailed the authority and legitimacy of the Provisional Government. The Germans were not sympathetic with his communist ideas, but with his promise to end what he called a war of imperialism. They reasoned that if they could close down the eastern front, they could in theory transfer their armies from the eastern part of Europe to the western front and overcome the English and French armies before the American army could reach Europe. The Germans calculated that it would take the Americans about one year to train and then transport an army across the Atlantic Ocean, which turned out to be right, so they had one year to knock the Russians out of the war. They put Lenin and his fellow Bolshevik leaders on a sealed train (sealed because they did not want any of his ideas to seep into German soil), sent him across Germany into Finland, and then on to Petrograd where he arrived at Finland Station in April 1917, just after the tsarist state had fallen and as the Provisional Government was attempting to establish its legitimacy and authority.

In the topsy-turvy days following Lenin's arrival, the Provisional Government attempted to organize an offensive against Germany in June. When that failed, the new leader of the Provisional Government, Alexander Kerensky, fearing a military coup led by General Lavr Kornilov in September, armed the Red Guard supporters of the Bolshevik Party to help block Kornilov, who never really made a serious attempt to topple the government. In October the Third or Communist Revolution transpired when the Provisional Government collapsed in the face of a Bolshevik coup. With Kerensky fleeing the country, Lenin set up the Russian Socialist Federated Soviet Republic (RSFSR) or Soviet Russia. The government was highly centralized with the Party leader controlling an executive committee called the Political Bureau or Politburo of the Central Committee. Key members of the Politburo included Joseph Stalin, Leon Trotsky, Grigory Zinoviev, Lev Kamenev, and Nikolai Bukharin. The Bolsheviks changed their name to the Communist Party in 1918.

The Communist coup d'état was successful because it was backed by soldiers and sailors attracted to the Communist pledge to end Russia's involvement in World War I. War dictated the course of events in Russia. The soldiers and sailors, who were mainly peasants, had no sympathy with communist ideology. They wanted peace and an opportunity to go home and take possession of the land.

The Bolshevik Revolution was disquieting to most Catholic leaders in Russia. They feared a communist government would reverse the gains the Catholic Church had made under the Provisional Government and begin a general persecution of religion. Their fears soon materialized.

On 8 November 1917, Lenin issued a decree on land that, among other things, declared that churches and other religious organizations could not own land. On 17 December, another decree placed all land, including that owned by religious organizations, under government ownership. On 24 December, all schools, including religious schools, theological academies, and seminaries, were nationalized and placed under the People's Commissar for Public Education. Religious instruction of those under eighteen was prohibited. On 31 December, the registration of births was transferred from religious organizations to the state and religious marriages were declared invalid, so only marriages licensed by the state were deemed legal. In addition, the government denounced the institution of marriage and what it called bourgeois morality, and encouraged free love, which had the dire consequence of increasing the number of illegitimate children and orphans. It claimed, too, that the family, rather than being a safe haven for protecting women and rearing children, was an institution that exploited them.[2]

On 23 January 1918, the government promulgated a new constitution that called for separation of church and state, but left the state deeply involved in religious affairs and basically reduced the ability of the organized religions to operate and survive. The new law reaffirmed that religious groups could not own property, teach religion in public or private schools and to minors, or be recognized as a legal person with juridical rights. On 23 January, the regime declared that church workers would not be paid a salary. On 2 February, it asserted again that churches could neither own property nor receive any state subsidy. It announced shortly thereafter that some historic church buildings would be turned into museums, no one associated with religious organizations could be paid a salary or stipend, and religious organizations could not have bank accounts.[3]

On 29 January, the Commissariat of War stipulated that all property of military church units was subject to confiscation by secular military units. In August the authorities nationalized church property and ruled that religious organizations had no legal rights. The government also ruled that henceforth for a religious organization to function, a group of twenty believers had to apply to the state for a license to register as a parish, to use a church building, and to hire a "cult servant." It started to close monasteries and convents and to replace religious instruction in schools with required courses on atheism.[4] It also began in 1918 to promote widespread, antireligious propaganda, and it soon substituted a new calendar of holidays and festivals associated with the Communist Revolution and the Communist Party leadership for religious holidays and worship days, and adopted the Gregorian calendar, which the Orthodox Church opposed. At the same time, the secret police began to arrest clergy and religious ministers. The Soviet government also began a general propaganda campaign to undermine religion and promote atheism.[5]

The Catholic leaders protested the antireligious laws, but were ambivalent about a course of action. Monsignor Konstantin Budkiewicz, the dean of the clergy in Petrograd, argued for defiance and a refusal to obey the rulings. Archbishop Eduard von der Ropp, the archbishop of Mogilev and metropolitan of the Catholic Church, pushed for compliance because he predicted that the Communists, who also wanted to abolish private property and stoke international revolution, would soon be toppled and replaced by a more tolerant government.[6]

Der Ropp's analysis had merit because the Communists were truly a fringe party with few supporters, but Lenin proved a brilliant politician. He quickly gained a measure of support among the rank-and-file soldiers and sailors by signing an armistice with Germany in December 1917 and then by opening up negotiations to terminate Russia's involvement in World War I. While the treaty negotiations were under way, he moved the capital from Petrograd to Moscow to gain a buffer against the Germans and created two key coercive institutions that boosted his hold on power – the Red Army and a secret police force called the Cheka (Emergency Commission).[7] Commissar of War Leon Trotsky organized the Red Army by persuading some 50,000 Russian army officers to serve as the nucleus of this new armed force. The regime bound the officers and new recruits to the regime by giving them decent wages and prerogatives and by setting up eventually a parallel structure of political officers who monitored the political allegiance of the professional military officers. Felix Dzerzhinsky, the Polish communist, organized and led the Cheka. Lenin used it to remove political rivals and opponents of the Communist regime and to build a totalitarian society. It introduced forced labor camps or gulags, which were chiefly located in Siberia, as a tool to control the population and to extract labor from real or imagined enemies of the new Communist order.[8] Intellectuals and liberals were some of the first prisoners of the gulags. The Solovetsky Islands in the White Sea also became part of the gulag, and it was the prison where many religious leaders were sent.

The Treaty of Brest-Litovsk was finally signed with the Germans on 3 March 1918. Under the terms of Brest-Litovsk, Soviet Russia lost Poland, the Baltic States, Ukraine, Bessarabia, and Finland. It was a draconian treaty to which many of Lenin's supporters objected, but Lenin sold it on the grounds that it would not last. He believed that the American involvement in the war would lead to Germany's defeat and the collapse of the German government. When that happened, Lenin argued, the Treaty of Brest-Litovsk would be nullified.

This treaty drastically affected the Catholic Church in Soviet Russia. It removed from the control of the Communists more than 11 million Catholics, reducing the number of Catholics in Soviet Russia from 13 million to about 1.6 million. The border changes called for major adjustments for the Catholic Church in Poland and in Soviet Russia.[9] The treaty also anticipated an independent Poland, which was confirmed when Germany surrendered in November 1918, and this new Polish state, with a population of some 27 million citizens, was an overwhelmingly Catholic country.

However, the Treaty of Brest-Litovsk, along with the other Soviet policies, soon precipitated civil war, which seemed to fulfill Archbishop der Ropp's prediction. The Russian Civil War pitted the former supporters of the old regime called the Whites against the Communist forces called the Reds. It was a seesaw affair that saw most of the populations – the peasants, the liberals, the minority nationalists, and other non-Communist socialists – sit on the sidelines. They liked neither the Reds nor the Whites. Communist policies on landownership, private business, national autonomy, and religious freedom were objectionable, but they were largely unenforceable because of the war. The Whites represented a return to the old order, but they, like the Communists, could not implement their platform. The vast majority of the people in the former Russian Empire bided their time and perhaps hoped that the Reds and Whites would destroy one another. Many, however, did not trust the Whites, particularly after the Entente Powers – the former allies of the toppled tsarist government, including England, France, Japan, and, as of April 1917, the United States – intervened in the Civil War in favor of the Whites because they thought the Whites held out the promise of taking Russia back into World War I and of reestablishing the eastern front, which would prevent the Germans from transferring troops from Eastern Europe to Western Europe, where the battle was stalemated. The Entente states also wanted to prevent weapons and ammunition that they had stockpiled in ports like Murmansk and Archangel from falling into the hands of the Reds and aimed to protect the Czech Legion, which was trying to cross Russia to exit from Vladivostok after the eastern front was closed.

The leadership of the Orthodox Church, including Patriarch Tikhon, openly sympathized with and supported the Whites, which distinguished it from the equivocating masses and made the Orthodox Church vulnerable to charges of backing the old order and of foreign intervention.[10] In May 1918 the Communists, in the face of protests from foreign governments and Pope Benedict XV, executed the Romanov family of Nicholas II, fearing perhaps a White push toward Yekaterinburg, where the family was held in prison.

When World War I ended in November 1918 with Germany's surrender and subsequent evacuation from Ukraine, Lenin immediately tore up the Treaty of Brest-Litovsk and had the Red Army occupy and claim Ukraine for Soviet Russia. He did not try to reclaim Poland, the Baltic states, Finland, and Bessarabia for fear of provoking the French and British, who were monitoring Russian affairs from Versailles, where peace negotiations related to the end of World War I were under way. In 1919 the Entente Powers, except Japan and the United States, withdrew their forces from Russia. The Americans had to wait until the ice around Vladivostok melted in spring 1920. The Japanese did not want to depart, but eventually evacuated the Maritime Province and Vladivostok in 1922 and Sakhalin Island in 1925.[11]

Meanwhile, the Civil War in Russia continued and the outcome was far from certain. The Reds had an advantage because of the quality of their leadership, flexibility based on their belief in the inevitability of their cause, and the mistakes of the hidebound Whites. However, the Whites had the support of the Russian Orthodox Church and Patriarch Tikhon. The patriarch made clear his objections to the Communists and their continuing antireligious legislation. In 1919 the Soviet government outlawed religious instruction of children under the age of eighteen and closed additional monasteries. However, it could show flexibility when it saw an advantage. In the summer of 1919, for example, the Red Army captured Omsk, which was the capital of White opposition in Siberia. The Communists, who had supine support in Siberia, decided to keep the White regime's "Orthodox, Catholic, Lutheran, 'Jewish' Old Believer, and Muslim" workers in place and to bind them to the Soviet government by an oath of loyalty, sworn, surprisingly, in the name of "almighty God."[12]

As the antireligious fight between the Soviet government and the Orthodox Church escalated, Pope Benedict XV decided to protest publicly the intensifying attacks on the Orthodox Church.[13] The regime retaliated by arresting Archbishop der Ropp on 17 November 1919. It then sent him to Poland as part of a prisoner exchange that brought Karl Radek, a key Communist leader, to Soviet Russia.[14] In January 1920 a Catholic clerical conference in Petrograd passed a resolution stating that Catholics could not be members of the Communist Party. The declaration, while understandable, was unnecessary, and in the eyes of one observer confirmed the government's opinion of the Catholic Church as a counterrevolutionary institution.[15]

By 1920 the Civil War had clearly shifted in favor of the Red Army. It was then that the newly independent nation of Poland decided to strike the Red Army in order to reclaim territory that it had lost to Russia as a result of the famous Partitions of Poland that took place in the eighteenth century. The Polish and Red Armies battled back and forth and the Red Army nearly captured Warsaw, but eventually the Poles, with help from the French, forced the Treaty of Riga on the Communist government in March 1921. The Communists agreed to move their border east, giving Poland control of a part of western Ukraine and western Belorussia, but most of Ukraine and Belorussia stayed under the control of the Communists, which was an outcome that the Poles regretted but lacked the power to change. As for the Communists, they resented giving any territory to the Poles and vowed to retake it.

The Treaty of Riga further reduced the size and structure of the Catholic Church in Soviet Russia. It transferred to Poland the western part of Ukraine (including the cities of Ternopol, Stanislaw, and Lviv) and the western part of Belorussia (including the city of Pinsk), and split the dioceses of Lutsk, Vilna, Lublin, and Samogitia and part of the dioceses of Zhytomyr, Kamieniec-Podolski, and Minsk. Three bishops who found their dioceses divided by the new boundary set by the Treaty of Riga were caught in the middle. Bishop Zygmunt Łoziński of Minsk was arrested by the Soviet regime in 1920 and then deported to Poland in 1922. Bishop Piotr Mańkowski of Kamieniec-Podolski and Archbishop Ignacy Dub-Dubowski of Lutsk-Zhytomyr departed Soviet Russia with the Polish troops who left after the Treaty of Riga. Their auxiliary bishops and most of the priests in their dioceses joined them.[16] Their decision was prompted by the fact that they had publicly supported Poland during the Soviet–Polish War and it was clear that they were persona non grata in Soviet Russia, which formally expelled them. Bishop Joseph Kessler of the diocese of Tiraspol found himself in Bessarabia on the Romanian side of the Romanian–Russian border and the Soviet government refused to allow him to move to the Soviet side.[17]

What was left of the hierarchy of the Catholic Church was centered in Petrograd and consisted of Archbishop Jan Cieplak, who assumed leadership of the Latin Rite archdiocese of Mogilev after der Ropp's deportation to Poland, and the previously mentioned Monsignor Konstantin Budkiewicz, the dean of the clergy. In addition, Exarch Leonid Fedorov, the head of the newly formed Russian Catholic Church, which had nine Russian priests and perhaps a few hundred followers, resided in Petrograd.[18] The Mogilev archdiocese had 331 parishes and 400 priests, most of whom were non-Russian. The Catholic Church set up another diocese in Vladivostok under Bishop Karol Sliwowski in 1923, just after the Japanese vacated the city, and it had approximately 30,000 Catholics and a few priests. One retired bishop, Anton Zerr, lived in Tiraspol on the Soviet side of the Romanian–Soviet border. The total number of Catholics dwelling in post-Riga Soviet Russia was about 1,160,000, and of that total about 600,000 were Poles and the other 560,000 or so were Lithuanians, Ukrainians, Belorussians, Latvians, Volga Germans, and a few Italians.

With the conclusion of the Polish–Soviet War, the Reds mopped up the rest of the White forces. In 1921 the last White army of any significance under General Petr Wrangel boarded French and Greek ships and evacuated from the Crimea. The Communists now wielded uncontested power.

Communist government and the Catholic Church, 1921

The Communist attitude toward the small Catholic Church was decidedly malevolent, an attitude based on atheist ideology, Russian tradition, and experience. Although the Russian Orthodox Church was by far the major victim of the Soviet government's antireligious effort, the Catholic Church was the largest and most influential Christian religion in the world. It was also a leading evolver and supporter of the Western value system that underpinned the capitalist global order. In short, it was the major religious challenge to the international communist movement and held the distinction of being the Kremlin's principal, international religious enemy. Specifically, the Communist hostility to the Catholic Church hinged on seven overlapping reasons, some of which applied to religion in general and others of which were unique to the Catholic Church. As mentioned, the Communists were Marxists who believed that there was no God, no afterlife, no absolute morality, and no immortal soul. The only reality was the physical, material world and the condition of economic exploitation. Religion was a product of exploitation, superstition, and ignorance. They were convinced that its demise would clarify reality for and improve the life of the masses.

Second, religion in Soviet Russia was a problem in the mind of the Communists because it kept the peasants, the majority of the population, ignorant of history's drive toward an unexploitative society, toward communism. Although religion was a declining and antiquated force, it was a drag on progress in a backward society like Soviet Russia, where it was a tool exploiters used to keep the masses impervious to social and economic injustice. It was, as Marx declared, the "opium of the people." The Communists held that its departure would accelerate the coming revolution in Soviet Russia.

Third, Lenin was a will-to-power politician. He and the Communist elite agreed with a growing number of political philosophers in Western Europe that willpower dictated the pace of events in history. Although Marx and Engels had stipulated that revolution or the social movement from a backward to a more advanced socioeconomic system, from capitalism to communism, would take place only when conditions were ripe for that transition – namely, when society was industrialized and had a large majority working class – Lenin believed that it was indeed possible to accelerate that change if there were a group of iron-willed, dedicated leaders who would not stop at anything in order to push a given society forward. He thought that a direct attack on religion would help propel the whole revolutionary process, particularly in a country like Soviet Russia.

Fourth, the Catholic Church was a world religion. It had an independent leader in the pope who had international standing. It was very influential in the capitalist and the developing world, where it could move people and some governments. It directly competed with and opposed the communist worldview of human nature and reality, which all religions did, but the Catholic Church, with its missionaries, churches, schools, and hospitals was the largest Christian denomination in the world and was on every continent. It provided the main spiritual and moral underpinning of the capitalist world order and of Western values. An attack on it not only weakened a strong and intrinsic foe, but also could help move forward the international revolution.

Fifth, the Catholic Church was viewed as a long-term enemy of the Russian nation because of its role in helping to evolve the national identities of the Ukrainian and Belorussian peoples and in growing Western values among the East Slavs. The Communist Party included many Russian nationalists who identified with this traditional anti-Catholic bias and who wanted to continue the tsarist policy of persecuting the Catholic Church.

Sixth, Catholicism was the religion of the majority of Poles, Lithuanians, Hungarians, Czechs, Slovaks, Austrians, and about one-third of the Germans and Latvians, who shared or were very close to the western border of Soviet Russia. The Russian Communist government had border disagreements with some of these nations, considered some of them fertile ground for revolutionary activity, and considered others potential threats. Damaging the Catholic Church could destabilize these governments and open opportunities for pushing the international revolution, enlarging Soviet Russia's borders, and improving Soviet security.

Finally, Catholics in Soviet Russia were largely non-Russians, mainly Poles, Lithuanians, Ukrainians, and Belorussians, who were concentrated in the western part of the Soviet state along the borders with Poland and the Baltic states. From the Kremlin's perspective, the Catholic Church in Soviet Russia, although minute, was a security concern – a group of citizens who might cooperate with their coreligionists on the other side of the border and who, in any event, had an allegiance to a foreigner, the pope, whom the Soviet government could not control. Attacking, repressing, and forcibly removing Catholics from the borderlands enhanced Soviet security.

In March 1919 Lenin set up the Communist International or Comintern. Its purpose was to spread the Communist Revolution internationally, to knock down Western values and global order and, with them, the Catholic Church, and to replace the Western system with a Communist world system that answered to Moscow. Its strategy to achieve that purpose was to set up Communist parties around the globe that were subordinate to Soviet Russia and that would do Soviet bidding in helping to start revolutionary activity.[19] Soon small Communist parties were set up in Germany, Italy, France, Turkey, China, Iran, England, India, the United States, and other developed and developing countries. The international revolution was the ultimate guarantee of Soviet power. The Communists knew that they had come to power in a non-industrialized country where most citizens were peasants engaged in agriculture rather than workers involved in industry, so they were keen to start the international fire that would allow Communists to take power in the industrial West and help the Communists in Russia quickly industrialize and grow a working class, the natural constituency of the Communists.

The Comintern's initial focus was on countries in Europe and Asia because they were geographically proximate to Soviet Russia. In Europe, the Communists organized uprisings or tried to overthrow governments in Germany, Bulgaria, and Hungary in the immediate post–World War I period. In Italy, their activities helped bring Benito Mussolini and his anti-Communist Fascist Party to power in 1922. They worked to infiltrate the British trade unions and the Labour Party, and they set up strong Communist parties in France under Maurice Thorez, in Italy under Palmiro Togliatti, in Germany under Ernst Thälmann, and in the United States under Earl Browder. They also cultivated and found supporters and agents among intellectuals in these countries.

In Asia, the Comintern also worked to stimulate revolution. It tried to penetrate Islamic societies, but generally speaking its avowed atheism abhorred Muslims. It found the Arab regions impenetrable. In Iran the Comintern tried to foster the

Communist Party of Iran, but that effort proved abortive. It was able to attach itself to Kemal Ataturk's movement in Turkey that aimed to set up a Turkish state in the face of British and French opposition after the Ottoman Empire fell at the end of World War I, but once Ataturk achieved his goal, he turned on the Communist Party of Turkey and beheaded it. He rounded up its leaders, all of them, and put them on a boat in the Black Sea and the boat mysteriously sank. In non-Muslim regions, the Communists had somewhat more success. In India, the freedom movement disconcerted the Communists because it took the line of passive resistance. The Communists could think only in terms of violence, and they didn't know what to do with Indian passive resistance. For example, they might get together a big crowd, but instead of going where they wanted it to go, it wandered off to temples and started praying, and so India was hard to deal with, although the horse did not throw the rider as in Persia. In Outer Mongolia, the Communists were able to take power and set up a satellite in 1921 that answered to Moscow. It became the prototype that Moscow used for satellites in Eastern Europe after World War II.

The Comintern also brought Korean and Vietnamese Communists to the Soviet Union for training with the intention of using them to revolt against Japanese and French colonial rule when the time was right. It was a puzzle to many outsiders at the time as to why the Soviet Union was investing so much time and resources on educating nationals from remote countries that were ground down under foreign rule and seemed inert and helpless. The time would come when these people would be neither helpless nor inert, and that time would come quickly – in a single generation, illustrative of the powerful regenerative force of awakened nationalism.

In China, too, the Communists had great success, at least for a while. In 1921 the Comintern organized the Chinese Communist Party (CCP), and one year later the Comintern arranged to have the CCP join the popular Kuomintang Party (KMT) of Sun Yat-sen, a fateful decision that Sun endorsed because he could find no Western allies to help China move forward.[20] The KMT hoped to dislodge foreigners from China, including the British who were in Hong Kong. The Communists provided weapons and training and the KMT provided popular support and soldiers. In 1927 Chiang Kai-shek, Sun's successor, turned on the Communists and tried to wipe them out in the so-called Shanghai massacre.[21] A few escaped, including Mao Zedong, who carried on a low-level civil war against the KMT and was eventually forced to take refuge in the far northwest, in Shensi Province, an event called "the Long March," where the Comintern could extend an umbilical cord across the Gobi Desert from the Soviet satellite in Outer Mongolia in order to keep the CCP alive so that it could be used at a later and more opportune time.

Leaders of the Catholic Church around the globe were alert to Moscow's effort to expand communism, which some of them saw as an attempt to halt the advance of Western values around the world and posit in their stead a totalitarian system of government, a sort of dynamic Byzantine-Mongol model of authoritarianism, driven by class warfare, without the moderating influence of Orthodoxy. Cardinal Aleksander Kakowski, the archbishop of Warsaw, called communism the antithesis of civilization and Cardinal August Hlond, the primate of Poland, saw it as the work of Satan. Leading Catholic intellectuals and writers, including Jacques Maritain in France, Fritz Gerlich in Germany, and Hilaire Belloc, G. K. Chesterton, Graham Greene, Evelyn Waugh, Christopher Dawson, and J. R. R. Tolkien in Great Britain assailed communism as a dire threat to Western civilization. Chesterton recalled that Catholic culture throughout history had stood against the barbarians from the East, who were now gathering under the banner of "Bolshevism." He and others looked to Poland as the first line of defense.[22]

Catholic leaders did what they could to block and frustrate the Communists. The Vatican knew that communism thrived in an environment of instability, so it worked to stabilize countries in Eastern Europe near the Soviet border. It signed concordats with Latvia in 1922, Poland in 1925, and Lithuania and Romania in 1927, and a modus vivendi with Czechoslovakia in 1928. In addition it signed the Lateran Treaty with Mussolini in 1929, which regularized relations between the Vatican and the Italian government and set up Vatican City as a sovereign state. The Holy See hoped that stabilizing church–state relations in Italy would remove an issue that the Communists could exploit.

The Vatican also diligently worked on a concordat with the German Weimar government. The challenge was that the Treaty of Versailles had changed the borders and required delicate negotiations to replace German bishops with bishops of the nations that now controlled what had been German territory. The Vatican wanted a countrywide concordat because one-third of Germany's population was Roman Catholic, which per capita gave Germany the largest number of Catholics in Central and Eastern Europe. Although most Germans were Protestant, mainly Lutherans, the Catholic population was still larger than that of Poland, Hungary, and Lithuania combined. The Vatican approached the problem through a *divide et impera* strategy, signing separate concordats with various German *länder*, with Prussia in 1929, and with Baden in 1932. Finally, it reached an agreement with the German government on 10 September 1933, but by then the Nazis were in power, so it signed a concordat (*Reichskondordat*) with the Third Reich, what it called a *malum necessarium*, because it did not want to appear as endorsing Nazi policies, but it wanted the agreement to settle ecclesiastical administration.[23]

The Vatican and other Catholic representatives also frequently briefed governments about the Communist menace, particularly in Germany and in various Eastern European countries. The Church also encouraged Catholics to become involved in politics, labor unions, and youth organizations to block or balance Communist influence.[24] Pope Pius' first encyclical, *Ubi Arcano*, issued in December 1922, decried false ideologies and asked Catholics and others to take civil and political action to promote international justice and peace, a clarion call that gave birth to the Catholic Action movement. Although Catholics were split by national, social, class, and educational differences, there was a common sense among believing Catholics in Europe that the faith, the papacy, and the Western tradition were under attack by the Communists and other secularizing forces and had to be shielded. Numerous Catholics became involved in Catholic Action activities, politics, and political parties in the interwar period and adopted staunch anti-Communist positions that in some Eastern European countries led them to back far right zealots who were not only anti-Communist, but also anti-Semitic.[25] Within the Vatican were powerful philo- and anti-Semitic voices, which ended up publicly producing an equivocal condemnation of anti-Semitism in 1928.[26]

The Vatican was also interested in promoting Catholic–Orthodox cooperation in the new Eastern European countries that had a predominately Orthodox population, particularly in Romania because its intellectual elite had a Western orientation. Rome was interested in improving ties not only to curb communism and instability, but also to build bridges between faith communities. Generally speaking, the Romanian Orthodox Church was receptive to good relations with the Roman Catholic Church. It was a way for it to maintain and secure its autonomy in the world of Orthodoxy and to contain the Romanian Greek Catholic Church, which it viewed as a rival that might siphon off some of its believers. Although Rome was certainly interested in uniting with the Romanian Orthodox Church, the two Churches concentrated in the interwar period on cooperation to maintain social order and harmony.[27]

Despite the Soviet government's rivalry with the Catholic Church internationally and its persecution domestically, the Kremlin did not appreciably intensify attacks on the Catholic Church in 1921. There seemed to be two reasons for the hiatus. There was an internal debate in the Communist Party between hardliners who wanted to spill blood in the streets and pragmatists who saw an advantage in tolerating the religious groups in return for support. The pragmatists had the upper hand in 1921.[28] More important, however, was the massive uprising of peasants in early 1921 just as the Civil War and Russo–Polish War ended.

Lenin wanted to build a Communist society in Russia. Part of that goal could be achieved by destroying religion, including the Catholic Church. Above all, it meant the abolition of private property, which was central to Westernization and capitalism and at the heart of the Communist Revolution. Lenin's conundrum was that peasants, who constituted about 83 percent of the population, had grabbed land during the chaos of the abdication of the tsarist government, the fall of the Provisional Government, and the Civil War. He planned to take it away from them so that he could use the land and its products to finance the industrialization of society and to create a large working class. Lenin wanted to force collective labor, working in common instead of individual enterprise. To further this basic aim of communism, it was believed that all industrial workers could be trusted because they were not contaminated by the ownership of property. The nature or plan of factory labor specialized the workers, that is, they neither made all of what they worked on nor owned any part of the finished product. Whereas peasants either owned their land or aspired to own it, and the product of their labor, what they produced, was their own. So the Communists from the start held that peasants could not be claimed for socialism, that they were sure to resist it, and that the only peasants who could be counted on were the agricultural laborers or hired hands, and only so long as they remained without property. The Communists abhorred peasants, whom they thought of as petit bourgeoisie – grasping rustics who yearned for private land and middle-class status and who were deeply religious and utterly clueless that history was ushering in the advanced order of communism in place of capitalism. Marx spoke of the stupidity of farmers, and he would have liked to do away with them, but his followers were unable to do so because no regime can do without producers of food.

When Lenin attempted to expand his policy of collectivization in early 1921 as the Civil War ended, he ran into massive peasant opposition, more threatening than the White movement. The peasants were not about to see Russia drift back to the days of Muscovite absolutism where they did the work and the government and its supporters benefited. They wanted private property and economic freedom. Sailors from the Kronstadt naval base joined the peasants, which put a sharp point on the population's discontent with Communist policies because the sailors had been so instrumental in the success of the Communist coup in October 1917. The non-Communist political parties and intellectuals also joined the mounting chorus of resistance and demanded reforms, civil and political rights, the rule of law, individual freedom, and representative government. Minority nationality groups also pushed for independence. The religious organizations began to organize, too, with some like the Catholic Church advocating religious freedom and separation of church and state, and others like the Russian Orthodox Church demanding an end of persecution and antireligious legislation. The peasant rebellion now promised to make the Communist victory in the Civil War pyrrhic.

In a novel and expedient move Lenin backed off of complete collectivization of the land and allowed the peasants to control (not own) the land, hire labor, and sell their produce for a profit after they paid a tax. Lenin did the same thing for small businesses. This policy was called the New Economic Policy (NEP), and the results soon produced a new class of people who were not dependent on the government and had some independent income. The NEP started Russia back on the road to stability and the beginning of a middle class – entrepreneurial farmers called *kulaks* and businessmen called Nepmen. NEP produced more than 25,000,000 peasant-farmer proprietors, each household with a small individual plot. It was a great economic success. In a few years agriculture had recovered to its prewar levels, although industry lagged seriously behind. In theory the NEP policy had the potential, if left in place, to produce a rural and town middle class, which could curb the Communist monopoly on power over time, and to grow Western values across Soviet Russia.

The peasant majority accepted the compromise and eased their revolt against the regime, but Lenin and most of the other Communist leaders had no intention of allowing such a fundamental repudiation of communism, which opposed all private property, to stay in place. However, until the regime's coercive institutions – the secret police and Red Army – were strengthened, the government had little choice but to continue with the NEP. So the Communists could not nullify the fruit of the Second and Third Revolutions, the peasant takeover of the land. In 1922 the Cheka was renamed the GPU (Gosudarstvennoye politicheskoye upravlenie or State Political Directorate) of the NKVD (Narodinii Kommissariate Vnutrennykh Del or People's Commissariat of Internal Affairs).

Lenin also made a concession to minority nationalists. Before he held power, Lenin had always argued for the right of the subject nationalities to secede from the Russian Empire. He had called Imperial Russia "the prison house of nations." Now in charge of the Soviet government, he changed his position, arguing that Soviet Russia did not repress national groups but welded them together in a higher stage of unity called Soviet comradeship, which looked very much like a form of Russian nationalism, and that any nationalist who agitated for secession or independence from Soviet Russia was an enemy of the people and an ally of the capitalist foe. He threw the nationalists a bone by reorganizing the RSFSR and creating in 1922 national republics that had the façade of national governments joined in fraternal unity with the dominant Soviet Russian government. The top leader in each republic was a coopted member of the minority nationality, but real power operated below that figurehead and was consolidated in the hands of Communists in Moscow. The new construct was called the Union of Soviet Socialist Republics or the USSR or the Soviet Union, which was a reconstitution of the tsarist empire minus the nations that had gained their freedom at the end of World War I. It was enough of a concession, when added to the state's monopoly on force and propaganda, to rein in the force of nationalism for decades.

As for the liberals and moderate socialists, he did virtually nothing. He outlawed the Kadet Party in 1918 on the grounds that it represented class enemies of the state and he arrested and imprisoned most of the leaders of the other political parties. He did set up a political system that seemed to reflect Western values in that there was a constitution, elections, and elected representatives, but the Communist Party held real power and decided, in any event, who could stand for office. There was only an appearance of representation and division of power.

Lenin did make one small concession to Russian Orthodoxy. In September 1922 he permitted an influential group of Orthodox intellectuals to leave Soviet Russia. They relocated mainly in Paris and included Nikolai Berdyaev, George Florovsky, Boris Vysheslavtsev, Vasilii Zenkovsky, Vladimir Ilyin, Sergius Bulgakov, Lev Shestov, Nicolas Zernov, George Fedotov, Nikolai Lossky, Simeon Frank, Nikola Arseniev, Mother Maria Skobtsova, and Sergei Bezobrazen. These philosophers and theologians eventually offered new insights on Christian theology and published a fascinating journal called *Put'* or *The Way*, to which Catholic and Protestant theologians contributed.[29] Protestant organizations such as the YMCA, the World Student Christian Federation, and the Anglican Church largely financed this Russian Orthodox community in Paris.

Notes

1 See the dated but still cogent Moorehead 1958, pp. 178–82; and Tooze 2014, pp. 71–72.
2 For early antireligious laws and policies, see Kuroedov and Pankratov 1971, pp. 29–31, 53–66.
3 For a good overview of the antireligious legislation, see Czaplicki 2000, pp. 2–4.
4 Pospelovsky 1995, p. 50.
5 Pospelovsky 1987–88, 1, p. 28. Also see Ramet 1983, p. 4.
6 McCullagh 1924, pp. 159, 210, 233.

7 The secret police actually had multiple name changes and increasing responsibilities. See Shearer and Khaustov 2014, p. 2.

8 Applebaum 2004.

9 On the disposition of Catholic churches, monasteries, and property in the borderlands between independent Poland, Lithuania, and Soviet Russia, see GARF, f. R1041, op. 1, d. 84, (1917), l. 4; d. 637 (1918); d. 638 (1918), d. 639 (1918); d. 640 (1918). Independence for Poland and the Baltic states came when the Germans surrendered in November 1918.

10 See the valuable memoir of Archbishop Basile Krivochéine (Krivochéine 2010), who fought for the White forces during the civil war and then, after leaving Russia with the Communist victory and being ordained an Orthodox priest, struggled with the Communist government once he became a bishop and leader of Orthodox diaspora until his death in 1985.

11 Japan's allies, particularly the United States, objected to the Japanese occupation of eastern Siberia and demanded that the Japanese evacuate the territory. The Japanese resented the pressure from the United States, which strained Japanese–U.S. relations.

12 GARF, f. 176, op. 6, d. 19 (18 July 1919), l. 4.

13 Pospelovsky 1987–88, 2, pp. 13–14.

14 Dunn 1977, pp. 31–32; Stehle 1981, pp. 21–24; Zatko 1965, pp. 76–77, 79; Zugger 2001, p. 97. Der Ropp had been imprisoned by Nicholas II, but was freed by the Provisional Government and made archbishop of Mogilev in July 1917.

15 McCullagh 1924, pp. 157, 205.

16 Czaplicki and Osipova 2014, "Biography of Servant of God, Zygmunt Łoziński," at https://biographies.library.nd.edu/catalog/biography-1843; "Biography of Piotr Mańkowski," at https://biographies.library.nd.edu/catalog/biography-1212, "Biography of Archbishop Ignacy Dub-dubowski," at https://biographies.library.nd.edu/catalog/biography-0933 (accessed 2 April 2016).
Also see Dunn 2004, p. 75; McCullagh 1924, pp. 157, 161–62, 202–03; Zatko 1965, pp. 96–97.

17 Czaplicki 2000, p. xxvi.

18 Osipova [1999] 2014, p. 16.

19 Ulam 1974, pp. 123, 144.

20 Mitter 2013, p. 44.

21 Mitter 2013, p. 49.

22 G. K. Chesterton 1929, pp. 60–62; Pease 2009, pp. 111, 114, 126–30.

23 The Vatican's concordat with Hitler's government in 1933 was controversial. For an excellent survey of diplomatic activity between Weimar Germany and the Vatican, see Stehlim 1983.

24 For examples of the Catholic effort, see Bodó 2008, p. 217; Pease 2009, p. 114; Whitney 2009, pp. 3–4.

25 Conway 1997; Dunn 2004, p. 90.

26 Pettinaroli 2011, p. 85. Also see Deffayet 2005, pp. 831–51; Wolf 2010, pp. 87–131.

27 Kent 2002, p. 51; Leustean 2014, pp. 154–60.

28 Bociurkiw 1969, pp. 77, 81–82.

29 Arjakovsky 2013.

References

Applebaum, Anne 2004, *Gulag: A History*, New York: Doubleday.

Arjakovsky, Antoine 2013, *The Way: Religious Thinkers of the Russian Immigration in Paris and Their Journal, 1925–1940*, John A. Jillions and Michael Plekon (eds.), Jerry Ryan (trans.), Notre Dame, IN: University of Notre Dame Press.

Bociurkiw, Bohdan 1969, "Church–State Relations in the USSR," in *Religion and the Soviet State: A Dilemma of Power*, Max Haywood and William C. Fletcher (eds.), New York: Praeger, pp. 71–104.

Bodó, B. 2008, "'Do Not Lead Us Into (Fascist) Temptation': The Catholic Church in Interwar Hungary," in *Clerical Fascism in Interwar Europe*, Matthew Feldman and Marius Turda with Tudor Georgescu (eds.), New York: Routledge, pp. 201–20.

Chesterton, G. K. 1929, *Generally Speaking*, at www.gkc.org.uk/gkc/books/Generally_ Speaking_scan.pdf, (accessed 2 April 2016).

Conway, Martin 1997, *Catholic Parties in Europe 1918–1945*, New York: Routledge, 1997.

Czaplicki, Bronisław 2000, "A History of the Persecution," from *Kniga pomiati* 2000 Found at a History of the Persecutions: Catholic Church in Russia, pp. 1–42 (accessed 2 April 2016).

Czaplicki, Bronisław and Osipova, Irina 2014, *Book of Remembrance: Biography of Catholic Clergy and Laity in the Soviet Union (USSR) from 1918 to 1953*, Geraldine Kelly (trans.), and made available by University of Notre Dame at https://biographies.library. nd.edu/catalog/biography-0004 (accessed 2 April 2016).

Deffayet, L. 2005, "Amici Israël: les raisons d'in échec: des elements nouveaux apporté par l'ouverture des archives du Saint-Office," in *Mélanges de l'École français de Rome – Italie et Méditerranée*, 117, no. 2, pp. 831–51.

Dunn, Dennis J. 1977, *The Catholic Church and the Soviet Government, 1939–1949*, New York: *East European Quarterly* Series, distributed by Columbia University Press.

Dunn, Dennis J. 2004, *The Catholic Church and Russia: Popes, Patriarchs, Tsars and Commissars*, Aldershot, UK: Ashgate.

GARF (Gosudarstennyi arkiv Rossiiskoi Federatsii) 1917–19, f. 176, f. R1041, Moscow.

Kent, Peter C. 2002, *The Lonely Cold War of Pope Pius XII: The Roman Catholic Church and the Division of Europe, 1943–1950*, Montreal: McGill-Queen's University Press.

Krivochéine, Archevêque Basile 2010, *Mémoire des deux mondes De la revolution* à *l'Église captive*, préface du Métropolite Hilarion (Alfeyev) de Volokolamsk, Paris: Les Éditions de Cerf.

Kuroedov, V. A. and Pankratov, A. S. (eds.) 1971, *Zakolnodal'stvo o religioznych kul'takh: sbornik materialov i dokumentov*, Moscow: Yuridicheskaia Literatura.

Leustean, Lucian N. 2014, "The Romanian Orthodox Church," in *Orthodox Christianity and Nationalism in Nineteenth-Century Southeastern Europe*, Lucian N. Leustean (ed.), New York: Fordham University Press, pp. 154–60.

McCullagh, Francis 1924, *The Bolshevik Persecution of Christianity*, New York: L. E. P. Dutton and Co.

Mitter, Rana 2013, *Forgotten Ally: China's World War II, 1937–1945*, New York: Houghton Mifflin, Harcourt.

Moorehead, Alan 1958, *The Russian Revolution*, New York: Harper & Brothers.

Osipova, Irina (comp. and ed.) [1999] 2014, *Brides of Christ, Martyrs for Russia: Mother Catherine Abrikosova and the Eastern Rite Dominican Sisters*, Geraldine Kelley (trans.), published by Geraldine Kelley, originally published as *Vozliubiv Boga i sleduia za Nim: Goneniia na russkikh katolikov v SSSR*, Moscow: Serebrianye niti, 1999.

Pease, Neal 2009, *Rome's Most Faithful Daughter: The Catholic Church and Independent Poland, 1914–1935*, Athens: Ohio University Press.

Pettinaroli, Laura 2011, "Afterword," in *The Holy See and the Holodomor Documents from the Vatican Secret Archive on the Great Famine of 1932–1933 in Soviet Ukraine*, Athanasius D. McVay and Lubomyr Y. Luciuk (eds. and intro), Toronto: University of Toronto Press, pp. 83–87.

Pospelovsky, Dmitri V. 1987–88, *A History of Soviet Atheism in Theory and Practice and the Believer*, 2 vols., vol. 1: *A History of Marxist-Leninist Atheism and Soviet Antireligious Policies*, vol. 2: *Soviet Antireligious Campaign and Persecutions*, New York: St. Martin's Press.

Pospelovsky, Dmitri V. 1995, *The Russian Orthodox Church in the Twentieth Century* Crestwood, NY: St. Vladimir's Seminary.

Ramet, Sabrina Petra (ed.) 1983, *Religion in the Soviet Union*, Cambridge: Cambridge University Press.

Shearer, David R. and Khaustov, Vladimir 2014, *Stalin and the Lubianka: A Documentary History of the Political Police and Security Organs in the Soviet Union, 1922–1953*, New Haven, CT: Yale University Press.

Stehle, Hansjakob 1981, *Eastern Politics of Vatican, 1917–1979*, Athens: Ohio University Press.

Stehlim, Stewart A. 1983, *Weimar and the Vatican, 1919–1939: German–Vatican Diplomatic Relations in the Interwar Years*, Princeton, NJ: Princeton University Press.

Tooze, Adam 2014, *The Deluge: The Great War and the Reordering of Global Order, 1916–1931*, New York: Viking.

Ulam, Adam 1974, *Expansion and Coexistence: The History of Soviet Foreign Policy, 1917–1973*, New York: Praeger.

Whitney, Susan 2009, *Mobilizing Youth: Communists and Catholics in Interwar France*, Durham, NC: Duke University Press.

Wolf, Hubert 2010, *Pope and Devil: The Vatican Archives and the Third Reich*, Kenneth Kronenberg (trans.), Cambridge, MA: Harvard University Press.

Zatko, James 1965, *Descent Into Darkness: The Destruction of the Roman Catholic Church in Russia, 1917–1923*, Notre Dame, IN: University of Notre Dame Press.

Zugger, Rev. Christopher Lawrence 2001, *The Forgotten: Catholics of the Soviet Empire From Lenin Through Stalin*, Syracuse, NY: Syracuse University Press.

4 Soviet Russia and the Catholic Church, 1921–1924

Communist government and the Vatican, 1921–1924

Although Catholic leaders in the Soviet Union were pessimistic about the future of the Catholic Church in the USSR, Pope Benedict XV and Catholic leaders connected to Rome were optimistic. To be sure, the Vatican and Catholic leaders were deeply disturbed by Moscow's anti-Catholic and anti-Western policies in Soviet Russia and elsewhere, but they hoped that the Communists, with the Civil War behind them, would relax their stand against religion and busy themselves with the task of government and return to the path of Westernization that Nicholas II and the Provisional Government had been on. After all, Lenin reversed Communist core doctrine when in March 1921 he announced the New Economic Policy, which was a major concession to the peasants that gave them the right to control private property.

But the pope and Catholic leaders were ebullient for another reason. In spite of the persecution and the Soviet government's avowed atheism, they believed that Russia's conversion to Catholicism was at hand. Their belief hinged on four developments. As mentioned, Pope Benedict set up on 11 May 1917 the Congregation for Eastern Churches, dedicated to fostering the growth of Catholicism in the East. This institution seemed a God-inspired idea that would facilitate the unification of the Catholic and Orthodox Churches. Second, two days after the Congregation for Eastern Churches was established, three Portuguese children claimed that the Blessed Virgin had appeared to them at Fatima in the first of a series of revelations in which she revealed that Russia would be converted to Catholicism if Catholics followed her advice. For Catholic leaders outside of Soviet Russia, the Fatima revelations were a halcyon premonition of Russia's turning to Rome. Third, the pope and others thought that the Communist coup in October 1917 was an opportunity. To be sure, they were appalled and pained that the Communists were attempting to annihilate religion, but they concluded that the Bolsheviks would eventually change policies or be replaced. In the interim, Lenin was damaging not just the Catholic Church, but also "the colossus of Orthodoxy" with its virulent anti-Catholicism. In that circumstance, the Orthodox Russians might be open to the idea of papal leadership and union with the Catholic Church. Finally, Poland, an overwhelmingly Catholic country on the border of

Soviet Russia, gained its independence in 1918. For Church leaders, this was a miracle and yet another serene sign that the stars were aligning for Soviet Russia's embrace of the Catholic faith. They could imagine that Poland would be a forward base from which to launch the proselytization of Soviet Russia.[1]

In the last years of his papacy, Pope Benedict XV looked for a way to reach out to the Soviet government. He thought contact and dialogue might start the process for what was one of the Catholic Church's long sought objectives: the end of the Great Schism of 1054. In 1920 he sent greetings and a prayer to Patriarch Tikhon on his feast day. The Soviet government interpreted the message as an anti-Soviet act.[2] Prospects for an improvement in Catholic–Soviet relations did not look auspicious. However, in 1921 Pope Benedict discovered what he thought was another way to open a bridge to the Soviet government.

In post–World War I Eastern Europe, famine mushroomed as a general problem because of the breakdown of general order, damage to the agricultural sector, and the wartime embargoes that the victorious Entente Powers refused to lift when hostilities ceased. In Soviet Russia, the famine was worse because of the Civil War and the government's policies of "War Communism" and collectivization of the land. By 1920–21 millions of peasants were dying of cholera and typhus because of their compromised resistance related to starvation, particularly in the Volga and North Caucasus regions. The United States had set up the American Relief Administration (ARA) under Herbert Hoover to address the famine problem in Europe, but the effort did not extend to Soviet Russia because of its diplomatic isolation, revolutionary policies, and abject hostility to capitalist nations. In 1921 Patriarch Tikhon, Maxim Gorky, and other Russian leaders not associated with the government appealed to the West to help feed the Soviet people.[3] The United States immediately agreed to extend famine relief to Soviet Russia. It set up a subsidiary of the ARA called the Russian Relief Program under Colonel William Haskell in order to provide and coordinate aid, but specifically emphasized that such assistance was not de facto recognition of the Soviet government.[4]

Pope Benedict decided that the famine in Soviet Russia and the American initiative to help the Russians gave the Catholic Church a way to show its love of the Russian people and perhaps to influence the Soviet government to modify its antireligious policies. In 1921 he began planning for a Papal Famine Relief Mission that could operate under the umbrella of the American-led Russian Relief Program. However, he died in January 1922 before the Mission was created.

Benedict's successor was Achille Ratti who took the name of Pope Pius XI (r. 1922–39). Ratti was the former archbishop of Milan and the papal nuncio to the newly independent country of Poland. He considered himself a diplomat, a catalyst, a mediator, a peacemaker, and somewhat of an expert on Catholic–Orthodox relations in Eastern Europe and Soviet Russia. He was later called the *papa poloca* (the Polish pope) because of his work and interest in Poland, but he was just as passionate about Soviet Russia. From his perch as the papal nuncio in Warsaw, he observed Soviet society. He knew the Communist threat personally because he lived in Warsaw during the Communist siege of the capital during the Soviet–Polish War. He despised the Communists but loved the Russian people.

Ratti shared Pope Benedict's confidence that Russia was on the verge of accepting Catholicism and took his election as pope as yet another sign that God wanted the Church to continue Benedict's initiative and to focus on Eastern Europe and Russia. In many ways, his papacy was consumed by policies aimed at converting the Russians and persuading the Communists to abandon their persecution of the Catholic Church. For years, no matter what outrages and attacks the Communists delivered on the Catholic Church and religion in general, Pius XI remained optimistic that a new day would soon dawn for the Church in Russia.

His hopefulness was put to the test almost immediately upon being named pope. In March 1922 Lenin blamed the Orthodox Church, the Catholic Church, and other religions for magnifying the famine because they refused to turn over their religious vessels to pay for food for the starving masses. "It is precisely now and only now," Lenin announced, "when in the starving regions people are eating human flesh, and hundreds if not thousands of corpses are littering the roads, that we can (and therefore must) carry out the confiscation of church valuables with the most savage and merciless energy." He added, "the greater the number of representatives of the reactionary clergy and reactionary bourgeoisie we succeed in executing for this reason, the better."[5] It was classic Lenin, using a crisis to further the goal of creating a Communist society, in this case by weakening religion.

The pope was taken aback at Lenin's charges and policy. He immediately offered to buy the religious aids and paraphernalia as a way of defusing the issue. The Polish government protested the confiscation to Georgi Chicherin, the Soviet foreign minister. However, the Soviet government rejected the pope's offer, spurned the Poles, and carried on with its campaign of confiscation and misinformation in order to damage the churches in the eyes of the people.[6]

Lenin's cold, calculating approach of using the famine to assail religion did not augur well for the Catholic Church's desire to impress the Soviet government with an offer of famine relief. Nonetheless, Pius was nonplussed and thought that the situation could improve. He looked for a convenient, non-controversial way to offer famine relief to the Soviet government.

In the first months of 1922 the international scene did not look promising for a Vatican demarche toward Communist Russia. International relations were conflicted, anxious, and insecure.[7] Many countries were stressed by postwar unemployment, the cost of the war, and disappointment over the outcome of the war. In addition, insecurity and anxiety grew partly as the result of Soviet Russia's policy of promoting international revolution through the Comintern, breaking international agreements and refusing to pay the foreign debts of the tsarist government, and putting its own citizens at risk by a range of ideological policies. The Communists reveled in their uncompromising hostility to the West and certain awareness that soon the capitalist governments would collapse and Communist regimes would take power. Virtually no government in the world extended diplomatic recognition to Lenin's regime. Russia, one of the world's major powers, was the home of a radical left political movement that amounted to an organized conspiracy that pushed war, anarchy, and revolution, and helped precipitate the growth of anti-Communist radical right groups across Europe and Asia that were as extreme as the Communists and pushed their own policies of racism, war, and ultra-nationalism.

Germany, another of the world's major powers, was dispirited and gloomy. It had high unemployment. Radical left and radical right political movements fought for support, including the German Communist Party and the right-wing Freikorps. The democratic Weimar government, which had replaced the kaiser and had been forced to sign the Versailles Treaty, was weak and without popular support. It desperately wanted to revise the terms of the Versailles Treaty, particularly the annual reparations payments that it was obligated to make to the victorious powers in World War I. The Germans were very disturbed over the Polish Corridor that gave Poland access to the Baltic Sea and separated East Prussia from Germany proper. They also chafed at the demilitarized western borders, which kept the Rhineland and Ruhr Valley defenseless against French political and military pressure. They were also suffering from food shortages and from the national humiliation of being held accountable for causing World War I. The German industrial base was largely unscathed by the war, but mainly idle because the postwar global economy was in shambles. The German military was restricted, but its officer corps was intact and deeply resentful over the wartime defeat. It acted as a virtual parallel and destabilizing government to the Weimar government, which it loathed and unjustly blamed for Versailles and the German defeat.

The United States, which was the largest creditor nation in the world, drifted in the postwar period into an isolationist phase. It refused to join the League of Nations and to take a leadership role in stabilizing international trade and the global economy. Its leaders were inexperienced, uncertain, and preoccupied with domestic issues. It looked upon Europe as a source of war, entangling alliances, and myopic and self-serving policies, and upon the Soviet Union as the antithesis of everything the United States stood for. The United States girded itself against the so-called Red Scare and the possibility that Communists or their sympathizers might try to promote revolution in the United States. It was especially vexed that the Soviet government persecuted religion and opposed private property. It also looked with great suspicion upon Japan, which was carving out a sphere of influence across Asia and in the Pacific.

The English and the French were presumed to be major powers, but they were in debt, had weak economies, and were stressed by the human and financial cost of World War I. They were preoccupied with extending their sphere of influence in newly acquired protectorates in the Middle East and in consolidating power in their Asian and African colonies. They faced national liberation movements in Asia, which the Communists tried to exploit. The British were troubled about the Kuomintang in China and the French about Comintern activities in Southeast Asia. The French were discombobulated because they were weaker than the Germans, even though they had won the war. They tried to level the Germans with the demilitarization provisions and reparation payments of the Versailles Treaty, but Germany remained fundamentally strong and a constant source of uneasiness for the French. The British were more diffident about the Germans and some British leaders publicly stated that the Versailles Treaty was unfair to the Germans and should be revised.

Then there was the dozen new or newly revised states of Eastern Europe that emerged as a result of the collapse of the Russian Empire, the Austrian-Hungarian Empire, the German Empire, and the Ottoman Empire, and included Lithuania, Latvia, Estonia, Finland, Poland, Austria, Albania, Yugoslavia (the result of a merger of Serbia, Croatia, Montenegro, Macedonia, Slovenia, and Bosnia-Hercegovina), Czechoslovakia, Romania, Bulgaria, and Kemalist Turkey. Many of these states suffered from ultra-nationalism, broken or disrupted market and trade patterns, irredentism, boundary disagreements, economies that rested on agricultural exports, intolerance of religious and national minorities, anti-Semitism, and inexperienced politicians and bureaucrats. Many of them also looked to France as a model of government and a trading partner, hoping that France would buy their exports and protect them against the two hegemons of Germany and Soviet Russia that rued their loss of imperial sway and resented the very existence of many of the new Eastern European states that nestled between them.

The Central and Eastern European states were particularly vexed about Communist Russia and its policy of promoting revolution against Western values. France, however, was weakened by World War I and was engaged in supporting its own agricultural sector and not that of the new states, which were overwhelmingly agricultural economies, with the exception of Czechoslovakia, that needed export markets. France could offer the example of its social democracy, and many of the new governments tried to set up democratic regimes, but the internal and external challenges were too great for politicians who lacked experience with democracy. Many of the new regimes soon moved toward dictatorships. Soviet Russia and Germany wanted to control the weak Eastern European states separating them, but in the immediate post–World War I environment, they were restrained from doing so – Russia by civil war and its rancorous ideology, and Germany by the Versailles Treaty and its defeat in World War I.

Any move by the Vatican toward Moscow risked adding confusion to the already strained world order, particularly in Eastern Europe where anti-Communism was one of the few issues that united the region's disparate governments and factions. Pope Pius XI, however, was convinced that such an overture would help, not hurt, Europe and the Catholic Church, and he urged governments to connect diplomatically with the Soviet regime, providing the Kremlin would grant religious liberty to its people.[8]

On 10 April 1922, the Genoa Conference was convened to deal with some of the many problems confronting the postwar world. The major issue at hand was Germany's request for a reduction of its reparation payments. Another issue was the debt of the tsarist government that the Soviet government had repudiated. Genoa was the first international gathering to which the Communist government was invited since the end of World War I. Even though Moscow was organizing or attempting to organize revolutions against the world capitalist order and even though it had broken just about every rule of customary international behavior, from publishing secret treaties to repudiating tsarist government debts, it was still invited by the Great Powers to attend Genoa. For the Soviets, their presence at Genoa was a vindication of their ideology and policies. It was also an opportunity to advance the revolution globally, to divide the Western powers, and to gain diplomatic recognition and legitimacy as a shield against Western capitalist politicians whom they feared might be conspiring against it.

Pope Pius XI decided to approach the Soviet delegation at the Genoa Conference and offer to send a Papal Famine Relief Mission to Soviet Russia. The offer included food and financial aid and a request that the Kremlin grant toleration to the Catholic Church and the right to carry on missionary work in Soviet Russia. The Vatican's proposal was facilitated by the German government, which had taken the controversial step of recognizing the Soviet government by signing the Treaty of Rapallo in the middle of the Genoa Conference.[9] The pope hoped that the effort to expend the Catholic Church's resources on behalf of the Russian people would open their hearts to the Catholic faith.[10]

The Communists quickly accepted the Vatican's offer of financial and food aid. It was a concrete offer to help alleviate the plight of Soviet Russia's starving citizens. It brought a measure of prestige and recognition to the isolated Communist regime and held out the possibility of undercutting Catholics who were anti-Communist and of dampening any involvement of Catholic-leaning countries in an anti-Communist coalition of Western states. In addition, it was validation. It indicated that perhaps even the Catholic Church, the archenemy of the communist worldview, was waking up to the staying power of the Soviet government and to the coming victory of international communism. Finally, it allowed the Soviets to please the Germans, who wanted the Kremlin to accept the Vatican's offer because it gave the Germans some cover for taking the controversial step of being the first major Western state to recognize a government that was anti-capitalist, antireligious, and pro-revolutionary.

To the great disappointment of Pope Pius, the Soviets ruled out any missionary work and boldly asserted that the Catholic Church was already tolerated. The pope was not deterred by the Soviets' meretricious claim of toleration or refusal to allow missionary work. He believed that once his envoys set foot on Soviet soil, there would be opportunities for missionary work and changes in the relationship.[11]

The man Pius XI chose to head the Papal Famine Relief Mission was an American Jesuit priest by the name of Father Edmund Walsh, who was well connected in Washington and who was a friend of Colonel Haskell, which was critical since the ARA's Russian Program could provide coordination, direction, and protection for the Papal Mission. Father Louis Gallagher, another American Jesuit, was named Fr. Walsh's assistant.[12] In late 1923 a German priest, Father Eduard Gehrmann, succeeded Fr. Walsh as head of the Mission.

The Papal Famine Relief Mission under Fr. Walsh arrived in Soviet Russia in the summer of 1922 and included twelve other clerics (four Jesuits, three Steylers, three Salesians, and two Claretians), who kept a low profile and wore civilian clothes as opposed to clerical garb.[13] It was an amazing outreach effort for the Catholic Church – feeding Soviet citizens in the hope that its effort would persuade the government to be tolerant of the Catholic Church in Soviet Russia and open the door to the conversion of the Orthodox to Catholicism. By some accounts the Papal Mission helped save more than 150,000 citizens from starvation.[14] As a small token of its appreciation, the Soviet government released the remains of Andrew Bobola, SJ, who had been martyred in 1657 in Polotsk during a Cossack uprising and buried in Polotsk.[15] Pope Pius XI canonized Andrew Bobola, who was known as the apostle of Lithuania, on 17 April 1938.

Communist government and the Catholic Church, 1922–1924

By late 1922, with the Papal Famine Relief Mission hard at work, the Vatican expected that the Catholic Church would finally be accorded some measure of toleration. To its surprise, the Soviet government ramped up its attack on the Catholic Church. In November the Kremlin announced that it planned to put the Catholic leaders and priests in Petrograd on trial for anti-Soviet and counterrevolutionary acts. In December it shut the Catholic Church's two seminaries, theological academy, and many parish churches.[16] It also arrested many priests. In the course of 1923 it closed many but not all Catholic churches. It eventually allowed only two Catholic churches to remain open in the two major cities of Petrograd and Moscow – Notre Dame Church in Petrograd, which was owned by the French government and pastored by a French Dominican by the name of Jean-Baptiste Amoudru, and St. Louis des Français Church in Moscow, which was also owned by the French and administered by a French Assumptionist priest by the name of Eugene Neveu as of 1926.

   On 21–25 March 1923, the Soviet government followed through on its plan to try the Catholic clergy in Petrograd, who constituted the leadership of the Catholic Church in Soviet Russia. Archbishop Jan Cieplak, the head of the Church, and Monsignor Konstantin Budkiewicz, the dean of the clergy, were tried and convicted of a broad range of anti-Soviet activities, including planning a counterrevolution and turning citizens against the government. They were sentenced to death. Cieplak's sentence was commuted to a term in prison for ten years that included a stipulation that he not say Mass.[17] In April 1924 he was deported to Latvia at the request of the small Irish Communist Party that was embarrassed over the persecution of Catholics. He eventually ended up in Warsaw, where he advised Pius XI on Eastern Europe and Soviet Russia until his death in 1926.[18]

   Budkiewicz was not as fortunate as Cieplak. He was executed on 31 March 1923.[19] There was some evidence that the Soviets hinted at a prisoner exchange with Poland for Budkiewicz, but, if so, it was not acted upon.[20] Tried with Cieplak and Budkiewicz were Monsignor Antoni Malecki and seven other priests. They were found guilty of working with Cieplak and Budkiewicz's counterrevolutionary movement and sentenced to three years in prison and the forfeiture of civil rights.[21] Malecki had organized a seminary of sorts in a private apartment after the Communists had closed the Catholic seminary in Petrograd, and his arrest stifled that initiative. However, Father Michał Rutkowski managed to restart the training and eventually reported that retired Bishop Anton Zerr (b. 1849) of Tiraspol ordained two priests in 1925–26, Boleslaw Jurewicz and Julian Cimaszkiewicz.[22]

Exarch Leonid Fedorov and four priests of the new Eastern Rite were convicted of participating in a counterrevolutionary group and sentenced to imprisonment for ten years. Exarch Fedorov was released in 1926, arrested in 1926 and sent to Solovetsky Prison, released in 1929, arrested in 1931, and released at the end of 1933 and exiled to Arkhangelsk oblast. In January 1934 he was permitted to live in Vyatka, where he died on 7 March 1934.[23] It is impossible to say exactly what happened to the priests who were tried with Fedorov and to many other priests and nuns who were arrested, but it is safe to say that many of them were sent to the gulag in Siberia or to the prison on the Solovetsky Islands, where they did forced labor. Some priests were forced to renounce their priesthood and sign documents stating that there was no persecution of religion in the Soviet Union. Some like Father Józef Bielogołowy of Minsk were offered leadership roles if they would organize splintering churches. The GPU asked him to lead a version of the schismatic Old Catholic Church in Belorussia. He turned down the offer and was then arrested and jailed in Lubyanka Prison in Moscow, where he died.[24] Others were exchanged for Communist prisoners and some were released for payment. A few were expelled or allowed to leave the Soviet Union. Among the latter was Fr. Vladimir Abrikosov, the leader of a small Eastern-Rite Dominican community, who was expelled in 1922. Sister Julia Danzas, who was with the Eastern-Rite Sisters of the Order of St. Basil, was released from Solovetsky Prison and sent to France in 1933. Her brother apparently paid the Soviet government to release her.

More typical of the plight of clergy was the story of Fr. Abrikosov's wife, Mother Catherine Abrikosova. After Fr. Abrikosov was expelled, she remained in Moscow where she continued to build up the Dominican religious community. Fr. Nikolai Alexandrov (Archbishop Cieplak ordained him in 1922) replaced her husband as the spiritual director of the community, which by 1923 had twenty-eight members and had spawned a Dominican Third Order of laypersons.[25] In November 1923 the GPU arrested Mother Catherine, Fr. Nikolai, half of the sisters, and various laity. The last sisters were arrested and imprisoned in March 1924 with the exception of Sister Catherine de Ricci (Tatyana Galkina), who was quite ill, and two other sisters who were nursing her.[26] The nuns were tried and convicted of promoting "a monarchist organization with ties to the Vatican" and distributing abroad anti-Soviet information. Their sentences varied from five to ten years in prison with Mother Catherine given ten years.[27]

In April 1923 the Catholic Church was a topic of discussion at the 12th Party Congress where a resolution was passed to reduce "the growth of nationalist-clerical influence among the Polish minority in the USSR," especially among school-aged children. Discussions were also held in July about the possibility of diluting the nexus between Catholicism and Polish national identity by placing non-Polish priests in Polish communities.[28] The GPU did corrupt some priests and appointed some of its own agents as priests in order to compromise the Church and scandalize parishioners. Neveu, the French cleric in Moscow, noted in a letter to the Vatican in October 1934 that there were clerical agents provocateurs in various cities, including Minsk.[29] In November 1923 the Soviet Ministry of Justice propounded that the decree separating church and state had been implemented regarding the

Catholic Church, which was a euphemism for the destruction of the hierarchy of the Church.[30]

Patriarch Tikhon was put on trial in 1923 at the same time as the Catholic leaders. He was found guilty of anti-Soviet activities and placed under house arrest, where he died in 1925. His trial and the trials of Catholic and Orthodox leaders indicated that the Soviet government was determined to move simultaneously against the leadership of both Churches.[31] When Patriarch Tikhon died, the Communists allowed Metropolitan Sergius to be *locum tenens*, but refused to permit him to be elected patriarch and, instead, promoted the so-called Renovationist Church, which was an Orthodox faction created to splinter and weaken the Russian Orthodox Church and which the Communists supported between 1922 and 1946, when it was ended.

At the same time that the Soviet government intensified its attack on the Catholic Church in Russia, the Comintern increased its activities to expand the international revolution. In fact, from the Soviet point of view, the international expansion of communism was more critical than a clubbing of Catholicism or Orthodoxy in Soviet Russia because the international revolution would simultaneously guarantee the security of the Soviet government and sever religion's lifeline. In 1923 the Comintern seized on a crisis in Germany in order to try to overthrow the German government and move the international revolution forward.

The crisis of 1923 had roots stretching back to the Versailles Treaty and the Genoa Conference of 1922. Versailles stipulated that Germany had to pay annual reparations to the victorious powers. The Germans found the payments arduous. They asked for relief at Genoa. The French and English refused to modify the terms. The Germans tried to intimidate Paris and London by signing the Rapallo Treaty with the Soviet Union on 16 April 1922. This treaty established diplomatic and commercial ties between Germany and the USSR. It implied that Germany was moving closer to the world's leading anti-capitalist and pariah state. The Soviets were euphoric over Rapallo. It gave Moscow a unique partnership with a major industrial state with a large working class and that was the home of Karl Marx. The agreement would diminish any chance of an anti-Communist coalition of capitalist states lining up against the Soviet Union.

The French and British, however, were not cowed and rejected any modification of the reparations formula. In early 1923 Berlin decided to escalate the issue with the French and British by refusing to make a required annual payment. In response, French and Belgian troops occupied the demilitarized Ruhr Valley and planned to take the payment in the form of coal. The Weimar regime responded by ordering the miners to halt work and guaranteeing their salaries, which it accomplished by printing money and stimulating inflation, which soon got out of hand. By the summer of 1923 the German government was on the verge of collapse amidst growing inflation, unemployment, and angst over Versailles, the war, and radical communism.

Lenin and the Communists perceived in the German crisis the destabilizing and anarchic conditions that brought them to power in Russia and the opportunity to jumpstart the international revolution they had been anticipating since the end of

World War I. The Comintern issued orders to the Communist Party of Germany to make a play for power, which it did by organizing revolts in a number of German cities, with a major effort in Hamburg. In the face of the Communist challenge, the Weimar government rallied and smashed the Communist-led rebellion. It also had to put down in November a putsch in Munich led by Adolph Hitler, the leader of the radical right National Socialist or Nazi Party. Hitler was thrown into prison, where he served five months and managed to pen *Mein Kampf,* the guidebook that anchored Nazism on anti-Communism, anti-Semitism, racism, war, and *lebensraum* – space and territory for the Aryan master race to grow.

Chastened by the growth of left and right extremism, the Western powers now decided to make an accommodation to Germany. The Americans produced in 1924 the Dawes Plan, which extended credits to Germany that enabled the Germans to revive their economy and begin to pay reparations. In addition, the English, French, Italians, Belgians, and Germans agreed to the Locarno Treaty in 1925, which reduced tension in Europe by defining the western borders of Germany and gave Germany membership in the League of Nations. Together, Dawes and Locarno brought Germany back into the Western community of nations and tended to isolate the Soviet Union.

The Communists were disappointed that Germany settled down and did not become the focal point for the international revolution, but they had no regrets. They persisted in their policy of trying to promote international revolution and increasingly focused their attention on inflaming China, which Lenin had predicted would lead to the expansion of communism in the West. They also still had a tie to Germany, and it soon evolved into a military relationship when General Hans von Seeckt and the Reichswehr established their own partnership with the Soviet government, apparently without the initial knowledge of the Weimar government, that allowed the German military to start rearming by building weapons and training facilities in Soviet Russia and gave the Soviets access to German military products and training. The Soviets were not chagrined in the least about the anti-Communist movements that appeared in Germany and elsewhere in Europe and Asia. They held that the future belonged to communism, and anti-Communist movements, whether Hitler, Mussolini, or the Vatican's international anti-Communist activities, were ersatz phantoms on the road to an inevitable Communist-dominated world. They were oblivious to the fact that anarchic conditions, which they precipitated and exacerbated as ideal conditions for their radical left movement, also created opportunities for the radical right.

Amazingly, throughout the Comintern's activities in Germany and elsewhere and during the Kremlin's escalating attack on the Catholic Church in the Soviet Union, the Papal Famine Relief Mission continued to help starving people in the Soviet Union. Such perseverance was strong evidence that Pope Pius XI was convinced that the Church had to stay the course of trying to work with the Soviet government or, at least, hang on to something in Soviet Russia in order to be ready for the possibility of Russia's conversion.

In 1924 the Papal Famine Relief Mission had finally fulfilled its commitment and was due to end, but the Vatican and the Kremlin decided to explore the possibility of continuing the Mission and of establishing diplomatic relations. Talks opened in early 1924 in Berlin and quickly reached an impasse. The Vatican's chief negotiator and eventual nuncio to Germany was Eugenio Pacelli, the future Pope Pius XII.[32] The Kremlin demanded that the Papal Famine Relief Mission increase its budget and distribute more food.[33] It also wanted diplomatic relations. Pacelli made clear that the Soviets had to stop the persecution of the Catholic Church before the Vatican would consider either request. It soon became obvious to Pacelli that the Communists had no intention of making any accommodation to the Catholic Church. In August 1924, after two arduous years in the Soviet Union, the Vatican withdrew its relief mission.[34]

In the mid-1920s the position of the Catholic Church in Soviet Russia continued to deteriorate. The number of clergy declined. A NKVD report in 1924 listed only a handful of active priests and parish councils. Other sources indicated that between 116 and about 200 priests were free, which, nonetheless, indicated a more than 50 percent reduction from the number of priests at the end of March 1921.[35] The only bishop who was not in prison was the previously mentioned Anton Zerr, who lived in Tiraspol. He was retired and in poor health, but could still function. Bishop Karol Sliwowski of Vladivostok was under house arrest and died in 1933.[36]

Anti-Catholic and antireligious propaganda also increased and became more sophisticated during the middle of the 1920s. In 1925 Emelian Iaroslavsky started the League of Atheists (Militant Atheists as of 1929), which produced newspapers (*Bezbozhnik* and *Antireligioznik*), journals, and books that promoted atheism, the Marxist-Leninist worldview, and anti-Catholicism.[37] The Catholic Church was routinely denounced and pilloried in these and other Soviet publications. In addition, the secularization and vulgarization of the culture intensified and stretched to such absurdities as forbidding as of 1927 the performance of Rakhmaninov's "Night Service" and Mozart's "Requiem."[38]

The Comintern also sought ways to undermine the Catholic Church. In the mid-1920s the Communists in Europe became active in the Proletarian Freethinkers, an organization socialists had founded to diminish the impact of religion, particularly the Catholic Church, in the political life of Europe. The Communists or the Russian Bezbozhniki (Godless) joined various national affiliates of the Freethinkers and pushed a confrontational policy with churches and clergy.

Notes

1 Pease 2009, p. 149.
2 Dunn 2004, p. 80.
3 For primary source materials related to the famine in Soviet Russia, including appeals for help, see Famine of 1921–22, in "Seventeen Moments in Soviet History: 1921."
4 Patenaude 2002.
5 Lenin to Molotov and members of the Politburo, 19 March 1922, in Pipes 1996, pp. 152–54. For examples of Soviet documents relating to the seizure of church valuables, see Corley 1996, pp. 26–30; also see G. Shtrikker 1995, 1: 39, 156.
6 McCullough 1924, pp. 112–13; Walsh 1931, pp. 182–83; Zatko 1965, p. 125.

7 For first-rate studies of the end of the war and interwar period, see Macmillan 2002; Tooze 2014.

8 McVay and Luciuk 2011, p. vi.

9 Stehle 1981, pp. 36–37.

10 Pease 2009, pp. 4, 37, 137, 152–53.

11 Stehle 1981, p. 30.

12 For details on Walsh and his Mission, see Gallagher 1962.

13 Stehle 1981, pp. 32–33, 41, 44, 48–53, 59–60.

14 Alekseev 1991, pp. 220–22; Stehle 1981, pp. 33, 43–44. See Pettinaroli 2015, pp. 464–71, on Mission details and statistics.

15 GARF, f, A353, op. 6, d. 17(1922–23), l.

16 Dunn 1977, p. 35; Galter 1957, pp. 39–40; Szczesniak 1959, pp. 226–33; Walsh 1931, pp. 184–87; Zatko 1965, pp. 171, 183.

17 RGASPI, Moscow, Protokol (12 January 1924), f. 89, op. 4, d. 115, l. 8.

18 L'Archivio della Sacra Congregazione degli Affari Ecclesiastici Straordinari, Pontificia Commissione, Pro Russia, scatola (box) 1, fascicolo (file) 12/28, d'Herbigny to Secretary of State, 30 November 1926, Vatican, fogli (sheet(s) 25 (Blue 17) (henceforth cited as AES, Pro Russia, s., fasc., f.).

19 Walter Duranty, the notoriously pro-Soviet bureau chief for the *New York Times* in Moscow from 1922 to 1936, believed that the execution helped "to retard American recognition of the U.S.S.R. for ten years." See Duranty 1935, p. 205; also see Walsh 1931, p. 184.

20 Pease 2009, p. 155.

21 Dunn 2004, pp. 79–80.

22 Fr. Michał Rutkowski was arrested in 1923 and sent to Poland in 1926 as part of a prisoner exchange. See Czaplicki and Osipova 2014, "Biography of Father Michał Rutkowski," at https://biographies.library.nd.edu/catalog/biography-1843. Fr. Jurewicz was arrested in 1929, sent to Solovetsky Prison, and executed in 1937. See Czaplicki and Osipova 2014, "Biography of Father Boleslaw Jurewicz," at https://biographies. library.nd.edu/catalog/biography-1588. See Czaplicki and Osipova 2014, "Biography of Fr. Julian Cimaszkiewicz," at https://biographies.library.nd.edu/catalog/biography-1514 (all accessed 4 April 2016).

23 See Czaplicki and Osipova 2014, "Biography of Blessed Leonid Fedorov, Exarch of Russian Greek-Catholic Church in Russia," at https://biographies.library.nd.edu/catalog/biography-0264 (accessed 4 April 2016).

24 Fr. Józef Biełogołowy was arrested in 1922, released in 1924, met with d'Herbigny in 1926, arrested in 1926, sent to Solovetsky Prison and then transferred to Lubyanka Prison, where he died in 1928. See Czaplicki and Osipova 2014, "Biography of Father Józef Biełogołowy," at https://biographies.library.nd.edu/catalog/biography-0121 (accessed 4 April 2016).

25 Osipova [1999] 2014, pp. 23–24, 38.

26 Osipova [1999] 2014, pp. 18, 40–41.

27 Osipova [1999] 2014, pp. 18, 42.

28 *KPSS v resoliutsiiakh sezdov, konferentsii I plenumov tseka* 1953, 1: 742; on Polish priests, see RGASPI, Protokol No. 28, f. 89, op. 4, d. 115 (4 July 1923), l. 30.

29 AES, *Pro Russia*, s. 43, fasc. 250, Neveu to Giobbe, Moscow, 23 October 1934, f. 43, prot. 166/28.

30 GARF, f. A353, op. 3, d. 752 (22 April–9 November 1923).

31 RGASPI, Protokol Nos. 12–16, f. 89, op. 4, d. 115 (30 January 1923), (6 February 1923), (27 February 1923), (6 March 1923), l. 2–2a, 3, 6–7, 8; Dunn 2004, p. 80.

32 Stehle 1981, pp. 73–79.

33 Stehle 1981, pp. 59–60.

34 In the wake of the departure of the Papal Famine Relief Mission, Pius XI issued a special allocution denouncing communism. See P.P. Pius XI 1924, "Allocutio," *Acta*

Apostolicae Sedis, Vatican City, 1917–1939 (Acts of the Holy See),16: 494; also see Stehle 1981, pp. 49, 59–66.
35 GARF, f. R393, op. 43, d. 484 (1924). On the figure of 200 priests, see Alvarez 2002, p. 142.
36 Zugger 2001, p. 137.
37 For information on the League, see Peris 1998.
38 RGASPI, Protokol No. 82, f. 17, op. 113, d. 353 (29 January 1927), l. 9–10.

References

Acta Apostolicae Sedis, Vatican City, 1917–1939 (Acts of the Holy See), cited as *AAS*.

Alekseev, V. A. 1991, *Illiuziy i dogmy*, Moscow: Politizdat.

Alvarez, David 2002, *Spies in the Vatican: Espionage and Intrigue from Napoleon to the Holocaust*, Lawrence: University Press of Kansas.

Corley, Felix 1996, *Religion in the Soviet Union: An Archival Reader*, New York: New York University Press.

Czaplicki, Bronisław and Osipova, Irina 2014, *Book of Remembrance: Biography of Catholic Clergy and Laity in the Soviet Union (USSR) from 1918 to 1953*, Geraldine Kelly (trans.), and made available by University of Notre Dame at https://biographies.library. nd.edu/catalog/biography-0004 (accessed 2 April 2016).

Dunn, Dennis J. 1977, *The Catholic Church and the Soviet Government, 1939–1949*, New York: *East European Quarterly* Series, distributed by Columbia University Press.

Dunn, Dennis J. 2004, *The Catholic Church and Russia: Popes, Patriarchs, Tsars and Commissars*, Aldershot, UK: Ashgate.

Duranty, Walter 1935, *I Write as I Please*, New York: Simon and Schuster.

Gallagher, Louis Jr. 1962, *Edmund Walsh, S.J.: A Biography*, New York: Benziger Brothers.

Galter, Albert 1957, *The Red Book of the Persecuted Church*, Westminster, MD: The Newman Press.

GARF (Gosudarstennyi arkiv Rossiiskoi Federatsii) f. A353, Moscow.

KPSS v resoliutsiiakh sezdov, konferentsii I plenumov tseka 1953, vol. 1, Moscow: Gos. Izd-vo. Polit. Lit-ry.

L'Archivio della Sacra Congregazione degli Affari Ecclesiastici Straordinari, Pontificia Commissione, *Pro Russia*, scatola (box), fascicolo (file), fogli (sheet(s), Archivio Segreto Vaticano (cited as AES, *Pro Russia*, s., fasc., f.).

Macmillan, Margaret 2002, *Paris 1919*, New York: Random House.

McCullagh, Francis, 1924, *The Bolshevik Persecution of Christianity*, New York: L E. P. Dutton and Co.

McVay, Athanasius D. and Luciuk, Lubomyr Y. 2011, "Introduction: The Holy See and the Holodomor," in *The Holy See and the Holodomor Documents from the Vatican Secret Archive on the Great Famine of 1932–1933 in Soviet Ukraine*, Athanasius D. McVay and Lubomyr Y. Luciuk (eds. and intro.), Toronto: University of Toronto, pp. iii–xxii.

Osipova, Irina (comp. and ed.) [1999] 2014, *Brides of Christ, Martyrs for Russia: Mother Catherine Abrikosova and the Eastern Rite Dominican Sisters*, Geraldine Kelley (trans.), published by Geraldine Kelley, originally published as *Vozliubiv Boga i sleduia za Nim: Goneniia na russkikh katolikov v SSSR*, Moscow: Serebrianye niti, 1999.

Patenaude, Bernard M. 2002, *The Big Show in Bololand: The American Relief Expedition to Soviet Russia in the Famine of 1921*, Stanford, CA: Stanford University Press.

Pease, Neal 2009, *Rome's Most Faithful Daughter: The Catholic Church and Independent Poland, 1914–1935*, Athens: Ohio University Press.

Peris, Daniel 1998, *Storming the Heavens: The Soviet League of the Militant Godless*, Ithaca, NY: Cornell University Press.

Pettinaroli, Laura 2015, *La Politique Russie du Saint-Siège (1905–1939)*, Rome: École française de Rome.

Pipes, Richard 1996, *The Unknown Lenin: From the Secret Archives*, New Haven, CT: Yale University Press.

RGASPI (Rossiiskii gosudarstvennyi arkiv sotsial'no-politcheskoi istorii), fund 17, 89, Moscow.

"Seventeen Moments in Soviet History: 1921," at http://soviethistory.msu.edu (accessed 4 April 2016).

Shtrikker, G. (ed.) 1995, *Russkaia pravoslavnaia Tserkov'v sovetskoe vremia (1917–1991): Materialy i documenty po istorii? otnoshenii? mezhdu gosudarstvom i Tserkov'iu*, 2 vols., Moscow: Propilei.

Stehle, Hansjakob 1981, *Eastern Politics of Vatican, 1917–1979*, Athens: Ohio University Press.

Szczesniak, Boleslaw R. 1959, *The Russian Revolution and Religion*, Notre Dame, IN: University of Notre Dame Press.

Tooze, Adam 2014, *The Deluge: The Great War and the Reordering of Global Order, 1916–1931*, New York: Viking.

Walsh, Edmund A. 1931, *The Last Stand: An Interpretation of the Soviet Five-Year Plan*, Boston, MA: Little, Brown and Co.

Zatko, James, 1965, *Descent into Darkness: The Destruction of the Roman Catholic Church in Russia, 1917–1923*, Notre Dame, IN: University of Notre Dame Press.

Zugger, Rev. Christopher Lawrence 2001, *The Forgotten: Catholics of the Soviet Empire from Lenin through Stalin*, Syracuse, NY: Syracuse University Press.

5   The Catholic Church and Vatican initiatives, mid-1920s–1930

Orthodox–Catholic ties and the Albertyn experiment

The Soviet government's continuing policy of persecution disturbed Pius XI, but his optimism about Catholicism's future in Soviet Russia did not flag. He looked for new ways to penetrate Soviet Russia. In 1924 the Vatican officially reorganized and sanctioned an organization it called Catholica Unio, which had the goal of unifying the Orthodox and Catholic Churches. The movement started in Vienna in 1922 and was initially called the Ukrainian Religious Committee. Catholica Unio had branches in Europe, particularly in Germany, and in the United States, where it became part of the Catholic Near East Welfare Association.[1] Its main activity was raising funds to help improve Catholic–Orthodox relations for the purpose of unifying the Churches under the pope. It helped improve communication between Orthodox and Catholics in Europe, but the Soviet government's vicious and unmitigated persecution of both the Orthodox and Catholic Churches in the USSR proscribed any hope of establishing an opportunity, let alone a basis, for interfaith dialogue. It did make a major effort during the famine in 1932–33 to collect funds to feed starving Catholics in the USSR.[2]

In Paris, there was a separate but very important ecumenical dialogue between Catholics and Orthodox Russians in emigration. They searched for a common Christian response to nihilism and communism throughout the 1920s and 1930s. The leaders of the dialogue included Catholic theologian Jacques Maritain and such Orthodox intellectuals as Sergei Bulgakov and Nikolai Berdyaev. The Russian émigrés, influenced by Fyodor Dostoevsky, Alexei Khomiakhov, Vladimir Soloviev, and a range of fin-de-siècle French and German philosophers, were prolific and provided in their journal called *The Way*, mentioned earlier, new insights on a rich variety of theological subjects, including ideas on God's personalism, ever-present holy wisdom (*sophia*), and constant centrality in human existence and life. Their work constituted a major development in the history of Orthodox thought.[3] One question that they that did not solve, although they tried, was to offer a satisfying explanation for why Orthodox Russia produced communism or Leninism-Stalinism. The Orthodox community increased significantly in the interwar period, and so did Orthodox and Catholic understanding. Eventually, some Orthodox intellectuals converted to Catholicism.[4] Many of the leading

Orthodox philosophers, however, like Berdyaev, while they worked earnestly for cooperation with the pope, could not find a way to reconcile their hard and fast certainty in Russia's spirituality and exceptionalism with Rome's leadership.

In 1925 Pope Pius hit on yet another strategy for advancing the unification of the Catholic and Orthodox Churches. He decided that the Catholic Church should experiment with a new kind of Eastern Rite that would appeal to Orthodox Christians who lived in the eastern borderlands or *kresy* of Poland (Galicia and Volhynia). If such a Rite were successful in converting Poland's Orthodox, then it might be attractive to the Orthodox of the Soviet Union. The new Rite Pius conceived was a hybrid Eastern Rite that he called the Byzantine-Slavonic Rite. It allowed the Orthodox to keep being Orthodox in every way, just like the Ukrainian Catholic Rite, except the clergy would be celibate and would report to a local Latin bishop, who inevitably would be a Pole.

To implement his plan, Pius recruited a close friend who shared his views, the French Jesuit priest Michel d'Herbigny. Pius met d'Herbigny when he was archbishop of Milan. Both men had decided that the Orthodox East was fertile ground for growing the Catholic Church and particularly the Uniate form of Catholicism. D'Herbigny, who was fluent in Russian, had made a career of studying the Russian Orthodox Church. Pius was deeply impressed by him. In March 1925 Pius named him general consultant or relator to the Vatican's Pontifical Institute of Oriental Studies, sometimes called the Pro Russia Commission, a new agency under the Congregation of Eastern Churches. To d'Herbigny and to the Jesuit order, Pius gave the specific job of building the new Rite. The Jesuits had a sizeable presence in Poland and their general, Father Włodzimierz Ledóchowski, SJ, was a Polish native. Fr. Ledóchowski was pleased that his order was entrusted with the pope's pet project, but he was a Pole, suspicious of papal involvement in issues that touched on Poland's vital interests, and he was the leader of the Jesuits, who undoubtedly resented the fact that his subordinate was a confidant of the pope.[5] The Pro Russia Commission was to coordinate the effort to build the new rite, but its charge was more general – to serve the pastoral needs of all Catholics of all Rites in the USSR and of Eastern rite Catholics in the Polish *kresy* and in emigration.[6]

The first step to implement the pope's plan was the creation of a model parish to find out if the new rite would appeal to the Orthodox. In 1925 in the town Albertyn on the Polish side of the Polish–Soviet border, the Byzantine-Slavonic Rite was set up among a group of willing Orthodox.[7] Pope Pius and d'Herbigny were hopeful that the new rite would be the catalyst for the unification of the Catholic and Orthodox Churches.

Unfortunately divisions within Poland complicated the plan. Poland was not a monolithic Catholic country. Poland's population was roughly 25 percent non-Catholic. There were more than 3 million Jews and 4 million Orthodox Christians who were mainly Ukrainian and Belorussian. The remaining 75 percent of the population was mainly Catholic, but the Catholics were of different Rites that were at times at loggerheads and associated with divisive political agendas. The two major Rites were the Latin Catholics, who constituted roughly 17 million souls and who were largely ethnic Poles, and the Greek or Ukrainian Catholic Uniate Rite, which numbered about 3 million believers and who were largely Ukrainians living in western Ukraine, which had been part of the Austrian Empire before it collapsed at the end of World War I. When the new Poland was created after World War I and the Russo–Polish War, it included Lviv and western Ukraine.[8] In addition a small Armenian Catholic Rite existed in western Ukraine and there were more than 100,000 Lithuanian Latin Catholics who were mainly centered in Vilna, the historical capital of Lithuania that Poland took by force at the end of World War I, thus embittering relations between Poland and the new Baltic state of Lithuania.

The Polish Latin Catholics were led by Polish religious leaders who thought of the Eastern Rite as a Trojan horse for a Ukrainian separatist movement that hoped to establish a western Ukrainian state. They also thought that Ukrainian Eastern Catholicism was an inferior form of Catholicism and that the Ukrainian Catholics should forego their tradition and embrace Latin Catholicism. Polish politicians felt the same way and opposed the growth of Catholicism in its Uniate form because they thought it would hurt Polish unity, would not be effective against the Russians who had resisted calls for unity with Catholicism for some 900 years, and would actually irritate the Russians and stir up trouble between the Soviet Union and Poland at a time when the Poles wanted no trouble on their eastern border.[9]

The Ukrainian Catholic Church, on the other hand, was proud of its tradition and very much excited about expanding its form of Catholicism. It thought that it was the natural bridge between the Orthodox and Catholic worlds. Its leader was the previously mentioned and highly respected Metropolitan Andrei Sheptytsky. He was sensitive to the Polish politicians' fears of Ukrainian separatism and tried not to associate Greek Catholicism with Ukrainian nationalism, but his efforts, in the mind of Polish officials, fell woefully short, and, in any event, the Ukrainian Church, perhaps unwittingly, became a nucleus for western Ukrainian nationalism.[10]

Sheptytsky had hoped that Pope Pius XI would support a plan that would use him and the Ukrainian Catholic Church as the medium through which the Orthodox in Poland and eventually in Russia would be converted. Pius rejected the Ukrainian plan because he knew it would alienate the Poles. Sheptytsky was disappointed, but understood the necessity of finding an approach that might not upset the Poles and might appeal to Russian and Belorussian Orthodox the way a Ukrainian Catholic Church that had nationalist overtones could not.

The Poles, however, not only objected to the Ukrainian plan, but to Pius' hybrid plan. They thought that the pope's effort would alienate the Orthodox Christians who were under their control, a group whom they were trying to cultivate to be loyal citizens, because the new Rite smacked of Latin trickery – a kind of Rube Goldberg contraption with an Orthodox liturgy but led by celibate priests who answered to a Latin ordinary. They, therefore, decided against giving any support to the new Rite. Instead, they pursued their own idea of backing the creation of an independent Orthodox Church, free of Russian leadership, which would be dependent on the Poles and be grateful to the Poles for supporting Orthodox autocephaly. Ideally, they wanted the Orthodox to convert to Latin Catholicism, but since the Orthodox showed no affection for conversion, they opted for a solution that would at least separate the Orthodox within Poland from Russian leadership and perhaps set up a barrier between the Orthodox in Poland and the Communist government of Soviet Russia.[11]

Complicating the Polish plan, however, was the issue of ownership of church property. When the tsarist government ruled the eastern borderlands in the nineteenth century, it suppressed the Ukrainian Catholic Church there and turned over its property to the Orthodox Church. Now that the eastern borderlands were in the hands of the Poles, the Catholic Church laid claim to all former Uniate property. There was no attempt to negotiate a fair or reasonable settlement with the Orthodox Church. If the property were already in the hands of the Catholic Church, the Church simply took title to the property with the backing of the Polish government. If the Orthodox Church was using the property, the Catholic Church demanded and received compensation from the Orthodox Church. If the property were vacant and not in use, the title was transferred to the Catholic Church. However, the Polish government feared that the vacant Orthodox churches and chapels might strengthen the Ukrainian Uniate Church, which it was suspicious of, and so it decided to burn the empty buildings to the ground before the Ukrainian Catholics could take them. Complicating the situation even more, the Polish Latin Rite sent priests among the Ukrainian Orthodox and Ukrainian Catholics and tried to convert them to the Latin Rite. The Ukrainian Uniate leadership objected to the burnings and the proselytism.

The Vatican was aghast. No one was on the same page, and each group pursued its own agenda without reference to the political and national realities in the borderlands or in the Soviet Union.[12] The Orthodox under Polish control were utterly confused and alienated by the contradictory policies of the government and the Vatican, and so neither the new Rite nor Orthodox autocephaly took root in the Polish *kresy*.[13]

The d'Herbigny mission

Pope Pius XI and d'Herbigny were disappointed, but did not abandon their plan for the new Byzantine-Slavonic Rite. They thought it needed more time and fine-tuning. In the meantime, they searched for a strategy to strengthen Catholicism in Soviet Russia. It was decided that Father d'Herbigny should travel to the USSR on a tourist visa in 1925 to assess the status of the Catholic Church and Soviet policy toward religion. D'Herbigny arrived in Moscow on 4 October 1925. The Soviet government treated him with some importance and thought that he might be a facilitator for the establishment of diplomatic relations between the USSR and the Vatican. It allowed him to meet with the head of the Renovationist Church, who impressed the Jesuit. D'Herbigny naïvely thought that the existence of the Renovationist Church was a sign that Moscow was changing its position toward religion. He similarly concluded that the NEP indicated that the Communists were no longer hostile to private property.[14]

D'Herbigny departed the USSR on 20 October 1925 full of enthusiasm for the possibility of growing and strengthening Catholicism in the USSR. He thought that the time was ripe to reconstruct the Catholic hierarchy. The pope shared his confidence. Both Pope Pius and d'Herbigny were upset about the decimation of the Catholic hierarchy in Soviet Russia that had occurred in 1923. Together they devised a furtive plan to rebuild the Catholic hierarchy in Soviet Russia. They decided that d'Herbigny should return to the USSR, but now as a bishop with full powers to ordain bishops, restructure the Catholic Church, and possibly begin to grow the new Byzantine-Slavonic Rite, which showed the pope's willingness to be flexible on canonical issues.[15] The pope had d'Herbigny secretly consecrated a bishop on 29 March 1926 (Papal Nuncio Eugenio Pacelli in Berlin consecrated him), and d'Herbigny then returned to the USSR on 1 April 1926. The Soviet government again allowed him some freedom to move around the USSR because it believed he might help with the establishment of diplomatic relations between Moscow and the Vatican. In addition, he was French and the French government sponsored him, and Moscow was interested in improving its ties with Paris.

D'Herbigny's first stop was Moscow. Here he waited for Pie Eugène-Joseph Neveu (b. 1877), the French Assumptionist priest who had been toiling in Russia since 1907. Through the intercession of the French government, Neveu was permitted on 21 April to go from Kharkov to Moscow and assume the pastorate of St. Louis des Français, which was owned by the French and which provided religious services to the Catholic foreign community. When Neveu arrived in Moscow, d'Herbigny surprised him by ordaining him a bishop and naming him Apostolic Delegate in the Soviet Union with full authority to manage the Catholic Church and to set up new structures and jurisdictions for the Catholic Church within the Soviet Union. D'Herbigny also showed Neveu a map that divided the huge Soviet territory into ten apostolic administrations. Each administration was to have an apostolic administrator. Neveu gave D'Herbigny the names of priests who might be suitable candidates for the positions. D'Herbigny planned to travel to designate as many apostolic administrators as he could, and he told Neveu that he could fill in vacancies. Neveu's appointment was incredibly important and perhaps justified the pope and d'Herbigny's wild gambit to rebuild the Catholic hierarchy. Bishop Neveu proved a shrewd administrator and sharp analyst of Soviet religious and political policies, whom the Soviet regime was unwilling to touch because the French government supported him.[16] He also had the advantage of living in the French diplomatic compound and having access to the diplomatic pouches of France and other countries.

On 22 April, Bishop d'Herbigny left Moscow and visited over the span of almost three weeks various cities and towns where there were sizeable Catholic congregations and priests, including Kharkov, Odessa, Kiev, and Leningrad. On 1 May, he was in Kiev, where he named Theophilus Skalski (b. 1877) the apostolic administrator for the Lutsk-Zhitomir diocese. On 10 May, he was again in Moscow at St. Louis des Français Church, where he ordained Boleslas Sloskans (b. 1893), a Latvian, the bishop and apostolic administrator of the combined diocese of Mogilev-Minsk with residency in Minsk. On that same day, he ordained Alexander Frison (b. 1875) the bishop and the apostolic administrator of Odessa and Crimea and apostolic visitor to the diocese of Tiraspol. Frison, who was German, eventually reorganized the Tiraspol diocese into four subdivisions: central (head-quartered at Odessa), north (Volga region anchored on Saratov), south (Caucasus centered on Piatigorsk), and Tbilisi (for Catholics living in the Georgian Soviet Republic).[17] D'Herbigny also named two other apostolic administrators before he left the USSR: Augustin Baumtrog (b. 1882) for the Volga region and John Roth (b. 1881) for the Caucasus and Transcaucasia except for Georgia. On 16 May 1926, the Jesuit departed the USSR for Rome.

Bishop d'Herbigny returned to the USSR on 4 August 1926, but this time Moscow, now very suspicious of him, restricted his travels to the Russian region of the Soviet Union where there were few Catholics. On 13 August 1926, he ordained in Moscow Monsignor Antoni Malecki (b. 1861) bishop and named him apostolic administrator of Leningrad. Malecki, a deeply revered leader of Polish Catholics in Russia, had been released from prison in 1925.[18] The Church now had its full complement of four bishops (Neveu, Sloskans, Frison, and Malecki) and considered its hierarchy reconstituted. D'Herbigny also named the following apostolic administrators: Wincenty Ilgin (b. 1886) on 15 August 1926 for Kharkov (including part of the diocese of Mogilev) and on 1 September 1926 Mieczystaw [Mikhail] Joudokas (b. 1891) for Kazan, Samara, and Simbirsk, and Giuliani Gronski (b. 1873) for Irkutsk and East Siberia. He confirmed that Bishop Neveu was the highest Catholic authority in the USSR with full powers over all Catholics and with the right to appoint apostolic administrators and ordain bishops without the Holy See's approval if a death or vacancy occurred among the four living bishops. Neveu also supplied the Catholic clergy – bishops, priests, and nuns – with modest financial support and rudimentary care packages throughout his tenure as apostolic administrator in Moscow. On 4 September 1926, the Kremlin, which had closely watched d'Herbigny's activities, canceled his visa and expelled him.[19]

After d'Herbigny's departure from the Soviet Union, additional apostolic administrator appointments were announced, including Joseph Kruschinsky (b. 1865) for Odessa (co-apostolic administrator with Bishop Frison), Jan Swiderski for Kamieniec (part of the diocese of Mogilev), Stefan Demurov for Georgia and Azerbaizhan, Casmir Naskreski for Kamieniec-Podolski, who worked with Bishop Skalski, and Karapet Dilurgian and Akop Bakaratian for Armenian Rite Catholics.[20]

Apparently d'Herbigny was unaware that the Soviets had monitored closely his actions and knew very early of his effort to rebuild the hierarchy of the Catholic Church.[21] Reports emerged that one of his assistants in Rome, Father Alexander Deubner, was a Soviet agent who informed the Kremlin of what d'Herbigny was doing, but that was unlikely and the evidence is very circumstantial. It was more likely a case of Bishop d'Herbigny being naïve and careless in the face of a regime that had declared its opposition to religion and had shown consistently that it wanted to destroy the Catholic Church.[22]

Even before Bishop d'Herbigny was expelled from the Soviet Union, the Soviet regime started to move against the new Catholic leadership. In June 1926 Bishop Skalski, dean of St. Alexander Church in Kiev and apostolic administrator of the Zhitomir diocese, was arrested. He was charged with and found guilty of counterrevolutionary activities and sentenced to ten years' imprisonment. Skalski was more than simply a new bishop. He was a major figure, like Bishop Malecki, among the Polish Catholic minority living in the Soviet Union, which was virtually synonymous with Moscow's "Catholic problem." He was revered among the Polish Catholics in Ukraine (some 476,000 believers), and the Poles viewed him as a martyr.[23] The Soviet government wanted him gone because it viewed him as a barrier to the "sovietization" of the Poles. In 1930 he was sent to Poland as part of a prisoner exchange for Polish Communists.[24]

From the Soviet point of view, the Catholic Church was a barrier to absorbing Poles in the USSR and thus a bitter rebuttal to Communist claims to be the wave of the future. Moscow wanted to cut all ties to Catholic leaders in Poland, particularly the exiled Bishop der Ropp.[25] On 24 July 1926, Felix Dzerzhinsky, the head of the secret police (GPU), formerly the Cheka, informed the Politburo about the dangers of "Catholic religious circles." The Politburo then condemned the Catholic Church as "harmful" because it spread and harbored an "anti-Soviet character."[26] It was clear that the Kremlin was not about to allow the Catholic Church to reestablish its hierarchy and organizational structure.

In October 1926 Wincenty Ilgin, the new apostolic administrator of Kharkov, was arrested, found guilty of counterrevolutionary activity, and imprisoned. He was deported to Lithuania in 1933. Monsignor Michael Iodakas was arrested in 1926, released and arrested again in 1929, released and arrested again in 1933, and apparently died in 1937. Bishop Boleslas Sloskans was arrested in 1929 and sent to Latvia in 1932. Monsignor Dilurgian was arrested in 1929 and apparently died in prison. Bishop Frison was arrested in 1929, released, rearrested in 1930, and released. According to information from the Italian ambassador in Moscow, he was able to stabilize his ministry in the Crimea in 1933.[27] However, he was rearrested in 1935, released, arrested in 1936, and was executed in prison in 1937. In 1930 the Soviets arrested Monsignors Skalski and Swiderski, who were sent to Poland in 1932 in a prisoner exchange, and Monsignors Baumtrog and Roth, who both apparently died in prison.[28]

In 1930 Bishop Malecki was arrested and sent to Dubinino, near Bratsk, in Siberia. On 12 July 1933, the apostolic nuncio in Warsaw, Msgr. Francisco Margaggio, informed Bishop d'Herbigny that the former secretary of the Polish legation in Moscow, Alfredo Poninski, told him that the Polish government on 1 November 1932 had asked the Soviet government to release Bishop Malecki to improve relations and to fulfill the Treaty of Riga guarantees regarding the religious rights of the Polish minority in the USSR. Warsaw also suggested that Malecki's death in prison would be a major issue not just for Poland, but also for the entire world. Margaggio wrote that Poninski relayed the fact that the Polish ambassador in Moscow was working with the German, French, and Italian ambassadors to try to save and maintain historical Catholic churches in the major cities of the Soviet Union, including St. Peter and Paul in Moscow, St. Catherine in Leningrad, and other churches in Moscow, Kiev, and Kharkov, and that Poninski had kept Bishop Neveu informed of all of these activities.[29] Apparently, nothing came of the plan to preserve historical Catholic churches because they were closed in the course of the 1930s. However, the Soviet government did agree to allow Bishop Malecki, who was now quite ill and exhausted, to depart for Poland on 27 February 1934. He died in Warsaw on 15 January 1935.[30]

Neveu secretly ordained in 1932 another bishop, Father Bartholemew Remov, who had converted to Catholicism and who had been an Orthodox priest and rector of the Moscow Ecclesiastical Academy. Bishop Neveu gave him the title of archbishop and apostolic administrator of Eastern Rite Catholics in Moscow. Archbishop Bartholemew believed that the Catholic and Orthodox Churches should unite and forge a coalition against the Bolsheviks. Bishop d'Herbigny was thrilled about this development. He wanted Archbishop Remov to persuade other Orthodox bishops to come together to elect a patriarch who then might flee the Soviet Union for Rome, where he could declare a union of the Catholic and Orthodox Churches under the pope.[31]

On 23 May 1933, Bishop Skalski sent a report to Nuncio Margaggio that described the situation of the Catholic Church in Soviet Russia as dire. He divulged that that many priests were imprisoned in Solovetsky prison, including Exarch Leonid Fedorov.[32] Sometime in September or October 1933 Bishop Neveu sent d'Herbigny a list of Catholic priests exiled to Lithuania. Neveu said a Protestant pastor was also exiled and that most of his information came from the German ambassador in Moscow.[33] Apostolic Administrator Demurov communicated on 30 October 1933 from Baku that the Catholic Church's condition in the Caucasus region had not improved but had not yet deteriorated.[34]

In May 1932, Mother Catherine Abrikosova was sent to Butyrka Prison Hospital, where she was operated on for breast cancer. The Soviet regime released her in August 1932 and Bishop Neveu met her then for the first time when she visited St. Louis des Français Church. He wrote, "This genuine confessor of the Faith is very courageous; before such a well-tempered soul one feels small. She still looks ill. She uses only her right arm; she no longer has the use of her left arm." Mother Catherine was forced to leave Moscow and live in Kostroma from 1932 to 1933, where she was arrested again and sentenced to ten years in Butyrka Prison, where she died of cancer on 23 July 1936.[35]

The only Catholic official who was largely unhampered and unpressured was Bishop Neveu, who was the apostolic administrator in Moscow and pastor of St. Louis des Français Church. He became the chief broadcaster of what was happening to the Catholic Church in the Soviet Union in the 1930s until he had to depart the USSR to receive medical treatment in France in 1936.

As late as 1930 Pope Pius XI and Bishop d'Herbigny did not know the extent of what had happened and was happening to its newly designated hierarchy, mainly because communication was so poor and information so sparse. When the reality finally sunk in, however, Pope Pius XI and Bishop d'Herbigny remained confident that the conversion of Soviet Russia to Catholicism was still close at hand.[36] They also had faith in the new Byzantine-Slavonic Rite as a solid way to achieve union between the Orthodox and the Catholic Churches. In 1929 the pope named Bishop d'Herbigny the head of yet a new organization called the Collegium Russicum, a center in Rome dedicated to train priests for the new Byzantine-Slavonic

Rite. In 1930 he appointed him head of the Pro Russia Commission, which was now independent of the Congregation of Eastern Churches.[37]

Meanwhile, the Soviet campaign against the Catholic Church and religion persisted. In 1929 the import of religious and ethical literature was proscribed. In addition, a constitutional amendment prohibited religious organizations from publicly displaying their beliefs and rituals and engaging in religious propaganda. New laws also reiterated that priests had no civil rights and churches needed licenses to operate and remain open. On 8 April 1929, a new Law on Religious Associations stressed that religious associations had to register with the government and list a council of twenty adults. It also outlawed religious instruction of children, the sponsorship of religious events for young people, holding religious services outside of an approved and licensed religious building, promotion of public lectures on the Bible, and visitations to the sick and infirmed without government permission. In August 1929 Sundays and other holy days were declared regular workdays and their place was taken by new government-sanctioned holidays that celebrated the revolution and Communist leaders.[38]

The Kremlin also proceeded to close most of the lingering Catholic churches. Many of the buildings were converted into cinemas, cultural centers, and social spaces for children, and church bells were removed and used to support the industrialization fund under the First Five-Year Plan, which started in late 1928.[39] The Soviet archives detailed the government's use of propaganda, workers' petitions, class divisions, safety concerns, and claims of disloyalty to close the churches. A typical example was the story of a mainly Polish Catholic congregation whose church building in Samara was taken over by the local *soviet* and turned into a children's theater and movie house. On 24 May, the Soviet journal *Kommunist* declared that the Polish Catholic Church in Samara was an ideal building and location for a sorely needed children's cultural center. In the early summer of 1929 petitions from workers were gathered requesting that the Church be converted into such a cultural venue. On 15 July, workers from the Dzerzhinsky Polish Club of Samara declared that the Church worked on behalf of "Nepmen and fanatics," who opposed the interests of workers. On 7 December 1929, the Dzerzhinsky Club met again and voted eighty-five in favor of the petitioners with no one against and two abstentions, because, they resolved, the church and its priests were "counterrevolutionaries and spies" of Poland's Piłsudski government, "religion and the church" were "weapons of the class struggle against Soviet power," and, finally "God and the Church were not needed." On 1 January 1930, workers from the Middle Volga plant met and recommended that the Polish Church in Samara be closed and converted into a cultural center and that its bells and the bells of other churches be confiscated and used to help fund the industrialization drive.[40]

In 1931, after the Samara Church was closed, Polish believers petitioned for permission to use the chapel of the Catholic cemetery in Samara for religious services because their church was closed. On 23 April 1931, the Standing Committee on Religious Affairs under the Presidium of the Central Executive Committee in Moscow rejected the petition because the chapel did not meet the canonical regulations of Catholic Church buildings and was too small and thus unsafe to accommodate the number of petitioners. In addition, the Committee declared that other premises in Samara could be used for "Catholic worship."[41]

There was also an effort to spread atheism, including a special attempt in 1928–29 to turn the some 600,000 Polish Catholics on the Soviet side of the Soviet–Polish border into atheists so that they could then use them as agents to undermine the Catholic Church and spread atheism into Poland. Special zones called *Markhlevshchina* in Ukraine and *Dzerzhinshchina* in Belorussia were created where the Polish language was used and where organized, abiding programs spread atheism, assailed Catholicism, and promoted loyalty to the Soviet Union.[42] The Soviet plan could have been a response to the Vatican's advocacy of the new Byzantine-Slavonic rite among Orthodox Christians on the Polish side of the Polish–Soviet border.

Besides efforts to spread atheism, the Soviet government intensified anti-Catholic propaganda, which during the First Five-Year Plan and the hyperbolic collectivization drive blanketed Ukraine, Crimea, Belorussia, North Caucasus, and the Volga German region.[43] Much of it was uninspired and artless. One example in December 1929 urged Poles to forget Christmas and celebrate "a Day of Industrialization and Collectivization!" Another slogan announced, "Priests are faithful servants of Polish Fascists, capitalists and land owners!"[44]

However, some of the propaganda was more biting and hinted at unrest among the Catholic population. One example was a newspaper article from 15 January 1930 called "Gothic." It claimed that all churches were "false and corrupt," supported slavery, and groveled before the rich and powerful exploiting class, but that the worst religion by far was the Catholic Church. The article maintained that the Catholic Church exercised a powerful influence on world affairs and even moved Catherine the Great, but that its impact was always perverse and reactionary. It argued that the Church introduced the Inquisition, tortured and killed scientists and dissidents who did not agree with its "holy nonsense," slaughtered Huguenots during the St. Bartholomew's Day massacre, and frustrated the progress of science. It further claimed that the Catholic Church, with its signature "Gothic" cathedrals, was a tower of hypocrisy, immorality, and deception and that its clergy, from the pope down to the parish priest, who claimed to be celibate and chaste, engaged in sex. The article cited the case of one priest in Samara, who was identified as forty-three-year-old Father Władislav Kunda. The paper alleged that he was secretly married to a woman whom he had passed off as his sister and was, like Catholic priests everywhere, from Madrid to New York to Samara, hypocritical, deceitful, and "not alien to the tradition of Pope Alexander Borgia." The article went on to decry the Poles of Samara for inciting "religious fanaticism" because the government had closed the "Gothic" cathedral that housed such a clerical hypocrite.[45]

The Soviet report did not say what happened to Fr. Kunda. According to the Memorial Society, he left Samara and became pastor of another parish in Rogaczów. On 5 December 1935, he was arrested as "the leader of a counter-revolutionary nationalistic group of Catholic Poles" and sentenced on 20 May 1936 to eight years of hard labor and shot for "systematic, insurgent, anti-Soviet agitation among the convicts" on 31 August 1937.[46]

The Kremlin's animus against the Catholic Church also had an international aspect. The Comintern and the Society of Militant Atheism, whose followers were often called Bezbozhniki, intensified their vilification of the Catholic Church abroad. In November 1930 the Russian Bezbozhniki finally separated from the European Freethinkers and organized their own Communist Freethinkers' International with branches in Germany, France, Belgium, Poland, Switzerland, and Czechoslovakia. They also formed a Mexican affiliate in 1931 and a Spanish organization called Liga Atea in 1932. From these different venues, the Communists published regular attacks on the Catholic Church. The addition of Mexico and Spain was especially significant because their populations were overwhelmingly Catholic.[47] Regular articles attacking the pope and the Catholic Church also appeared in Soviet journals that had an international circulation. The French ambassador to the Soviet Union reported to the Holy See that *Izvestiia*, the chief newspaper of the Soviet government, was full of antireligious and anti-Catholic articles in 1927, 1928, and 1929.[48] After he was transferred to Madrid in 1931, he continued to inform the Vatican of *Izvestiia*'s anti-Catholic diatribes.[49]

In response to the intensification of persecution in the USSR, Pope Pius XI on 8 February 1930 wrote an open letter that accused the Soviet government of killing priests, morally corrupting children, blackmailing believers, and orchestrating "horrible and sacrilegious outrages" against the Catholic Church. He announced that he would offer a mass on 19 March "for the salvation of so many souls put to such dire trials and for the release of our dear Russian people and that these great tribulations may cease" and called on believers around the world to join him in a World Day of Prayer for the persecuted believers in the USSR.[50] The pope stressed that the Vatican had tried to work with the Soviet government, but that the regime refused to make any accommodation and was imprisoning clergy, closing churches, and orchestrating a general attack on religious believers.[51] The Pope's plea for a Day of Prayer called international attention and publicity to Moscow's attack on religion and led the Anglican Church and the Lutheran Church of Germany to join with the Catholic Church on 19 March in praying for the persecuted believers of Soviet Russia.[52]

The Soviet government responded to the pope's protests by noting that the Catholic Church was a formidable enemy and was attempting to organize a coalition of Wall Street capitalists and Kerensky supporters against Moscow.[53] On 27 March 1930, *Izvestiia* wrote, "The idiots and simpletons who underrate the political significance of the most reactionary force of present-day capitalist society have received an object lesson. . . . The Catholic Church is a powerful motor capable of inducing journalists to write, politicians to deliver speeches and organizers to go into action."[54]

However, the Kremlin was not actually disturbed. It was not embarrassed over its patent persecution of believers, and actually celebrated its campaign against religion.[55] If anything, the pope's public censure of the Soviet government accelerated the arrest and incarceration of the last ecclesiastical leaders whom d'Herbigny had put in place, including Malecki, Swiderski, Baumtorg, Roth, Skalski, Dirlugian, and Bagratian, who were all imprisoned in 1930. Bishop Theophilis Maluanis, a Lithuanian who worked with Malecki in Leningrad, was secretly consecrated a bishop by Neveu in February 1929, but he, too, was arrested in 1930.

On 30 June 1930, Pope Pius XI announced that prayers after Low Mass throughout the Catholic world would henceforth have as their major goal the end of the evils being visited on the people of Soviet Russia. Still, in spite of the unequivocal assaults on religion and Catholicism, he remained sanguine about the future of the Catholic Church in the Soviet Union. Bishop d'Herbigny was similarly confident, but he eventually left his Vatican post in November 1933 and settled in Belgium and then France. He had fallen out of favor and was undercut, not because of events in Ukraine or the USSR, but primarily because his headstrong and undiplomatic approach to running the Pro Russia Commission alienated his Jesuit superior, Fr. Ledochoswky, Polish political leaders, and many Vatican insiders. It is hard to say who put the knife in d'Herbigny's back – there were many suspects – but Pease concluded that it was probably a combination of the Polish politicians and the Polish Jesuit general.[56]

Notes

1 McVay and Luciuk 2011a, p. 3 n.4.
2 L'Archivio della Sacra Congregazione degli Affari Ecclesiastici Straordinari, Pontificia Commissione, Pro Russia, scatola (box), 11, fascicolo (file) 74, Pius XI to d'Herbigny, audience note, 24 March 1933, fogli (sheet(s), 30r, prot. 134/28 (henceforth cited as AES, Pro Russia, s., fasc., f.).
3 Dunn 2014.
4 One of the leading converts was writer and philosopher Helene Iswolsky. See Iswolsky 1985. Most of the Russians who converted to Catholicism were from nonreligious families. See Filatov and Vorontsova 2000, p. 74.
5 Pease 2009, pp. 166–67.
6 AES, *Pro Russia*, s.1, fasc. 1, f.5 (red number 5), f. 25 (numbered in red 13), prot. 1/28, 4 June 1925, Vatican; McVay and Luciuk 2011, vii.
7 Pease 2009, p. 156.
8 On the transformation and importance of Lviv, see Amar 2015.
9 Pease 2009, pp. 152–53.
10 Bociurkiw 1996, pp. 13–14.
11 Pease 2009, pp. 152–53.
12 Pease 2009, p. 170.
13 Pease 2009, pp. 169–72
14 Zugger 2001, p. 228, 234.
15 Zugger 2001, pp. 228–29. For Bishop d'Herbigny's view of his experience and of the Soviet government, see d'Herbigny 1930a and 1930b.
16 A very good biography of Bishop Neveu can be found in Wenger 1987 and in Pettinaroli 2008. Apostolic administrator was a position the Church used to administer Church affairs in areas with few or no bishops. Such a person could be a bishop but did not have to hold that title. Neveu was the chief representative of the Catholic Church in the USSR from 1926 until his departure in 1936.
17 Zugger 2001, p. 233.

18 For details on his life, see Czaplicki and Osipova 2014, "Biography of Servant of God, Bishop Antoni Malecki," at https://biographies.library.nd.edu/catalog/biography-0467 (accessed 4 April 2016).

19 AES, *Pro Russia*, s.1, fasc. 4, d'Herbigny to Secretary of State, 30 November 1926, Vatican, f. 15 and 16 (2), prot. 12/28.

20 *Istina i zhizn'* 1994, No. 6: 27–30; Zugger 2001, pp. 233–34.

21 Pease 2009, p. 158.

22 Pease 2009, pp. 158, 165–67.

23 Dunn 1977, p. 37.

24 Czaplicki and Osipova 2014, "Biography on Monsignor Teofil Skalski," at https://biographies.library.nd.edu/catalog/biography-0614 (accessed 4 April 2016).

25 RGASPI, Protokol No. 66, f. 89, op. 4, d. 14 (11 November 1925), l. 11–12.

26 RGASPI, f. 17, op. 113, d. 353 (24 July 1926), l. 9–10.

27 AES, *Pro Russia*, s. 14, fasc. 91, Giobbe archival note, 23 July 1933, Vatican, f. 31rv, prot. 710/28.

28 Zugger 2001, pp. 237–39.

29 AES, *Pro Russia*, s. 11, fasc. 75, Margaggio to d'Herbigny, 12 July 1933, Warsaw, n. 12221, f. 20, f. 22, prot. 134/28.

30 Czaplicki and Osipova 2014, "Biography of Servant of God, Bishop Antoni Malecki," at https://biographies.library.nd.edu/catalog/biography-0467 (accessed 4 April 2016).

31 Dunn 2004, pp. 86–87.

32 AES, *Pro Russia*, s. 11, fasc. 74, Skalski to Margaggio, 23 May 1933, f. 73rv, prot. 134/28, f. 73rv.

33 AES, *Pro Russia*, s. 11, fasc. 76, Neveu to Pro Russia Commission (transmitted from d'Herbigny to Mon. Tardini), October 1933, Moscow, f. 21, prot. 134/28.

34 AES, *Pro Russia*, s. 48, fasc. 283, Demurov to Mons. Sarkis Der Abrahamian, 30 October 1933, f. 26r.

35 Osipova [1999] 2014, pp. 79–82.

36 AES, *Pro Russia*, s.1, fasc. 7, 1930, prot. 87, 124, 125. D'Herbigny indicated that Pope Pius realized in 1927 that the crackdown on the newly appointed hierarchy meant that the Church's plan for eastward expansion had to be put on hold. The archives and official acts of the Holy See indicated that Pope Pius condemned the Communist persecution and was losing his optimism, but remained hopeful for another decade. On d'Herbigny's testimony, see McVay and Luciuk 2011b, p. vi. General confusion reigned in Rome over who was a bishop and the organization of the hierarchy. See Pettinaroli 2015, pp. 549–52.

37 McVay and Luciuk 2011b, p. vii.

38 RGASPI, Protokol No. 113, f.117, op. 113, d. 871 (29 January 1929), l. 36; Dunn 2004, p. 89; and Orleanskii 1930. Bishop Skalski, who was freed from prison in 1932, reported on the new rules in 1933. See AES, *Pro Russia*, s. 11, fasc. 74, Skalski to Margaggio, 23 May 1933, f. 73rv. prot. 134/28, f. 74rv.

39 By the end of the 1930s most of the Catholic churches in the USSR had been closed. After World War II, new churches operated because of Soviet annexation of the Baltic states, eastern Poland, and Bessarabia. According to the Russian archives, the Catholic Church in the USSR in 1962 had 1,179 Catholic communities, 1,184 clergy, and 15,298 active lay leaders in the USSR. The number of churches was not listed, but was steadily declining. See GARF, f. 6991, op. 4, d. 194 (1946), l. 6–45; d. 428 (1962), l. 1.

40 GARF, f. 1235, op. 66, d. 427 (24 May 1929), l. 151(a); (15 July 1929), l. 151 (d and v); (16 July 1929), l. 120; (7 December 1929), l. 112 (2); (1 January 1930), l. 116 (2); (12 January 1930), l. 151 (g); and (18 March 1931), l. 90, 93. Personal statements of petitioners in summer 1929 are listed in f. 1235, op. 66, d. 427, l. 120–149. General Józef Piłsudski was the de facto military dictator of Poland since May 1926 and considered by Moscow an archenemy of the USSR.

41 GARF, f. 1235, op. 66, d. 427 (23 April 1931), l. 89, 90, 93.
42 Czaplicki 2000, p. 15.
43 See Garkavenko 1965; Iaroslavskii 1932; Koval'chuk 1929.
44 Czaplicki 2000, p. 16.
45 GARF, f. 1235, op. 66, d. 427 (15 January 1930), l. 151(b).
46 Czaplicki and Osipova 2014, "Biography of Father Władysław Kunda," at https://biographies.library.nd.edu/catalog/biography-1069, accessed 11 March 2016.
47 Kolarz 1961, pp. 187–88.
48 AES, *Pro Russia*, s.1, fasc. 9, Jean Herbette to Papal Secretary of State and to Bishop d'Herbigny, 15 November 1927, f. 3; and to Bishop d'Herbigny, 2 December 1927, 7 February 1928; 1 May 1928; September 1929; 18 February, 1931, Moscow, f. 1–6.
49 AES, *Pro Russia*, s.1 1925–1935, fasc. 9, Jean Herbette to d'Herbigny, 18 February 1931, Madrid, f. 1–6.
50 Pius XI, "De Divinis Iuribus in Ditione Russica Dire Laesis Reparandis," *Acta Apostolicae Sedis*,, Vatican City, 1917–1939 (Acts of the Holy See), vol. 22 (1930): 89–93 (henceforth cited as *AAS*); "De Precibus pro Russia in Liturgia no latina," *AAS*, vol. 22 (1930): 366, 89–93; Pontificia Commissio Pro Russia, "De Precibus pro Russia in Liturgia no latina," *AAS*, vol. 22 (1930): 366.
51 Dunn 1977, p. 39; *L'Osservatore romano*, 9 February 1930; Zugger 2001, p. 252.
52 Dunn 1977, p. 39; Kolarz 1961, pp. 185–86.
53 Zugger 2001, p. 252; also see Iaroslavskii 1935, p. 168 and Zaborov 1956, p. 276.
54 *Izvestiia*, 27 March 1930.
55 Zugger 2001, p. 252.
56 Pease 2009, p. 167; also see Pettinaroli 2008, pt. 2, pp. 468–71 and Pettinaroli 2015, pp. 560–2, 564, 570–2.

References

Acta Apostolicae Sedis, Vatican City, 1917–39 (Acts of the Holy See), cited as *AAS*.
Amar, Tarik Cyril 2015, *The Paradox of Ukrainian Lviv. A Borderland City Between Nazis, Stalinists, and Nationalists*, Ithaca, NY: Cornell University Press.
Bociurkiw, Bohdan R. 1996, *The Ukrainian Greek Catholic Church and the Soviet State, 1939–1950*, Edmonton: Canadian Institute of Ukrainian Studies Press.
Czaplicki, Bronisław 2000, "A History of the Persecution," from *Kniga pomiati* 2000 Found at a History of the Persecutions: Catholic Church in Russia, pp. 1–42 (accessed 2 April 2016).
Czaplicki, Bronisław and Osipova, Irina 2014, *Book of Remembrance: Biography of Catholic Clergy and Laity in the Soviet Union (USSR) from 1918 to 1953*, Geraldine Kelly (trans.), and made available by University of Notre Dame at https://biographies.library.nd.edu/catalog/biography-0004 (accessed 2 April 2016).
d'Herbigny, Michel 1930a, *Évêques russes en exil*, Rome: Institut Oriental.
d'Herbigny, Michel, 1930b, *La guerre antireligieuse en Russie soviétique*, Paris: Bussière.
Dunn, Dennis J. 1977, *The Catholic Church and the Soviet Government, 1939–1949*, New York: *East European Quarterly* Series, distributed by Columbia University Press.
Dunn, Dennis J. 2004, *The Catholic Church and Russia: Popes, Patriarchs, Tsars and Commissars*, Aldershot, UK: Ashgate.
Dunn, Dennis 2014, Review of Antoine Arajakovsky's *The Way: Religious Thinkers of the Russian Immigration in Paris and Their Journal, 1925–1940*, John A. Jillions and Michael Plekon (ed.), Jerry Ryan (trans.) Notre Dame, IN: University of Notre Dame Press, 2013, *Catholic Historical Review* 100, no. 3 (Summer): 627–28.

Filatov, Sergei and Vorontsova, Lyudmila 2000, "Catholic and Anti-Catholic Traditions in Russia," *Religion, State & Society* 28, no. 1: 69–84.

Garkavenko, F. (ed.) 1965, *O religii i tserkvi. Sbornik documentov*, Moscow: Izd.- vo. politicheskoi literatury.

GARF (Gosudarstennyi arkiv Rossiiskoi Federatsii) f. A353, f. 1235, f. 6991, Moscow.

Iaroslavskii, E. 1932, *Protiv religii i tservi*, Moscow: Ogiz.

Iaroslavskii, E. 1935, *Bor'ba za predelenie religii*, Moscow: Ogiz.

Istina i zhizn', 1994, no. 6, 27–30.

Iswolsky, Helene 1985, *No Time to Grieve: An Autobiographical Journey*, Philadelphia, PA: Winchell; Distributed by Hippocrene Books of New York.

Izvestiia, 1930, 27 March.

Kolarz, Walter 1961, *Religion in the Soviet Union*, New York, Macmillan.

Koval'chuk, I. 1929, *Ks'ondzy na Ukraini*, Kharkov: Derzh. Vid-vo Ukraini.

L'Archivio della Sacra Congregazione degli Affari Ecclesiastici Straordinari, Pontificia Commissione, *Pro Russia*, scatola (box), fascicolo (file), fogli (sheet(s), Archivio Segreto Vaticano (cited as AES, *Pro Russia*, s., fasc., f.).

L'Osservatore romano, 1930, 9 February.

McVay, Athanasius D. and Luciuk, Lubomyr Y. (eds. and intro.) 2011a, *The Holy See and the Holodomor Documents from the Vatican Secret Archive on the Great Famine of 1932–1933 in Soviet Ukraine*, Toronto: University of Toronto.

McVay, Athanasius D. and Luciuk, Lubomyr Y. 2011b, "Introduction: The Holy See and the Holodomor," in *The Holy See and the Holodomor Documents from the Vatican Secret Archive on the Great Famine of 1932–1933 in Soviet Ukraine*, Athanasius D. McVay and Lubomyr Y. Luciuk (eds. and intro.), Toronto: University of Toronto, pp. iii–xxii.

Orleanskii, Nikolai (ed.) 1930, *Zakon o religioznykh ob'edineniiakh RSFSR*, Moscow: Izddatel'stvo bezbozhnik.

Osipova, Irina (comp. and ed.) [1999] 2014, *Brides of Christ, Martyrs for Russia: Mother Catherine Abrikosova and the Eastern Rite Dominican Sisters*, Geraldine Kelley (trans.), published by Geraldine Kelley, originally published as *Vozliubiv Boga i sleduia za Nim: Goneniia na russkikh katolikov v SSSR*, Moscow: Serebrianye niti, 1999.

Pease, Neal 2009, *Rome's Most Faithful Daughter: The Catholic Church and Independent Poland, 1914–1935*, Athens: Ohio University Press.

Pettinaroli, Laura 2008, "*La politique russe du Saint-Siège (1905–1939)*," Université Lyon 2 (November 2008).

Pettinaroli, Laura 2015, La Politique Russie du Saint-Siège (1905–1939), Rome: École française de Rome.

RGASPI (Rossiiskii gosudarstvennyi arkiv sotsial'no-politcheskoi istorii), fund 17, 89, Moscow.

Wenger, Antoine 1987, *Rome et Moscou, 1900–1950*, Paris: Desclée de Brouwer.

Zaborov, M. A. 1956, *Krestovye pokhody*, Moscow: Izd-vo. Akademii nauk SSSR.

Zugger, Rev. Christopher Lawrence 2001, *The Forgotten: Catholics of the Soviet Empire from Lenin Through Stalin*, Syracuse, NY: Syracuse University Press.

6 The Kremlin, the Catholic Church, and collectivization, 1928–1933

The Soviet government, NEP, and collectivization (Fourth Revolution)

In 1924 Lenin died and a power struggle to succeed him ensued among the top Communist leaders who sat in the Politburo. The fray revolved around the NEP. The left wing of the Party demanded that this concession to private property, this fundamental repudiation of communism, be abandoned and replaced by collectivization and that the government's main focus should be on stimulating the international revolution and overturning the Western global order. The right wing of the Party supported the continuation of the NEP because it had been a resounding success and had restored the agricultural sector of the Russian economy. Citizens of the Soviet Union were no longer starving. Its effectiveness meant that a middle class would develop and that the process of industrialization and, thus, the formation of a working class would evolve more slowly, but the Communists would still be in charge and would guide the development of a balanced economy while presumably favoring policies that grew industry and the working class. The international revolution would be supported, but carefully and not at the risk of endangering the Soviet economy and security. Both wings supported the antireligious campaign, but the right wing would have inevitably moderated the effort because the peasants were very religious and any middle class arising from the peasantry would reflect that heritage.

Stalin, who held the position of general secretary, weighed into the struggle by adopting what he called a "center without wings," which implied that he was moderate and could be cultivated. Both wings appealed to Stalin for his support. He used his whip hand to isolate and get rid of Trotsky, Kamenev, and Zinoviev – the most influential voices in the left wing who themselves were rivals – and replace them in the Politburo with his own supporters. He then turned against the right wing and substituted its leaders – Bukharin, Tomsky, and Radek – with his own henchmen and thereby consolidated his position as the leader of the Soviet Union.

By 1927–28 the power struggle over Lenin's successor was over and Stalin was in full control. He put the Soviet Union on a new course. He decided that the international revolution was not going to happen as quickly as the Communists had expected. The capitalist powers appeared stable and strong. Germany was again part of the Western global structure. The League of Nations was up and functioning. In China the Communists suffered a major defeat when Chiang Kai-shek turned on the Comintern and the Chinese Communist Party in 1927 and nearly wiped out the Chinese Communists in the so-called Shanghai massacre.

Faced with the reality that revolution was not about to sweep the world, Stalin ordered the Comintern to switch policies at the Sixth Comintern Congress in 1928.[1] He now wanted the Communists to fight and discredit foreign socialist political parties that were competing with the Communists for the support of the working class. He thought that the Communists could use the hiatus in the revolutionary tide to remove all rivals on the left side of the political spectrum so that when the revolution did resume the workers would have no one to turn to except the Communists. This policy soon led to massive clashes between the socialists and Communists in Western countries, particularly in Germany, which made the anti-Communist Nazi Party look attractive as a force to balance the disruptive left and restore order. Stalin demanded that the Germans engage in violence and get rid of moderates and opportunists within the Party. He reminded the Germans at a meeting of the Presidium of the Executive Committee of the Communist International that the Bolsheviks had shown the way forward, clearly articulating the doctrine of Soviet primacy, which maintained that every Communist Party must follow the Soviet model and submit to Soviet leadership. He declared that Communists gain strength from "fierce battles" with any representative "of the counterrevolutionary imperialist bourgeoisie" and must root out all "instances of conciliatory vacillation."[2]

Stalin also decided that the time was ripe to launch the Fourth Revolution, to reverse the outcome of the February Revolution and to build what he called "socialism in one country." Stalin's touchstone, his basic Weltanschauung, was a profound and extreme hatred of the Western global order and a determination to push the revolution, what he called "the great break," at home and abroad.[3] On 9 September 1929, he wrote Molotov, "Remember, we are waging a struggle . . . with the whole capitalist world."[4] All of his policies flowed from that central tenet, whether it was religious persecution, ending NEP, negotiating with Hitler, or dealing with Churchill, Roosevelt, or the Catholic Church and its leaders. Above all, Stalin wanted to get rid of the NEP and launch the transformation of Soviet Russia into a communist society where there would be neither private property nor religion, only a powerful industrial society with a mammoth, secular working class led by the Communist Party. In 1921 the Communists lacked the power to take on and defeat the peasants. Now in control of a large secret police force, the gulag prison system, and a strengthened Red Army, Stalin looked for an opportunity to cut down the peasants and build a communist society on their bones.

By the late 1920s, a difficulty had developed under the New Economic Policy. The spectacular recovery of agriculture led to an abundance of produce and to low prices for agricultural products. On the other hand, the lag in industrial recovery and the relative inefficiency of Russian industry – its high cost of production – made for a scarcity of what the peasants wished to buy. But the real reason for the scarcity seemed to be that even during the New Economic Policy, the Soviet regime was concentrating on the industry that backed up the preparation for war. In other words, it was focused on military production either directly or indirectly and was not absorbed in the production of large amounts of reasonably priced consumer goods. So the peasants were selling what they produced at low prices, and they could not buy what they wanted or else they had to pay too high a price for it. They concluded that they were getting the short end of the deal, that they were being cut between the blades of scissors, one blade being low prices for what they sold and the other being high prices for what they bought. And so they became discontented and began to withhold grain from the market at the end of the 1920s. This was called the Grain or Scissors Crisis.

The obvious way to deal with the problem was to allow the farmers to get more money for their produce and to admit more consumer goods from abroad into the Russian market, but the Communists did not want to do that because it would have meant slowing down Communist plans to industrialize Soviet Russia. What they wanted to do was to render the peasantry helpless or, in their more brutal language, they planned to "defang" the peasantry by forcing it into collective farms or better still into state farms where the peasants would work together and either have only a small claim on what was produced, as in the collective farm (the *kolkhoz*), or no claim at all, as in the state farm (the *sovkhoz*). In short, the Communists wanted to make the peasant workers in the field similar to workers in the factory, who were paid only wages. The aim was the reduction of the peasantry to a landless, wage-earning class that owned nothing, either as to the means of production, that is land and tools, or as to what was produced, that is, grain, vegetables, fruit, and other products.[5]

Stalin opted to use the Scissors Crisis as the excuse to move forward. On 1 October 1928, he announced that he was scrapping the New Economic Policy and opening up the First Five-Year Plan, to be succeeded by others. This plan had two major aspects: forced collectivization of agriculture and a rapid, even horrid pace of industrial development, and the first was to pay for the second, that is, agriculture would bear the brunt of paying for industrialization.[6] In this way more than 25 million individual productive units of agriculture were to undergo a hundredfold reduction, to about a quarter of a million collective and state farms. Thus, the peasants could be corralled and regimented and bent to the will of the state, as they could not have been with more than 25 million individual units.[7] The administrative task of forcing the peasants to do something under the system of individually controlled farms would have been absolutely impossible.

Once the peasants were forced into the gigantean productive farm units, they would have to part with a large share of their produce at abnormally low prices and buy it back in common with all the consumers as finished products at abnormally high prices – much above what the same goods would have cost had German or British or American goods been purchased. And this difference, sometimes called the turnover tax, was to go to the state as the chief source of capital for investment in industry. What was to be taken from the peasants at a very low price were to be known as the procurement payments, that is, the state was to procure them from the peasants. Generally the state was to claim between 30 percent and 40 percent of what the peasants produced in the form of these procurement payments. The peasants were to live off of the rest. They would have to feed their livestock, take out seed for their next crop, and if anything were left after all of this they could sell it on the open market. The procurement payments did what the state wanted them to do. They ensured a steady source of food for the army, always the army first, for the bureaucracy, and for the town populations in general. And so the institution of these procurement payments ended the grain crisis. The peasants would no longer be able to withhold grain. The procurement payments were put to them as their "first commandment" – notice the biblical language.[8]

The collectivization of agriculture began on 1 October 1928 and endured to the middle of the 1930s. It was one of the epic struggles of world history. Stalin probably had no idea at all of what he was getting into or what kind of resistance he was going to meet. He should have, for what he was doing was overturning the results of the revolution that had given all the land to the peasants. And now all the land was to be reclaimed from them and they were to be put as workers in the field on what had been their property. In addition, the peasants' religious worldview, culture, and institutions, particularly churches, were to be destroyed and replaced by a secular outlook that hinged on Communist ideology and organizations.

The peasants resisted with all of their strength.[9] They had no weapons with which to fight. The population had been thoroughly disarmed. One of the very first decrees of the Soviet regime was to take weapons away from the civilian population. That was done in 1918, as far as the Soviet regime was able to do it, but increasingly so in later years. So peasants had no weapons to speak of. They used anything they could get to fight the Communists, even sharpened files, clubs, primitive bows and arrows, and a good many Communist officials were killed. The peasants also destroyed their livestock in vast numbers, taking the position that if they could not keep their animals, the state would not get them either. But their main weapon was the grain strike or the refusal to plant more grain than what they needed for themselves. And so they did this in 1931 and 1932, only to find out that the government collected the procurement payments anyway, and if they had not produced something above that level, then they starved. And so here was the second reason for killing animals. The peasants had to eat because they were starving. The loss of livestock was mindboggling, a disaster the magnitude of which was unlike any other in history save perhaps for the Thirty Years' War in Central Europe in the seventeenth century. Within a few years, the livestock of the former Russian Empire was cut in half – cows, pigs, sheep, and, particularly, horses, which the government had planned to replace with tractors, but the tractor production did not keep pace with the elimination of horses, and then when tractors finally started to come off the assembly lines, much of the production was shifted to the making of tanks instead of tractors because Hitler had come into power in Germany in January 1933.

In the end, the famine of 1932–33 did show the peasants – gave them an object lesson – that they would have to meet the procurement payments. The times were altogether terrible and harrowing. It was an upheaval without parallel and destruction on a scale to baffle the imagination.[10] Collectivization gave Stalin control of the food supply, and he used it to cage and discipline the Soviet population. It was the foundation of his dictatorship. Stalin announced in 1932 that the First Five-Year Plan was so successful that it had achieved its goals in four years and that he was launching the Second Five-Year Plan, which accelerated the growth of the *kolkhoz* and *sovkhoz* farms, quickened the pace of industrialization, and multiplied attacks on religion and the peasant population.[11]

The pace of collectivization was frantic and its costs were enormous. There was a huge loss of human life. The estimates all range in the millions, but a lack of records meant no exact accounting. Recent research has put the figure at between 5 million and 7.5 million lives lost mainly in Ukraine, which was the principal farming area and the epicenter of collectivization.[12] Ukrainian scholars call this tragedy the *Holodomor* ("murder by starvation") and compare it to the Holocaust.[13] In addition to Ukraine, the Volga and Northern Caucasus regions were severely hit. Most of the loss of life was among Ukrainian Orthodox Christians, but Catholics shared proportional to their numbers in this government-orchestrated disaster, and, given the fact that Catholics – Ukrainians, Poles, and Volga Germans – were concentrated in these regions, that proportion was significant and inevitably reduced the number of Catholics in the USSR. They suffered and died alongside the millions of Orthodox Ukrainians and Russians and the thousands of Protestants. Stalin did his best to hide the crime and ultimately declared that stories of famine were nothing but rumors and that the peasants had hidden grain and only feigned starvation, charges prominent Western writers like Pulitzer Prize–winning reporter Walter Duranty of the *New York Times* supported.[14]

Besides the quantitative loss of life, there was an equally significant qualitative loss of life. Under the program the *kulaks* were to be liquidated as a class, and very often as individuals as well. Even if somehow some survived, they were not allowed to be in agriculture. They were barred from the new collective and state farms through an internal passport system. It was considered too dangerous to let them in. But the *kulaks* were the best farmers in Russia, as Lenin frankly admitted. They were independent in spirit; they were capable, intelligent, and angry at being subjected to collectivization.[15] Ilya Ehrenburg, the poet laureate of Stalinism, when describing the *kulaks*, said, "Not one of them was guilty of anything; but they belonged to a class that was guilty of everything."[16] It was no wonder that Soviet agriculture was so unproductive and failed consistently to produce enough food to feed the population.

The destruction of the *kulaks* as a class removed not just economic entrepreneurs from the economy, but also many of the lay leaders within the various religious communities. Again, the Orthodox Ukrainian Church suffered the greatest loss here, but the Catholic Church also suffered a proportional decline in its lay leaders. Thousands upon thousands of Catholic lay leaders died and thus were lost to the Church that counted on their energy, example, and volunteerism to be the spark plugs and champions who, with the clergy, would inspire and lead by example the community of believers. The clergy, too, were wiped out and they were often the key leaders of the town and village communities in Ukraine and the Volga and North Caucasus regions. Of course, too, the Communists closed village churches, confiscated church bells, and replaced traditional observances of religious holidays with new, revolutionary celebrations.[17]

The third cost of collectivization was the damage it did to the psyche and souls of human beings. It was and is hard to measure this consequence, but collectivization turned people into wretches, murderers, beggars, robbers, and cannibals. It debased people, destroyed families and neighborhoods, and wiped out beauty, joy, love, innocence, and awe. It obliterated dignity, morality, order, security, and traditional culture.[18] A letter from a Catholic lady in Ukraine, written on 6 July 1933, described the condition: "There are always a great number of beggars. Before the May Day celebrations there was a veritable invasion of the dying: thieves and people without shelter who then ended up dying in the street. But because it is unseemly to show our poverty and our hunger to foreigners (since they say there is neither famine nor unemployment here) trucks were driven through the city streets to grab those wretches by force, like stray dogs. And thus they disappear without leaving a trace."[19] Another eyewitness from the Northern Caucasus region wrote, "A woman, unable to see the suffering of her children, killed them and ate them, because she had gone mad." The witness went on to say, "the basic necessities are lacking," and, "in general, there is a universal moral depression and the feeling of a terrible fatigue."[20]

The final cost of collectivization was the damage it did to the minds of the perpetrators of these pernicious deeds. The authorities came to believe that they had to impose upon the peasantry a hated system in order to make way for a better future and had to starve and shoot any recalcitrant peasants and, particularly, the "rich" *kulak* peasants, who were or might be in alliance with external capitalist foes, and who were, in any event, a vile class enemy who was threatening them.

Fear and suspicion clouded the mind of Stalin. He decided enemies were everywhere – in his family, in the Party, in the USSR, and in capitalist countries. Stalin knew that many in his own party had no liking at all for what he was doing and perhaps he convinced himself that there was a broad-based fifth column in the USSR working on behalf of potential foreign invaders, and so he resolved to eliminate all opposition inside and outside of the party, actual or potential.[21] He did not spare anyone, including Communist leaders and top military commanders. Stalin wielded terrible power and did terrible things.[22]

The paranoia erupted during the First Five-Year Plan and reached a crescendo during the mid- and late 1930s. Stalin installed in office as head of the secret police a man named Nikolai Yezhov ("hedgehog" in Russian). Yezhov became the faithful executor of Stalin's determination to exterminate all opposition, the executioner of Stalin's enemies. The purges of 1936, 1937, and 1938 soaked the Soviet Union in blood, but firm and reliable numbers are missing. What can be said is that no one ever killed as many Communists as Stalin. In three years, he reduced the celebrated Party to a hunk of bloody meat. In place of the strong men who tried to stay his hand came the sycophants, the toadies, the yes men, and the belly crawlers.

There were also trials of common and everyday citizens. These had the objective of instilling fear in the population and convincing the masses that there was indeed a vast and iniquitous conspiracy, that enemies were everywhere and that no one could be trusted. Such an atmosphere allowed the government to take extreme measures of repression and to demand unreasonable sacrifices from the masses. The Catholic Church was included in the paranoia.

Almost every year starting in 1931 there were cases and trials of Catholics charged and found guilty of an array of crimes, including conspiracy, money laundering, counterrevolution espionage, and contact with foreigners.[23] In January 1934, a small group of Catholics was arrested in Leningrad. Their case, tried on 12 March, was called "the case of [a] Catholic attempt on the life of Comrade Stalin."[24] There was not much information on this trial, but the objective of the random terror was to instill fear, mindless submission, and tireless loyalty to Stalin and the revolution he was heading.[25] By the end of the 1930s, the purges persisted but now they were less public because it apparently had dawned on Stalin that the public executions were conveying to the world an image of weakness and of a country in disarray.

Stalin fashioned a system of government that used intense fear to maintain control and brutalize the people through abject fear and unrestrained and arbitrary coercion.[26] Collectivization was so effective in controlling the population that the Nazis, who were committed to overthrowing communism, kept the collective farms in place when they invaded and occupied the USSR in 1941. Stalin also constructed a great propaganda myth that such suffering was necessary because the Soviet Union was surrounded by external and internal enemies – capitalist states and *kulaks* and Nepmen – but would prevail because it was led by Stalin, who was an infallible, godlike leader. The myth also maintained to the outside world that there was no famine, no terror, no violence, and no genocide. In the midst of catastrophic famine, the Soviet government exported grain because it wanted to earn hard currency for industrialization and to project the myth that communism was an advanced ideology that had made the USSR stronger and wealthier than capitalist countries that were suffering through the Great Depression. The myth led the Soviet government to reject all offers of help and to try to cover over the debilitating and self-inflicted bloodletting and writhing convulsion of the collectivization struggle because it did not want to look weak and vulnerable before capitalist states that might attack or take advantage of it. And so we have Stalinism, with its collectivization, violence, fear, personality cult, arbitrariness, malevolence, paranoia, regimentation, and xenophobia. This was the new model the Soviet Union offered to the world in the 1930s as an alternative to Western values.

Correspondence related to collectivization from the Vatican archives

Correspondence found in the Vatican archives provides a glimpse of the horrors that befell Catholics in the Soviet Union and, by inference, other religious believers. The Soviet government hid the crime of imposed famine, so little information appeared at the time on what was occurring. The Vatican only slowly learned of the atrocity in early 1933.

The first record in the Vatican archives related to the famine was a note from Msgr. Heinrich Wienken, who was the head of Catholic Charities (Caritasverband) in Berlin from 1922 to 1936. He wrote to Bishop d'Herbigny on 15 March 1933 that a terrible famine had raged in Soviet Russia since fall 1932 and was having a devastating impact on Catholics in Ukraine and the Volga region. He said the mortality rate was higher than in the famine of 1921–22.[27]

Father Wienken reported three days later to the Munich branch of Catholica Unio, the Catholic organization dedicated to promoting the union of the Orthodox and Catholic Churches, with a copy to d'Herbigny, that "a huge number of people have begun to die" in Soviet Russia because of famine and that 150,000 Volga German Catholics were starving. He went on to say that the German Ministry of Foreign Affairs was planning to inform the Soviet government that of the large amount of grain for which it had contracted, 25,000 tons could instead be distributed "to the starving residents of German origin."[28] Bishop d'Herbigny briefed Pius XI about news of the Soviet famine, and the pope expressed his deep compassion for those who were suffering and hoped that money could be collected "in Germany and in German-speaking countries" and that Catholica Unio could spend a portion of what it collected to alleviate the suffering in the Soviet Union. He further said that the Holy See was very sensitive to the crisis but "cannot assist" directly because different faith groups were involved in gathering funds.[29]

In April the pope reiterated his hope that funds could be raised to help the starving people of Russia.[30] On 7 April 1933, a close friend of Msgr. Wienken, who was unnamed, sent him a harrowing report of starvation and death in Ukraine, which was passed on to Bishop d'Herbigny and he, in turn, informed Pius XI. He wrote that "everywhere there are a large number of starving people and beggars" and that "looting and theft are inevitable. Above all they steal food." He continued that if someone had a piece of bread, others would attack and bite the bread and the hand holding the bread. He further recorded that "I have never seen faces so thin and savage, and bodies so little and covered with rags. And the whole suffering and oppressed populace dying without rebelling. It is something truly incomprehensible." He went on, "the country is in real chaos. The trains are late every day by six, seven or fifteen hours. Railway accidents are habitual but, naturally, it is forbidden to write this in the newspapers." He further wrote, "Outbreaks of typhoid occur throughout the country. Neither soap nor wood nor coal is to be found. There is more suffering in the villages than in the cities. People who come from villages often recount that, if they do not see an inhabitant of some house looking out for several days, they force the doors open and find rotting corpses, dead of starvation. It is necessary to live here to understand and believe the scope of this widespread disaster. . . . I am certain that so vile, thieving and lying a government has never existed before."[31]

In the weeks that followed, Pope Pius told d'Herbigny that the papal nuncio in Paris, Luigi Maglione, should approach the Soviet ambassador and find out if the government would be open to direct famine aid. Such an approach was necessary because Moscow was denying that there was a famine and that its citizens were dying of starvation. If Moscow should reject the offer of aid, the pope continued, on the grounds that there was no famine, then the disaster should be publicized in *L'Osservatore romano*, the Vatican's newspaper. Moreover, it should be reported to the "Ambassadors accredited to the Holy See" that the Soviet government was engaged in a great "act of cruelty" by exporting "food from Russia when it is known that poverty and hunger prevail in the USSR."[32]

D'Herbigny informed Papal Secretary of State Eugenio Pacelli of the pope's thoughts, but Pacelli presented a strong case against aid. He argued that because the Soviet government insisted that there was no famine and had declined aid from the Germans and other aid groups, it would reject Vatican aid. Furthermore, he pointed out, if a papal offer of assistance were accepted, there was no way that the papacy could be assured that the aid would reach the starving masses and not simply be confiscated by the Kremlin for its own purposes.[33]

Adding strength to Pacelli's arguments was a communication that came from the Italian ambassador to the USSR, Bernardo Attolico (1930–35), which claimed that Bishop Neveu in Moscow thought that it would be imprudent for the Vatican to offer aid when the Soviet government was adamantly denying that there was a famine in the Soviet Union. Attolico concurred with Bishop Neveu and added, "given that, officially, a famine *does not exist* in the USSR any offering of aid, from whatever side it came, would certainly be declined. But in the case of an offering coming from the Holy See, it would certainly be taken as somewhat insulting and would probably provoke the revival of anti-Catholic persecutions and demonstrations."[34] The pope decided against making an offer of direct aid to the Soviet ambassador in Paris and looked for more indirect ways of helping the starving masses. News of the catastrophe was published in *L'Osservatore romano* in the spring and summer of 1933.[35]

Meanwhile, reports of more deaths from starvation arrived in Rome. The French chargé d'affaires in Moscow sent a report to the French government on 23 May 1933 that was then presented to Pope Pius XI on 3 July. The report was based on an eyewitness, three-week auto tour to the Volga and North Caucasus regions by the German agricultural attaché at the German Embassy in Moscow, Mr. Otto Schiller. He said that there were "whole districts where there is no longer a single living soul" and that "the number of casualties of the food crisis is estimated at around three million." He noted that, unlike the famine in 1921, this one hit the rural villages the worst and that the Soviet government made sure that the cities had food and kept out "some people through the passport system." In Ukraine, he wrote that various foreign consuls reported that the situation "is barely more favorable" and that "there is even mention of fairly common incidents of cannibalism." The German attaché further recorded that "in the cities, sanitary services had to be organized to immediately remove people who are dying in the streets. In Siberia, typhus causes considerable havoc, especially in Novosibirsk and Chita." He went on to say that the Soviet government was attempting to increase the grain supply, but that the commissioner of agriculture complained that the peasants in the giant *sovkhoz* farms were inefficient, lacked a proper work ethic, and left work early. Ironically, Schiller noted, the Soviet government had filed a lawsuit "against the German concession, 'Drusag,' which is a model of prosperity in the North Caucasus, under the pretext that it violated the law limiting the workday to 8 hours."[36]

In late May 1933 reports from the directors of Caritasverband in Berlin and Munich to the Vatican reported on the lingering famine in the Soviet Union and described a proposal the new Reich government made "to bring aid to the German settlers of the Ukraine in the horrendous famine that still rages there."[37] A story from the *Regensberger Anziger*, dated 11 June 1933, which the Pro Russia Commission forwarded to *L'Osservatore romano*, reported that there was "news from all along the Russian–Romanian border on the Dniester that the relentless crackle of machine guns can be heard, mowing down the crowds trying to escape" to Romania.[38] In June Pope Pius XI consigned 40,000 French francs to Bishop Neveu to spend on "the hungry of the USSR," particularly "for prisoners." He was open to forwarding other money to aid the starving people of Soviet Russia if it could be sent via an ecclesiastic like Eastern Rite Bishop Alexander Everinov in Paris or Father Vladimir Dlusski, a Russian Catholic priest, in Berlin. He also wanted to send assistance through Bishop Angelo Giuseppe Roncalli, the apostolic visitor to Bulgaria and the future Pope John XXIII, or Bishop Stefan Kurtev, the leader of Greek Catholics in Bulgaria, and to help the Armenians in the USSR.[39]

In July the Pro Russia Commission received a letter from an eyewitness, probably located in Ukraine or the North Caucasus region and identified as Irene V., who claimed that beggars were everywhere, people were dying in the streets, and murder for food was commonplace. The government, Irene stated, claimed that there was no poverty, no unemployment, and no famine, and yet people were poor, famished, and dying unless they "enjoyed the benevolence of the authorities." She noted, "Our church is very pitiful now."[40]

Another note to the Holy See in July, from General Secretary of the European Federation of Ukrainians Abroad N. Hrabovych, declared, "The Muscovites trampled on their rights, their religion, and sought to imprison their spirit. By taxes, by plundering, by the insane experiments of industrialization and collectivization, they have ruined the national economy. The Ukraine has offered them a vigorous and armed resistance. In order to break it, they deported hundreds of thousands of millions of Ukrainians, and organized a famine in the country. At this moment the Ukraine is suffering terribly from hunger, from typhus, and from terror."[41] On 23 July Ambassador Attolico, who was in Rome, informed Bishop Giobbe of the Pro Russia Commission that "between three and ten million" deaths had occurred and, "despite the death rate (which the Soviets boast to be a just punishment for peasants who refuse to sow), . . . the regime has not lost its will and is moving ahead."[42] On 24 July an appeal from Ukrainian émigrés in Paris pleaded for help for Soviet Ukrainians who were dying of hunger in the streets "of Kiev and the other cities" and "eating corpses in the countryside."[43]

Msgr. Wienken wrote Bishop d'Herbigny on 26 July 1933 that, although the new Reich government refused to make a contribution to a fundraising effort by the Internal Evangelical Mission, Caritasverband, and the Mennonite World Society to aid the starving people of the Soviet Union, it did permit the "People's League for Germanism Abroad" to organize "a public collection throughout the

Reich in agreement with the German Ministry of Propaganda" between 9 July and 1 October for the relief of the starving in Soviet Russia. Wienken reported that the effort was so far a great success, but that the Soviet government reacted to the project by ridiculing it, declaring that no one was starving in the USSR, and initiating its own program to collect funds "to alleviate the hunger that exists in Germany."[44]

On 3 August Msgr. Wienken informed d'Herbigny that newspapers from around the world reported on the famine and the huge death toll resulting from starvation and thus diluted the Soviet claims that there was no famine. In addition, he said that a broad effort was being organized to rebut the Soviet claims and to appeal for financial and political support to establish humanitarian assistance in the Soviet Union. Wienken added that Theodor Cardinal Innitzer of Vienna would likely lead the appeal and that perhaps American Catholics could persuade President Franklin D. Roosevelt to insert a "'humanitarian clause' [to open the way for an aid initiative on a grand scale] in the projected agreement between Roosevelt and the Soviet government regarding the recognition of Soviet Russia by the United States."[45]

On 9 August, Msgr. Giobbe asked Nuncio Cesare Orseningo in Berlin to advise the Pro Russia Commission and Secretary Pacelli on the best way to make sure that money and food collected for the starving citizens of the Soviet Union, in which Catholic groups were involved, "will be distributed" impartially and "priests and centers of the Catholic faithful in the USSR will also benefit proportionally and in the appropriate measure." He also reviewed for the nuncio the hurdles to assistance, everything from the Soviet government's denial to the Kremlin using aid for its own benefit and refusing to guarantee that assistance would be fairly dispersed.[46]

In August an anonymous letter describing the famine in the North Caucasus region reached the Vatican and was published in *L'Osservatore romano*. It reported, "Our life is a frenzy, full of tears and blood. The famine is such that people are dying on the roads, ten at a time. Many people have turned purple from hunger, are swollen and covered with sores. Some desperate mothers abandon their children in the streets. . . . Others, in desperation, kill their children or kill themselves." The letter went on, "Everywhere you can see people lying around starving, in post offices, public gardens and in the markets. The state is not helping and is indifferent to all those who do not qualify under the category of worker. . . . The endless queues of beggars . . . look for anything to eat in the rubbish. They dig up the tombs of the dead in the cemeteries, exhuming the corpses as soon as they are buried to eat them. Deaths from the contagion of eating human flesh are common." The letter further noted that cannibals snatched children from the streets and ate them, murders and robberies were commonplace, disease was everywhere, prisoners died routinely, no one could leave the cities or towns without a permit, and "a formerly thriving country has now been turned into a cemetery, reduced by ruthless barbarians to the appearance of a desert." It further added that "an implacable hatred is growing against the authorities, and there have been cases in which the whole population rose up against the Communists soldiers to kill them." It went on, "the state has relentlessly taken everything, depriving the population of necessities. They took the last stores of maize and vegetables, and nothing remains in the orchards and gardens. Everything that remained to plant in the nearby town was also eaten. There is nothing left to sow and who is still able to sow? Murders and robberies have reached the maximum." The letter ended by pleading for help.[47]

In August and September various aid groups tried to raise funds for the famine victims. The pope expressed his support and sent 10,000 lire to Caritasverband in Berlin but cautioned, according to Msgr. Giobbe, that "he did not see how it would be possible to initiate a new collection for the starving of Russia while the current universal crisis is raging and all the more since there is no guarantee that the gifts will reach the starving." In September–October 1933 Msgr. Wienken thanked d'Herbigny for the pope's gift of 10,000 lire for the fund for the starving in Soviet Russia and informed him that the fundraising effort by Cardinal Innitzer and another one by Dr. Ewald Ammende of Vienna, the chief of the Conference of Minorities, had failed. He also noted that the German consul in Odessa, Dr. Roth, was attempting to find out what had happened to the Catholic clergy in the Odessa region.[48]

Catholic leaders in the West were incredulous, flummoxed, and numbed over Stalin's policy of deliberately starving to death his own citizens, indeed, some of the Soviet Union's most productive people. On 22 January 1934, *Time* magazine quoted Theodor Cardinal Innitzer, Archbishop of Vienna, as follows: "In spite of all efforts to minimize and deny that catastrophic starvation conditions ravaged the Soviet Union in the days previous to the harvest it is herewith emphatically declared and certified that in the course of the previous year (1933) millions of innocent persons, many of whom were residents of the best and most fruitful parts of Russia such as the Ukraine and the North Caucasus, died of starvation."[49]

In the wake of the end of the First Five-Year Plan and its collectivization drive, the Vatican was in shock. It was clear that the Vatican's effort to engage Soviet Russia and to create opportunities for the Catholic Church in the USSR had failed. The Catholic Church had again lost most of its hierarchy and many of its priests. It had also suffered a serious depletion of its believers because many of them were concentrated in the target regions of collectivization and the imposed famine.

However, Pope Pius XI was not yet fully persuaded to give up on Soviet Russia. Part of the reluctance was that powerful anti-Communist forces had emerged by 1933–34, most notably Adolph Hitler, and his Nazi movement was as threatening to the Catholic Church and Western values as communism. The pope had to be very careful not to do anything that could be "misconstrued as favoring Hitler over Stalin."[50] He abhorred both of these maniacal messiahs. Furthermore, he still, deep down, held on to a sliver of hope that Soviet Russia's conversion was a possibility.

The Vatican was not a major power. It could only influence world affairs through discreet and indirect diplomacy. It had moral authority in some quarters, but not in the Soviet Union and, increasingly, not in Germany after Hitler took power in 1933. By the mid-1930s Catholic leaders saw only an increasingly bleak future and were caught up in the vortex of a storm where the Scylla of communism and the Charybdis of Nazism moved the world toward Armageddon.

Notes

1 Stalin 1949, 11: 307–24. Bukharin, who temporarily resurfaced in 1928 with Stalin's blessing, initially suggested the change of policy. See McDermott and Agnew 1996, pp. 68–78, 98–100.
2 Stalin 1949, 11: 322.
3 Fitzpatrick 2015, pp. 41–63; Khlevniuk 2015, p. 7; Stalin 1952, 12: 124–41.
4 Stalin to Molotov, 9 September 1929, in Lih, Naumov, and Khlevniuk 1995, p. 178.
5 See Graziosi 1996; Ulam 1987, p. x; Viola 1996, p. 44.
6 Brzezinski 1960, p. 188; Khlevniuk 2015, p. 10; Nove 1969, pp. 158–59.
7 Duranty applauded the compression. See Duranty 1935, p. 287; also see Ulam 1987, p. ix.
8 Jasny 1949, p. 363.
9 On peasant resistance, see Viola 1996, pp. 24–29.
10 See Documents 52–57 in Shearer and Khaustov 2014, pp. 91–101.
11 Fitzpatrick 2015, p. 46; Khlevniuk 2015, pp. 109–22.
12 Davies and Wheatcroft 2009, pp. 412–15; Khlevniuk 2015, p. 349 n.31; Naimark 2010. Also see Conquest 1986; Ulam 1987, pp. vii–viii; and Conquest 2000, p. 96, where he puts the number killed at 10 million. Also see Mass 2013, pp. 36–39.
13 Luciuk 2008; Marples 2007; Shapoval 2005.
14 See Fitzpatrick 1994, pp. 74–75; Fitzpatrick 2015, pp. 45–47; 81–83. On Duranty, see his columns in the *New York Times*, 15 November 1931 and 23 August 1933.
15 More than 2 million of the *kulaks* were relocated in the Ural, Western Siberia, and Kazakh regions. See Shearer and Khaustov 2014, p. 100, and Documents 60–65, pp. 101–10. Also see Conquest 1986, pp. 4, 70; Ulam 1987, pp. vi–viii.
16 Conquest 2000, p. 94.
17 On the new antireligious legislation, see RGASPI, Protokol No. 113, f. 117, op. 113, d. 871 (29 January 1929), l. 36; Garkavenko 1965; Iaroslavskii 1932; Koval'chuk 1929; Orleanskii 1930; Teodorovich 1958, p. 214; also see Fitzpatrick 1999, pp. 204–08; and Viola 1996, p. vii.
18 The plight of one Catholic community in Samara was recounted in GARF, f. 1235, op. 66, d. 427 (24 May 1929), l. 151(a); (15 July 1929), l. 151 (d and v); (16 July 1929), l. 120; (7 December 1929), l. 112 (2); (1 January 1930), l. 116 (2); (12 January 1930), l. 151 (g); and (18 March 1931), l. 90, 93. Also see Fitzpatrick 1999, pp. 213–14, 218–24; Viola 1996, pp. 39–40, 46–47. See the documents from peasants caught up in collectivization in Siegelbaum and Sokolov 2000.
19 L'Archivio della Sacra Congregazione degli Affari Ecclesiastici Straordinari, Pontificia Commissione, Pro Russia, scatola (box) 14, fascicolo (file) 91, Irene V to Spacca, 6 July 1933, fogli (sheet(s) 22r, prot. 710/28 (edited copy fogli 24r-25r) (note that Spacca submitted document on 26 July 1933), (henceforth cited as AES, Pro Russia, s., fasc., f.).
20 AES, *Pro Russia*, s. 14, fasc. 91, Anonymous letter, August 1933, f. 35r (Italian translation f. 36r).
21 See commentary and Documents 101–03 in Shearer and Khaustov 2014, pp. 10, 187–92. Also see Fitzpatrick 2015, p. 44; Getty and Naumov 2002, particularly pp. 114–18, which described a new law of 7 August 1932 that established both state ownership of the land and the death penalty for peasants caught stealing food from the farms.
22 Milovan Djilas, the Yugoslav Communist who was with Stalin during World War II, wrote, "every crime was possible to Stalin for there was not one he had not committed." See Djilas 1962, p. 187.
23 See, for example, Czaplicki and Osipova 2014, https://biographies.library.nd.edu/catalog/biography-0632, https://biographies.library.nd.edu/catalog/biography-1069, and https://biographies.library.nd.edu/catalog/biography-0458 (accessed 11 March 2016).
24 See *Istina i zhizn'* 1996, No. 21: 32–39.
25 One can obtain a sense of the arbitrariness yet certainty of Stalin's infallibility in his relations with his subordinates. For example, he told Molotov in 1930 to shoot

common cashiers to bring order into the banking and finance ministry. Nikita Khrushchev recalled that he did whatever Stalin told him to do, even to the point of seeing "everything . . . through Stalin's eyes" and speaking with Stalin's "mouth." On Molotov, see Lih, Naumov, and Khlevniuk 1995, p. 31. On Khrushchev, see Khrushchev 1974, p. 31.

26 With the opening of the archives in Russia following the collapse of the USSR in 1991, researchers began to reveal the extent of the Russian nightmare. See Shearer and Khaustov 2014 on the secret police as the main tool of Stalinism; also see Figes 2007; Kuromiya 2007.

27 AES, *Pro Russia*, s. 11, fasc. 74, Wienken to d'Herbigny, Berlin, 15 March 1933, f. 27r–28v (Italian translation f. 29rv). My guide to selecting documents for the 1932–34 period for analysis rested in large part on the work of McVay and Luciuk 2011a, pp. 2–81; and Pettinaroli 2008, pt. 2, pp. 762–67. Also see Pettinaroli 2015, pp. 803–8.

28 AES, *Pro Russia*, s. 11, fasc. 74, Wienken to Müller, Berlin, 18 March 1933, f. 31rv–32r (Italian translation f. 33rv).

29 AES, *Pro Russia*, s. 11, fasc. 74, Pius XI to d'Herbigny, audience note, 24 March 1933, f. 30r, prot. 134/28.

30 AES, *Pro Russia*, s. 11, fasc. 74, Pius XI to d'Herbigny, minutes of Pro Russia Commission meeting, 5 April 1933, f.44r, prot. 134/28; Pius XI to d'Herbigny, audience note, 17 April 1933, f.37rv, prot. 134/28.

31 AES, *Pro Russia*, s. 11, fasc. 74, Anonymous to Wienken, 7 April 1933, f. 53–54v. McVay and Luciuk 2011a, p. 5, reported that the writer was describing events in Ukraine.

32 AES, *Pro Russia*, s. 11, fasc. 74, Pius XI to d'Herbigny, audience note, 17 April 1933, f. 37rv, prot. 134/28; AES, *Pro Russia*, s. 11, fasc. 74, Pius XI to d'Herbigny, audience note, 30 April 1933, f.78r-78v, prot. 160/29 (original prot. Number 51/1930); AES, *Pro Russia*, s. 11, fasc. 74, Pro Russia Commission to Maglione, 1 May 1933, f. 49r, prot. 134/28 (original prot. Number 160/29); AES, *Pro Russia*, s. 11, fasc. 74, Müller to d'Herbigny, Munich, 16 May 1933, f. 57r (Italian summary f. 58r); AES, *Pro Russia*, s. 11, fasc. 74, d'Herbigny to Pius XI, audience note, 21 May 1933, f. 55r, prot. 134/28; AES, *Pro Russia*, s. 11, fasc. 74, d'Herbigny to Pius XI, audience note, 21 May 1933, f. 60r, prot. 134/28.

33 AES, *Pro Russia*, s. 11, fasc. 74, d'Herbigny to Pacelli, Vatican, 4 May 1933, f. 50rv, prot. 160/1929; AES, *Pro Russia*, s. 11, fasc. 74, minutes of Pro Russia Commission meeting, 10 May 1933, f. 51r, prot. 160/29; AES, *Pro Russia*, s. 11, fasc. 74, d'Herbigny to Pius XI, audience note, 21 May 1933, f. 62rv, prot. 134/28; AES, *Pro Russia*, s. 11, fasc. 74, d'Herbigny to Pius XI, audience note, 21 May 1933, f. 61r, prot. 134/28.

34 AES, *Russia*, poss. 666, fasc. 74, Attolico to Grandi and De Vecchi, 12 May 1933, XIth (eleventh year of Fascist era), f. 61 (italics in original).

35 AES, *Pro Russia*, s. 11, fasc. 74, d'Herbigny to Pius XI, audience note, 21 May 1933, f. 61r, prot. 134/28; AES, *Pro Russia*, s. 14, fasc. 91, Irene V to Spacca, 6 July 1933, f. 22r, prot. 710/28 (edited copy f. 24r-25r) (note that Spacca submitted document on 26 July 1933); AES, *Pro Russia*, s. 14, fasc. 91, archival note, 7 July 1933, f. 23r.

36 AES, *Pro Russia*, s. 14, fasc. 91, French chargé d'affaires in Moscow to French Foreign Ministry, Europe N. 139; Moscow, 23 May 1933 (presented to Pius XI, 3 July 1933), f. 21b–21c.

37 AES, *Pro Russia*, s. 11, fasc. 74, Giobbe to Pacelli, 27 May 1933, f. 67r, prot. 17/32; AES, *Pro Russia*, s. 11, fasc. 74, Pacelli to d'Herbigny, 30 May 1933, f. 69r, prot. 1511/33.

38 AES, *Pro Russia*, s. 14, fasc. 91, Pro Russia Commission to *L'Osservatore romano*, July 1933 1933, f. 28r–30r.

39 AES, *Pro Russia*, s. 11, fasc. 74, d'Herbigny to Pius XI, audience note, 10 June 1933, f. 79r, prot. 134/28; AES, *Pro Russia*, s. 11, fasc. 75, minutes of Pro Russia Commission meeting, 14 June 1933, f. 3r, 4r, 6r, prot. 17/32.

40 AES, *Pro Russia*, s. 14, fasc. 91, Irene V to Spacca, 6 July 1933, f. 22r, prot. 710/28 (edited copy f. 24r–25r) (note that Spacca submitted document on 26 July 1933).
41 AES, *Russia*, poss. 664 P.O., fasc. 28, Hrabovych to the Holy See, 7 July 1933, f. 60r (prot. 950/33); also see f. 28r, 29r, 30r, 31rv, 32rv, 33r.
42 AES, *Pro Russia*, s. 14, fasc. 91, Giobbe archival note, 23 July 1933, f. 31rv, prot. 710/28.
43 AES, *Pro Russia*, s. 14, fasc. 91, Ilya Kossenko, Paris, 23 July 1933, f. 33rv (document was added to the archives on 18 August 1933).
44 AES, *Pro Russia*, s. 11, fasc. 75, Wienken to d'Herbigny, Berlin, 26 July 1933, f. 26rv–29r (Italian translation f. 30r-31v); AES, *Pro Russia*, s. 11, fasc. 75, Orsenigo to d'Herbigny, Berlin, 27 July 1933, f. 25r, prot. 7798.
45 AES, *Pro Russia*, s. 11, fasc. 75, Wienken to d'Herbigny, Berlin, 3 August 1933, f. 49rv–50r (Italian translation f. 51rv-52r).
46 AES, *Pro Russia*, s. 11, fasc. 75, Giobbe to Orsenigo, Vatican, 9 August 1933, f. 57r-59r, prot. 134/28.
47 AES, *Pro Russia*, s. 14, fasc. 91, Anonymous letter, August 1933, f. 35r (Italian translation f. 36r).
48 AES, *Pro Russia*, s. 11, fasc. 75, Giobbe to Orsenigo, Vatican, 31 August 1933, f. 60r, prot. 134/28; Wienken to d'Herbigny, Berlin, 5 September 1933, f. 79–81r (Italian translation f. 82rv–83r); d'Herbigny to Pius XI, audience note, 9 September 1933, f. 84r, prot. 134/28; AES, *Pro Russia*, s. 11, fasc. 76, Wienken to d'Herbigny, Berlin, circa September–October 1933 (perhaps 9 October), f. 28r–29v.
49 Quoted in McVay and Luciuk 2011b, p. xxviii, n. 87.
50 Pettinaroli 2011, p. 84.

References

Brzezinski, Zbigniew 1960, *The Soviet Bloc: Unity and Conflict*, Cambridge, MA: Harvard University Press.

Conquest, Robert 1986, *The Harvest of Sorrow: Soviet Collectivization and the Terror-Famine*, New York: Oxford University Press.

Conquest, Robert 2000, *Reflections on a Ravaged Century*, New York: W. W. Norton.

Czaplicki, Bronisław and Osipova, Irina 2014, *Book of Remembrance: Biography of Catholic Clergy and Laity in the Soviet Union (USSR) from 1918 to 1953*, Geraldine Kelly (trans.), and made available by University of Notre Dame at https://biographies.library.nd.edu/catalog/biography-0004 (accessed 2 April 2016).

Davies, W. and Wheatcroft, Stephen G. 2009, *The Years of Hunger: Soviet Agriculture, 1931–1933*, Basingstoke: Palgrave Macmillan.

Djilas, Milovan 1962, *Conversations with Stalin*, New York: Harcourt Brace and Company.

Duranty, Walter 1935, *I Write as I Please*, New York: Simon and Schuster.

Figes, Orlando 2007, *The Whisperers: Private Life in Stalin's Russia*, New Haven, CT: Yale University Press.

Fitzpatrick, Shelia 1994, *Stalin's Peasants: Resistance and Survival in the Russian Village After Collectivization*, New York: Oxford University Press.

Fitzpatrick, Shelia 1999, *Everyday Stalinism: Ordinary Life in Extraordinary Times: Soviet Russia in the 1930s*, New York: Oxford University Press.

Fitzpatrick, Shelia 2015, *On Stalin's Team: The Years of Living Dangerously in Soviet Politics*, Princeton, NJ: Princeton University Press.

GARF (Gosudarstennyi arkiv Rossiiskoi Federatsii) f. 1235, Moscow.

Garkavenko, F. (ed.) 1965, *O religii i tserkvi. Sbornik dokumentov*, Moscow: Izd.- vo. politicheskoi literatury.

Getty, J. Arch. 2013, *Practicing Stalinism: Bolsheviks, Boyars, and the Persistence of Tradition*, New Haven, CT: Yale University Press.

Graziosi, Andrea 1996, *The Great Soviet Peasant War: Bolsheviks and Peasants, 1917–1933*, Cambridge: Ukrainian Research Institute of Harvard University.

Iaroslavskii, E. 1932, *Protiv religii i tservi*, Moscow: Ogiz.

Istina i zhizn', 1996, no. 21, 32–39.

Jasny, Naum 1949, *The Socialized Agriculture of the USSR*, Stanford, CA: Stanford University Press.

Khlevniuk, Oleg V. 2015, *Stalin: New Biography of a Dictator*, Nora Seligman Favorov (trans.), New Haven, CT: Yale University Press.

Khrushchev, Nikita 1974, *Khrushchev Remembers: The Glasnost Tapes*, Jerrold L. Schecter (ed. and trans.), Boston, MA: Little, Brown.

Koval'chuk, I. 1929, *Ks'ondzy na Ukraini*, Kharkov: Derzh. Vid-vo Ukraini.

Kuromiya, Hiroaki 2007, *The Voices of the Dead: Stalin's Great Terror in the 1930s*, New Haven, CT: Yale University Press.

L'Archivio della Sacra Congregazione degli Affari Ecclesiastici Straordinari, Pontificia Commissione, *Pro Russia*, scatola (box), fascicolo (file), fogli (sheet(s), Archivio Segreto Vaticano (cited as AES, *Pro Russia*, s., fasc., f.).

Lih, Lars T., Naumov, Oleg V., and Khlevniuk, Oleg V. (eds.) 1995, *Stalin's Letters to Molotov*, Catherine A. Fitzpatrick (trans.), New Haven, CT: Yale University Press.

Luciuk, Lobomyr (ed.) 2008, *Holodomor: Reflections on the Great Famine of 1932–1933 in Soviet Ukraine*, Kingston, ON: Kashtan Press.

Marples, David 2007, *Heroes and Villains: Creating National History in Contemporary Ukraine*, Budapest: Central European University Press.

Mass, Warren 2013, "Holodomor: Stalin's Holocaust in the Ukraine," *New American* 29, no. 21 (4 November): 36–39.

McDermott, Kevin and Agnew, Jeremy 1996, *The Comintern: A History of International Communism from Lenin to Stalin*, Basingstoke: Palgrave Macmillan.

McVay, Athanasius D. and Luciuk, Lubomyr Y. (eds. and intro.) 2011a, *The Holy See and the Holodomor Documents from the Vatican Secret Archive on the Great Famine of 1932–1933 in Soviet Ukraine*, Toronto: University of Toronto.

McVay, Athanasius D. and Luciuk, Lubomyr Y. 2011b, "Introduction: The Holy See and the Holodomor," in *The Holy See and the Holodomor Documents from the Vatican Secret Archive on the Great Famine of 1932–1933 in Soviet Ukraine*, Athanasius D. McVay and Lubomyr Y. Luciuk (eds. and intro.), Toronto: University of Toronto, pp. iii–xxii.

Naimark, Norman M. 2010, *Stalin's Genocide*, Princeton, NJ: Princeton University Press.

Nove, Alec 1969, *An Economic History of the U.S.S.R.*, London: Penguin Press.

Orleanskii, Nikolai (ed.) 1930, *Zakon o religioznykh ob'edeneniiakh RSFSR*, Moscow: Izddatel'stvo bezbozhnik.

Pettinaroli, Laura 2008, "*La politique russe du Saint-Siège (1905–1939)*," Université Lyon 2 (November).

Pettinaroli, Laura 2011, "Afterword," in *The Holy See and the Holodomor Documents from the Vatican Secret Archive on the Great Famine of 1932–1933 in Soviet Ukraine*, Athanasius D. McVay and Lubomyr Y. Luciuk (eds. and intro.), Toronto: University of Toronto, pp. 83–87.

Pettinaroli, Laura 2015, La Politique Russie du Saint-Siège (1905–1939), Rome: École française de Rome.

RGASPI (Rossiiskii gosudarstvennyi arkiv sotsial'no-politcheskoi istorii), fund 117, Moscow.

Shapoval, Yuri (ed.) 2005, *The Famine Genocide of 1932–1933 in Ukraine: A Documentary Collection*, Kingston, ON: Kashtan Press.

Shearer, David R. and Khaustov, Vladimir 2014, *Stalin and the Lubianka: A Documentary History of the Political Police and Security Organs in the Soviet Union, 1922–1953*. New Haven, CT: Yale University Press.

Siegelbaum, Lewis and Sokolov, Andrei, Hoisington, Thomas and Shabad, Steven (compilers and commentators) 2000, *Stalinism as a Way of Life: A Narrative in Documents*, New Haven, CT: Yale University Press.

Stalin, J. V. 1949–52, *Sochineniia*, vols. 11 and 12, Moscow: Gos. izd-vo. polit. lit-ry.

Teodorovich, N. 1958, "The Roman Catholics," *Genocide in the USSR*. New York: Scarecrow Press for the Institute for the Study of the USSR in Munich, pp. 214–18.

Ulam, Adam 1987, "Introduction," in *Execution by Hunger: The Hidden Holocaust*, Miron Dolot (ed.), New York: W. W. Norton, pp. vii–xi.

Viola, Lynne 1996, *Peasant Rebels Under Stalin: Collectivization and the Culture of Peasant Resistance*, New York: Oxford University Press.

7   Soviet Russia and the Catholic Church under Stalin, 1933–1934

The international scene, 1933–1934

In October 1929, almost a year after the start of collectivization in the Soviet Union, the Great Depression struck the world. It undercut security, confidence in access to resources and markets, social stability, and international cooperation and harmony, and put the global economy into a deadly downward spiral of unemployment, trade embargoes, falling prices, bankruptcies, protective tariffs, bank runs, and life-sucking poverty.

Stalin interpreted the Great Depression as the beginning of the end of capitalism and the Western global order. Rather than deemphasize the collectivization drive, the advocacy of international revolution, the war on socialists in Europe, and the persecution of the Catholic Church and religion, Stalin now determined that these efforts had to be intensified because the international revolution was about to unfold and the Soviet Union had to be prepared to provide global leadership in the dawning age of communism.

The Soviet government's unmitigated penchant for violence at home and its contumelious push for revolution abroad led eventually to a massive international, anti-Communist reaction in Asia and in Europe. In Asia, Japan took the lead in the anti-Communist front. In the 1920s and 1930s it built up its war machine. It was leery of the United States and Western European regimes that seemed preoccupied mainly with restraining Japanese power and denying Japan what its leaders thought was its legitimate place in Asia, but Japan was particularly incensed that the Soviet Union, which signed the Kellogg-Briand Pact, by which all signatories agreed to resolve conflicts without recourse to war, was using force in China to push its agenda. In 1929 the Red Army temporarily occupied railroads in northern Manchuria and through the Comintern provoked protests against Japanese investments in Manchuria and Korea. The United States, England, and France tried to mediate the conflict between the USSR and China, but were rebuffed. Stalin, always attentive to China, confided to Molotov on 5 December 1929, "We rebuffed America and England and France rather harshly for their attempt to intervene. We couldn't have done otherwise. Let them know what the Bolsheviks are like! I think the Chinese landowners won't forget the object lesson taught them by the Far East Army. We decided not to withdraw our troops from China until our conditions are guaranteed."[1] In summer 1931 the Comintern declared, "China's transition to the socialist road of development demands the utmost expansion of the territorial basis of the Soviets and Red Army, their victory over the armed forces of counter-revolution, and the establishment of Soviet authority over an area of decisive significance in China."[2]

The Japanese were outraged that Soviet Russia openly violated international agreements and that the League of Nations, the international organization that many hoped would be able to resolve conflict through democratic procedures and negotiation before it led to war, did not address Soviet behavior. It appeared to be a hapless debating society. In September 1931 the Japanese decided to take matters into their own hands. They invaded Manchuria, changing the name of the Chinese province to Manchukuo. Once in Manchuria, Japan positioned its army on the Manchurian–Siberian border of the USSR near the maritime province from which Japan had evacuated only in 1922. The League of Nations did condemn the Japanese invasion and invoked embargoes against Japan, but they were not enforced. Radical right politicians, particularly in Germany and Italy, took note of the fact that Japan had acted decisively and had been able to take over the most developed part of China without any significant repercussion other than expulsion from the League of Nations.

Japan's proactive anti-Communism did not plague Stalin. He viewed the Japanese effort as another sign of capitalism's self-destructive, imperialist tendencies, which would ultimately help push the capitalist states into war and usher in the international revolution and the Communist era. However, until that happened, he did worry about the formation of an anti-Communist coalition against the Soviet Union and, specifically, about the presence of the Japanese army on the Soviet border in Siberia. He wanted to avoid war with Japan, particularly with the collectivization drive ripping a gaping wound into Soviet society and with the Red Army still being strengthened with the industrialization program. He pursued three policies to discourage the Japanese from attacking the USSR. The Comintern offered Chiang Kai-shek and the KMT military assistance if it would join with the Chinese Communist Party in a war against Japan. A Sino–Japanese war would help bog down the Japanese in China and potentially dissuade them from opening a new front against the USSR. Chiang Kai-shek, however, rejected the proposal. He preferred to defeat the Chinese Communists before he challenged the Japanese. The Chinese Communists did declare war on Japan, not to fight since they were far removed from Manchuria, but to try to embarrass the KMT into suspending the civil war and make common cause with them against the Japanese.

Second, Stalin placed the Red Army on the Manchurian border as a warning to Japan that any attack on the Soviet Union would be met with fierce resistance and battle. The Japanese probed the Soviet defense with a series of small skirmishes in the 1930s, but refrained from a major test while it consolidated its position in Manchuria and looked for potential allies.

Finally, Stalin reached out to the United States, which was a major Pacific power suspicious of Japanese intentions. Stalin thought that American interest in the Pacific, including the possibility of mineral consignments in Siberia, would lead the United States to work with the USSR to block Japan. In Stalin's mind, an intra-capitalist war between Japan and the United States was virtually inevitable and would buttress Soviet security in Asia. He made clear to Molotov on 19 June 1932 that the United States would like "to drag" the Soviet Union into war with Japan through "flattery," but "we can tell them to go to hell."[3] Instead, he wanted to have the United States check Japan.

Stalin's American demarche paid off with the signing of the Roosevelt-Litvinov Agreement in November 1933. The new government of Franklin D. Roosevelt that took power in 1933 was intent on two goals: first, developing policies to overcome the unemployment and economic turmoil of the Great Depression and, second, to check the predator nations of the world, particularly Japan in Asia. To achieve the latter goal, Roosevelt decided that the United States should establish diplomatic relations with the Soviet Union, which was achieved on 15 November 1933 with the signing of the Roosevelt-Litvinov Agreement. His action was intended to alert Japan that the United States and the Soviet Union, in spite of their ideological differences, might cooperate to check Japanese aggression in the Pacific. It was a warning shot across Japan's bow.

Stalin was hoping for more. When the new American ambassador, William C. Bullitt, arrived in Moscow in December 1933 for a brief visit, Stalin asked him if the Americans would help the USSR against Japan and in early 1934 had other Soviet officials pressure Bullitt on what the United States was going to do to curb Japan and suggest for starters that the United States should send a navel squadron to visit Vladivostok.[4]

All in all, Stalin's policies kept the Japanese at bay. It was not until 1938 that Japan made a move against the Red Army and then it discovered that the Red Army was a formidable force and that an invasion of Siberia would be difficult and so it pulled back and waited for its ally, Nazi Germany, to decide on future action against the USSR.

In Europe, Germany ended up being the major antagonist to communism and the Soviet Union. Initially, it was unclear if the radical left, the German Communist Party, or the radical right, Adolph Hitler's Nazi Party, would take power. Both political extremes worked to unhinge support for the democratic Weimar regime and found support among Germans upset over the outcome of World War I, the provisions of the Versailles Treaty, incompetent government, and the large-scale unemployment resulting from the onset of the Great Depression. The Nazis drew additional support from Germans aghast over the German Communist Party's Comintern-inspired violence against German socialists and the Kremlin's unprecedented, government-sanctioned famine and mass starvation of its citizens in the name of communist ideology.

In the 1930 and 1932 Reichstag elections the German Communist Party showed strength, capturing seventy-seven and eighty-nine seats, respectively. However, Hitler's Nazi Party manifested more vigor and captured 37.4 percent of the vote in 1932 and 230 seats in the Reichstag, the single largest voting bloc. In January 1933 Hitler was named chancellor of the German government. The political elite thought that it could use him to check the Communists and simultaneously attenuate his other extreme views on race and *lebensraum*. The German establishment soon discovered that it could not control Hitler. In short order, he suspended the constitution, removed rivals, and established a dictatorship.[5] He played the anti-Communist card to great advantage.

Anti-Communism enabled Hitler domestically to check liberals, moderate politicians, the middle class, and the Christian churches, which were more afraid of communism than Nazism. The horrendous stories of death, famine, carnage, mayhem, murder, and cannibalism flowing out of the Soviet Union provided concrete evidence that communism was an abomination beyond imagination and a menace to established order.

Anti-Communism also allowed Hitler to fan anti-Semitism, which already existed in the hyper-nationalistic Central and Eastern European states, because he equated the Communist threat with Jews. Nazi propaganda blazoned that many former and current top Communists were Jews, including Leon Trotsky, Lev Kamenev, Grigory Zinoviev, Mikhail Tomsky, Nikolai Bukharin, Alexei Rykov, Lazar Kaganovich, and Maxim Litvinov, the Soviet foreign minister.[6] Of course, most Jews were anti-Communist and became victims of Stalin just like other religious and national groups in the Soviet Union, but that fact was buried in the frenzied and polarized world of the 1930s. With cynicism and resolve, Hitler began to loosen the moral order of Germany and Central and Eastern Europe. Just as much as Stalin, he intended to choke the life out of the Judeo-Christian moral order, dim the beam of Western culture, and create a new world where, in the words of Modris Eksteins, "borders and limits became meaningless."[7]

Anti-Communism also permitted Hitler to keep the Versailles Treaty enforcers at bay and seduce them to appease some of his demands, both in the abandonment of the Versailles Treaty articles related to Germany's rearmament and in the annexation into Germany of Austria and the Sudetenland of Czechoslovakia. As Oleg Khlevniuk noted, the Western powers were open to Hitler's revisionism because of the "fundamental incompatibility" of Stalinism with Western values.[8]

Anti-Communism, in addition, gave Hitler a means to subvert the young, small, eponymous democracies that had appeared in Central and Eastern Europe after the breakup of the Russian, Austro-Hungarian, and Ottoman Empires at the conclusion of World War I – a beneficial fruit of Western religio-political values. These countries were afraid of Germany, but more fearful of Soviet Russia with its loathsome policies of collectivization, atheism, forced labor, and wholesale use of genocide to wipe out what it called class enemies and bourgeois nationalists.

Poland, Czechoslovakia, Hungary, Romania, Bulgaria, Yugoslavia, and the Baltic states should have cooperated with one another to promote their mutual security, but these new governments lost perspective on their own national interests in fits of ultra-nationalism and irredentism that led to tension among neighbors and exposed the whole region to manipulation by the Nazis.[9] Nazi Germany softened up the Eastern European governments by agreeing to buy their agricultural produce at market or above market prices in the wake of the Great Depression, when their foreign markets dried up. No state in Eastern Europe could resist the German offer, not even Poland, Czechoslovakia, and Yugoslavia, which were directly threatened by the Nazis. The Germans took over their economies and tied them to Germany's economy by paying high prices for food but placing the payments in German accounts that were blocked other than for purchases of German goods. In effect, the countries of Eastern Europe became part of the German war machine and economic engine.[10]

With growing support or at least acquiescence or indifference, Hitler prepared to halt and eliminate the Communist threat. In March 1935 he reintroduced the draft and started to rebuild the German military forces in violation of the Versailles Treaty. In March 1936, he remilitarized the Rhineland, which also violated the Versailles Treaty and neutralized France's military commitments to various Eastern European governments with which it had signed agreements of military cooperation. In July 1936 he supported Franco's forces in Spain against its Republican government, which was backed by the Comintern. Mussolini, who had attacked Abyssinia in October 1935 with Hitler's support, joined the Germans in support of Franco. The Spanish Civil War suddenly became a proxy war between the radical right and the radical left.[11] In November 1936 Japan and Germany signed the Anti-Comintern Pact, and Italy became a signatory a few months later. Italy was increasingly viewed as the junior partner to Germany. It followed the German lead on war and racism, including Hitler's anti-Semitism, although Mussolini's anti-Semitism was more pragmatic than ideological.[12]

When the anti-Communist reaction first mushroomed in the early 1930s, Stalin was untroubled. For him it was a sign of capitalism's denouement. As late as 1933, he was enthusiastic about the coming revolution and gave no quarter to the Western powers that might help check the radical right. In January 1933 he told Molotov that he liked his vitriolic and dismissive attack on the Western states, which was contained in an address Molotov gave to the Central Executive Committee and was published in *Pravda* on 24 January 1933. "The confident, contemptuous tone with respect to the 'great' powers," Stalin wrote, "the belief in our own strength, the delicate but plain spitting in the pot of the swaggering 'great powers' – very good. Let them eat it."[13]

Soviet government and the Catholic Church, 1933–1934

The growing tide of anti-Communism around the world and the threat of war in Asia and Europe did not lead Stalin to ameliorate treatment of the Catholic Church in the Soviet Union. In fact, Stalin intensified persecution of the Church. Bishop d'Herbigny wrote on 17 June 1933 that the pope anguished over the Soviet government's steadfast torture of Catholic priests in Soviet Russia and strongly supported the surviving priests in Soviet Russia and hoped that they would be able to persevere to guide the moral and spiritual path of the faithful in the face of the Bolshevik attack.[14] Bishop d'Herbigny in October 1933 gave to Msgr. Domenico Tardini, undersecretary of the Sacred Congregation for Extraordinary Ecclesiastical Affairs, a list of priests whom the Soviets deported to Lithuania, which he said the German ambassador had provided to him.[15]

A report from November 1933 in the Vatican archives, probably prepared by the Pro Russia Commission with information from Bishop Neveu, indicated that the condition of the Catholic Church in the USSR was stark and that the Polish ambassador in Moscow, Juliusz Łukasiewicz, reported widespread religious repression and a lack of priests in the western borderlands of the Soviet Union, conditions the Polish representative said were the result of Soviet government policies.[16]

One positive development for the Catholic Church in November 1933, which had nothing to do with Stalin, came as a result of President Roosevelt's desire to establish diplomatic relations with the Soviet Union. His plan was controversial in the United States because a significant part of the base of the Democratic Party, which was responsible for Roosevelt's election as president in 1932, was the labor unions and the Christian churches, particularly the Catholic Church. Both the unions and the Catholic Church were opposed to a diplomatic relationship with the Soviet Union because of its mistreatment of workers and its persecution of religion.

Roosevelt dealt with the opposition by lining up labor and religious leaders who supported his initiative, including Fr. Edmund Walsh, vice president of Georgetown University and former head of the Papal Famine Relief Mission to the USSR in 1922. He also threw the Catholic Church a bone. Inserted in the Roosevelt-Litvinov Agreement of 15 November 1933, which established diplomatic relations, was a clause that guaranteed that Americans assigned to the United States Embassy in the USSR could practice their religion and that American religious groups could assign religious personnel to provide pastoral services at the embassy. The Vatican archives had a copy of the correspondence between Roosevelt and Litvinov, including Roosevelt's stipulation that "clergymen, priests, rabbis or other ecclesiastical functionaries will be protected from all disability or persecution and will not be denied entry into the territory of the Soviet Union because of their ecclesiastical status," and Litvinov's disingenuous reply that Soviet law (Criminal Code, art. 137) prohibited any interference in the practice of religion, providing such practice does not endanger other citizens, and that all American citizens will have the same religious rights as Soviet citizens. As for visas, the Soviet government, Litvinov said, reserved the right to issue visas, but "will not discriminate on the basis of ecclesiastical status."[17]

The Soviet government desperately wanted diplomatic relations with the United States and, in its own chary way, tried to soften the Catholic Church's opposition in the United States. B. E. Skvirsky, an unofficial representative of the USSR in Washington, contacted Fr. Walsh and told him that U.S. diplomatic recognition might mean freedom for Catholic clergy in Soviet prisons. Without a hint of speciousness, he asked Fr. Walsh if he had a list of bishops and priests in Soviet prisons. Fr. Walsh told him that he thought there were three bishops and about 200 priests in prison, but he did not have certain information. Skvirsky wanted to know the names and locations of the prisoners. Walsh contacted Bishop d'Herbigny, but he was away from the Pro Russia Commission because of an illness, and so, receiving no reply, he informed Msgr. Amleto Giovanni Cicognani, who was the apostolic delegate in Washington, of Skvirsky's request. Cicognani then contacted Cardinal Tardini with the request but warned that if Fr. Walsh gave him a list that included deceased or free priests, then Skvirsky "would use it to discredit" Catholics in general and Fr. Walsh in particular. The Pro Russia Commission compiled a list, but it was not clear if Fr. Walsh received and communicated it to Skvirsky, but, in any event, no change came in the status of imprisoned Catholic clergy.[18] Perhaps, Skvirsky's goal was simply to distract the Church from its opposition to recognition by baiting it, but once recognition was obtained on 15 November, Moscow no longer had any concern in appearing to mollify the Catholic Church.[19]

The upshot of Roosevelt's maneuvering was the inclusion of a religious clause in the Roosevelt-Litvinov Agreement that permitted the Catholic Church to assign a priest to care for the spiritual needs of American Catholic diplomats in Moscow. The Vatican immediately assigned an American Assumptionist priest, Father Léopold Braun, to the new American Embassy.[20] The Assumptionist order was chosen because Bishop Neveu was an Assumptionist, and the Church thought that a priest from the same missionary order would establish a pattern of continuity and coordination. The French government wanted reassurance from Bishop Neveu that St. Louis des Français would remain a French church.[21]

Fr. Léopold Braun, who arrived in Moscow in March 1934, was a good man. He was a conservative Catholic priest who was knowledgeable about Catholic doctrine but largely unfamiliar with Soviet Russia, the Russian language, communism, Stalin, and international relations. His job was to provide religious ministry to American and other foreign Catholics in Moscow, who were usually associated with diplomatic service. At that he was good. He was not as good as Neveu at diplomacy, political analysis, or deflection of Soviet machinations, surveillance, and pressure, but his reports were valuable. When Bishop Neveu left Moscow in 1936 and was refused a reentry visa, Fr. Braun became the pastor of St. Louis des François Church, assumed the role of spiritual director for many foreign Catholics in the diplomatic community, and served, ipso facto, as the public representative of the Catholic Church in the Soviet Union. He witnessed the Soviets' self-flagellation during the purge trials, the tense events surrounding the Ribbentrop-Molotov Agreement, the start of World War II, the reaction of the Muscovites to the Nazi attack in 1941, and the resurgence of the Soviet Union after the Battle of Stalingrad. He left in December 1945, mainly being withdrawn because the Soviets complained to the U.S. government that he was persona non grata.[22]

Braun's experience was the subject of a memoir that was published in 2006.[23] The memoir recounted his day-to-day life as a priest and shed some light on the dramatic events unfolding in Moscow related to the purge trials in the mid- and late 1930s. In general, Braun discovered that the Soviets had no use or respect for him and only tolerated him because he was indirectly a part of the American delegation in Moscow, even though he had no diplomatic immunity. When Braun arrived in Moscow on 1 March 1934, Bishop Neveu was pleased with the addition of another priest in Moscow and took him under his wing.[24] He gave him a tutorial on Soviet reality and began to prepare Braun to write accurate reports on religious conditions in the USSR, and Braun eventually became fluent in Russian. In the meantime, the most cogent reports came from Bishop Neveu. Braun's presence did give Bishop Neveu an opportunity to take a one-week vacation to participate in a pilgrimage to Lourdes, France, and to brief the pope on the grim status of the Catholic Church in the USSR.[25]

The good news of Braun's arrival was quickly dampened by another development related to the USSR's application to join the League of Nations in 1934. Some Catholic countries like Switzerland and Portugal argued against Soviet membership because the USSR was persecuting religion, starving its own citizens, pushing revolution around the globe, and was largely responsible for the emergence and growth of the radical right menace. The French ambassador in Moscow informed Bishop Neveu that the Kremlin blamed the Vatican for the Swiss and Portuguese protests and retaliated by delaying a visa to Father Michel Clovis Florent, O. P., who had been approved by Moscow to come to Leningrad to replace to Father Amoudru in 1934, thus delaying the latter's departure.[26] The French government protested the delay, but to no avail.

On 8 October 1934, Bishop Neveu sent a long letter to the Vatican to report on the religious situation. He said that the current issue of *Bezbozhnik* ridiculed the Holy Father and claimed that the pope was attempting to lead a "crusade" against the USSR. He also noted that the Soviet government attacked religion constantly and that there was a need for more international publicity about the Soviet persecution. He wrote that he feared that "very soon there will not be a single Orthodox church in Moscow" because the Soviet government had penetrated the Russian Orthodox Church with leaders like Orthodox "Bishop Pitirim," who was "known to be an official of the GPU," and Orthodox Bishop Vladimir Poutiata, a "Rasputin-like" character, who was also "an agent of the GPU." He thought, too, that leaders like Metropolitan Sergius were being distracted by pompous titles. He ridiculed Soviet claims that it had eliminated prostitution and charged, "what is certain is that sodomy has increased to ungodly proportions among the men, especially in the Red Army."[27]

He wrote further that there was truth in newspaper reports that famine still raged in parts of Ukraine. He said that a German Catholic lady, the sister of a priest who had died in 1920, had visited "her village near Aleksandrovsk on the Dnieper two months ago" and reported that "the harvest was horrible; the wheat gave very little and the government took it all." He added that she further said, "We parishioners are forced to purchase food in order to eat. What's more, we were forced to do a lot of unnecessary repairs on the church. They know perfectly well that parishioners do not have the necessary funds for that, and this will be the excuse to turn the church into a cinema or some sort of grain storehouse."[28]

Neveu also updated the Vatican on the status of the Catholic clergy. He said that Father Franz Kuhn, who was arrested in 1933, had just been deported to Orel, that Father [Ferdinand] Pflug, the former priest of Yenakiyevo (near Makeyevka) in Ukraine, had been arrested and deported to a camp between Lake Ladoga and Lake Onega in 1933, and that Father Sergey Soloviev had been checked into an asylum, was dying, and was unreachable to give him the last rites. Neveu lamented, "Look at the ends to which we have been reduced."[29] He also chronicled that Mother Catherine Abrikosova, who had cancer and was in prison, had written that she was doing well and was in good spirits, and that her two "courageous Daughters," Sisters Philomena [Sophia] Eismont and Veronica [Vera] Tsvetkova, had been deported to Siberia. He gave the names of two nuns who had passed away, five who had been denied exit visas, and five who had been deported, and of three priests, one still in Minsk, one in prison, and one under house arrest.[30]

On 23 October 1934, Neveu wrote another long letter to the Vatican. He related that Father [Mesrab] Edidzhanian was in a work camp in Novosibirsk, but had written to say that he expected to be "transferred closer to us to work on the canal connecting the Moskva and the Volga Rivers." Neveu detailed that Fr. Pflug was in feeble condition and had lost an eye, but was required to "chop six cubic meters of wood in marshy lands where his feet are always in the water," lived on "650 grams of moldy bread every day, two or three spoonful of gruel, and nothing more," and slept on "bare boards." Neveu also relayed that a newspaper had published that Father Paul Schubert, aged sixty-two, was arrested in Odessa for espionage and that he was "suffering so much from hunger that his whole body is swollen." Neveu said it was impossible to send packages to prisoners because the prison administration moved prisoners who received packages and there was no forwarding address, which Neveu thought was "the height of cruelty." He also disclosed that Father Karol Alexander Łupinowitcz, who used to be at St. Peter and Paul parish in Moscow, "had been transferred to a location unreachable by any railway."[31]

Neveu also noted that Father [Kiriak] Reichart, who was at the Church of Saint Catherine (at the center of Odessa) and who said Mass "once a month" at the French Church of Saint Peter, had asked him for "balsam . . . for Mons. Frison," who had run out of sacramental oils, and "for 3000 rubles to pay the church taxes." He said an Orthodox priest in Odessa had converted to Catholicism and now lived "in extreme poverty." He asked the Vatican to supply the sacramental oils and to send money for the taxes, but advised that the funds should be dispatched via the Italian consulate in Odessa, where Italian ships often visited, because the post was unreliable and people "are often searched on trains in Ukraine."[32]

Neveu also revealed that he had given some assistance to Exarch Fedorov, who had communicated to him that he eventually wanted "to settle closer to Moscow and help the town of Roslavl in Smolensk Oblast." Neveu said that he suggested to Fedorov that he should go, instead, "to Vitebsk where there is but one priest for the city's two parishes, or that he should get closer to Leningrad to help Father Amoudru." Neveu also recorded that the three Franciscans of Mary sisters who had been deported to Danilov in the Kostroma Oblast had just received authorization to go to Poland and that he hoped that two other elderly and disabled sisters would be soon repatriated. Neveu confided that he had met recently with a Mr. Bagdonas, the councilor of the Lithuanian Legation who had come from Kaunas, who told him that Mons. [Teofilis] Matulianis was now in excellent health, but that Fr. [Józef] Kozakiewicz, who had been deported with Matulianis to Lithuania in 1933, had died.[33]

By the middle of the 1930s, it was clear that the Soviet government was convinced that the Western global order was in crisis, but that the last rites and burial had to be handled with care to avoid damage to the Soviet Union. The times called for a more balanced and moderate international policy, not a retreat from the clarion call of revolution, but a less aggressive Comintern policy that might not blow back on the USSR. Domestically, there was no slowing of the pace of collectivizing the land, destroying religion, including the Catholic Church, and purging enemies, recalcitrants, and heretics – real or imagined. The Age of Communism was dawning!

Notes

1 Stalin to Molotov, 5 December 1929, in Lih, Naumov, and Khlevniuk 1995, p. 183.
2 Degras 2014, p. 175. Also see correspondence between Stalin and head of Comintern in Dallin and Firsov 2000.
3 Stalin to Molotov, 19 June 1932, in Lih, Naumov, and Khlevniuk 1995, p. 229.
4 Dunn 1998, pp. 25–29. Evgenii Vladimirovich Rubdinin, "Conversations with Bullitt," 13 May 1934, f. 0129, op. 17, d. 1, l. 71–73; Troyanovsky to Litvinov, 3 March 1934, f. 0129, op. 17, d. 129 l. 127, Arkhiv vneshnei politiki R F (Archive of Foreign Affairs, Russian Federation), Moscow.
5 On Hitler and his rise to power, see Ian Kershaw 1998. The major biographies of Hitler include those by Alan Bullock, Werner Maser, Joachim Fest, and John Toland.
6 Christopher Browning reported that the training manual for Nazi workers taught that the main challenges to *lebensraum* and racial purity were Marxism/Bolshevism, liberalism, and Christianity. See Browning 1993, p. 180.
7 Eksteins 1989, p. 303.
8 Khlevniuk 2015, p. 163.
9 On the positive and negative effects of nationalism in Eastern Europe, see Rothschild and Wingfield 2000, pp. 1–21.
10 Rothschild and Wingfield 2000, p. 20.
11 The Church was alarmed at the influence of Nazi Germany in Spain. See Guasco and Perin 2010, pp. 107–29.
12 Michaelis 1978.
13 Stalin to Molotov, January 1933, in Lih, Naumov, and Khlevniuk 1995, p. 232.
14 L'Archivio della Sacra Congregazione degli Affari Ecclesiastici Straordinari, Pontificia Commissione, Pro Russia, scatola (box) 11, fascicolo (file) 74, Pius XI to d'Herbigny, audience note, 17 June 1933, fogli (sheet(s) 78r–78v, prot. 134/28 (henceforth cited as AES, Pro Russia, s., fasc., f.).
15 AES, *Pro Russia*, s. 11, Fasc. 76, d'Herbigny to Tardini, Rome, October 1933, f. 21, prot. 134/28.
16 AES, *Pro Russia*, s. 11, Fasc. 76, Pro Russia Commission, Rome, 21 November 1933, f. 44/33, 57rv, prot. 134/28.
17 AES, *Pro Russia*, s. 11, fasc. 76, FDR to Litvinov, Washington, DC, 16 November 1933, f. 64–65, prot. 134/28; Litvinov to Roosevelt, Washington, DC, 16 November 1933, f. 66–70, prot. 134/28; also see Dunn 1998, p. 22.
18 AES, *Pro Russia*, s. 11, Fasc. 76, Cicognani to Tardini, Washington, DC, 11 November 1933, f. 46, prot. 134/28; s. 11, Fasc. 48, Walsh to d'Herbigny, Washington, DC, 15 October 1933, f. 48; Pro Russia Commission, 27 November 1933, f. 51, f. 53–55.
19 Roosevelt's embrace of the USSR led Fr. Charles Coughlin, a radio priest from Detroit, to lead a large protest movement against Roosevelt's reelection. It failed in part because the Vatican opposed Coughlin. For information on Coughlin, see Brinkley 1982; Tull 1965; Warren 1996.

20 AES, *Pro Russia*, s. 48, fasc. 283, d'Herbigny to Pro Russia Commission, 7 May 1934, f. 10r.
21 AES, *Pro Russia*, s. 48, fasc. 284, Neveu to Pro Russia Commission, Moscow, 2 April 1936, f. 68; Dunn 1977, p. 41. Braun lived near Neveu in the French compound.
22 Dunn 1977, pp. 134–35. On the Nazi–Soviet alliance, see Read and Fisher 1989.
23 See Braun 2006.
24 Actually, there was another Catholic priest in the Italian Embassy, Fr. Garelli, but he served mainly Italian Catholics and, according to Neveu, "spends much time with the children of [Ambassador] Attolico." See AES, *Pro Russia*, s. 43, fasc. 251, Neveu to Giobbe, Moscow, 7 April 1935, f. 54, prot. 166/28.
25 AES, *Pro Russia*, s. 42, Fasc. 250, Neveu to Pro Russia Commission, Moscow, 23 September 1934, f. 31.
26 AES, *Pro Russia*, s. 42, Fasc. 250, Neveu to Pro Russia Commission, Moscow, 8 October 1933, f. 50; 24 September 1934, f. 32–33.
27 AES, *Pro Russia*, s. 43, fasc. 250, Neveu to Giobbe, Moscow, 8 October 1934, f. 41, prot. 166/28.
28 AES, *Pro Russia*, s. 43, fasc. 250, Neveu to Giobbe, Moscow, 8 October 1934, f. 40, prot. 166/28.
29 AES, *Pro Russia*, s. 43, fasc. 250, Neveu to Giobbe, Moscow, 8 October 1934, f. 40–41, prot. 166/28. Fr. Soloviev was a former Orthodox priest and nephew of famous Russian philosopher Vladimir Soloviev. He had also assumed the spiritual direction of the few nuns who remained in Mother Catherine's Dominican community in Moscow before his arrest in 1931. Fr. Soloviev survived his illness in 1934 and ultimately died in Kazan in 1942. See Czaplicki and Osipova 2014, "Biography of Father Sergey Soloviev," at https://biographies.library.nd.edu/catalog/biography-0632 (accessed 4 April 2016).
30 AES, *Pro Russia*, s. 43, fasc. 250, Neveu to Giobbe, Moscow, 8 October 1934, f.40–41, prot. 166/28. Mother Catherine eventually died in prison on 23 July 1936.
31 AES, *Pro Russia*, s. 43, fasc. 250, Neveu to Giobbe, Moscow, 23 October 1934, f. 43, prot. 166/28. Fr. Łupinowitcz was sentenced to death in 1937 and his exact date of death is unknown. See Czaplicki and Osipova 2014, "Biography of Fr. Karol Alexander Łupinowitcz," at https://biographies.library.nd.edu/catalog/biography-0458 (accessed 4 April 2016). Fr. Edidzhanian's fate is unknown. Fr. Schubert was arrested in 1933 and sentenced to death in 1937 and his fate is unknown.
32 AES, *Pro Russia*, s. 43, fasc. 250, Neveu to Giobbe, Moscow, 23 October 1934, f. 43, prot. 166/28. Fr. Reichart was arrested in 1935 and shot in 1938. See Czaplicki and Osipova 2014, "Biography of Father Kiriak Reichart," at https://biographies.library.nd.edu/catalog/biography-0558 (accessed 4 April 2016).
33 AES, *Pro Russia*, s. 43, fasc. 250, Neveu to Giobbe, Moscow, 23 October 1934, f. 43–44, prot. 166/28. Fedorov was released from prison at the end of 1933 and permitted to take up residence in Vyatka in January 1934, where he died on 7 March 1934.

References

Arkhiv vneshnei politiki R F (Archive of Foreign Affairs, Russian Federation), Moscow.
Braun, Léopold A. A. 2006, *In Lubianka's Shadow: The Memoirs of an American Priest in Stalin's Moscow, 1934–1945*, G. M. Hamburg (ed.), Notre Dame, IN: University of Notre Dame Press.
Brinkley, Alan 1982, *Voices of Protest: Huey Long, Father Coughlin, and the Great Depression*, New York: Alfred Knopf.
Browning, Christopher 1993, *Ordinary Men: Reserve Police Battalion 101 and the Final Solution in Poland*, New York: HarperPerennial.

Czaplicki, Bronisław and Osipova, Irina 2014, *Book of Remembrance: Biography of Catholic Clergy and Laity in the Soviet Union (USSR) from 1918 to 1953*, Geraldine Kelly (trans.), and made available by University of Notre Dame at https://biographies.library.nd.edu/catalog/biography-0004 (accessed 2 April 2016).

Dallin, A. and Firsov, F. I. (eds.) 2000, *Dimitrov and Stalin, 1934–43: Letters from the Soviet Archives*, New Haven, CT: Yale University Press.

Degras, Jane (ed.) 2014, *The Communist International 1919–1943: Documents*, Vol. III: *1929–1943*, New York: Routledge.

Dunn, Dennis J. 1977, *The Catholic Church and the Soviet Government, 1939–1949*, New York: *East European Quarterly* Series, distributed by Columbia University Press.

Dunn, Dennis J. 1998, *Caught Between Roosevelt and Stalin: America's Ambassadors in Moscow*, Lexington: University of Kentucky Press.

Eksteins, Modris 1989, *Rites of Spring: The Great War and the Birth of the Modern Age*, New York: Houghton Mifflin.

Guasco, Alberto and Perin, Raffaella (eds.) 2010, *Pius XI: Keywords*, Zürich-Berlin: LIT Verlag.

Kershaw, Ian 1998, *Hitler 1889–1936: Hubris*, New York: W. W. Norton.

Khlevniuk, Oleg V. 2015, *Stalin: New Biography of a Dictator*, Nora Seligman Favorov (trans.), New Haven, CT: Yale University Press.

L'Archivio della Sacra Congregazione degli Affari Ecclesiastici Straordinari, Pontificia Commissione, *Pro Russia*, scatola (box), fascicolo (file), fogli (sheet(s), Archivio Segreto Vaticano (cited as AES, *Pro Russia*, s., fasc., f.).

Lih, Lars T., Naumov, Oleg V., and Oleg V. Khlevniuk (eds.) 1995, *Stalin's Letters to Molotov*, Catherine A. Fitzpatrick (trans.), New Haven, CT: Yale University Press.

Michaelis, M. 1978, *Mussolini and the Jews: German–Italian Relations and the Jewish Question in Italy, 1922–1945*, New York: Oxford University Press.

Read, Anthony and Fisher, David 1989, *Deadly Embrace: Hitler, Stalin, and the Nazi–Soviet Pact, 1939–1941*, New York: W. W. Norton.

Rothschild, Joseph and Wingfield, Nancy M. 2000, *Return to Diversity: A Political History of East Central Europe Since World War II*, New York: Oxford University Press.

Tull, Charles J. 1965, *Father Coughlin and the New Deal*, Syracuse, NY: Syracuse University Press.

Warren, Donald 1996, *Radio Priest: Charles Coughlin, the Father of Hate Radio*, New York: The Free Press.

8 Soviet Russia and the Catholic Church under Stalin, 1935–1939

The international scene, 1935–1939

By 1934–35 the growing threat of war in Europe and Asia led Stalin to a reappraisal. He was still convinced that the international revolution was about to decapitate capitalist states, but he also feared an anti-capitalist coalition congealing against the Soviet Union. He wanted to contain Germany, Japan, and Italy, but not destroy them. These countries certainly pursued policies that were anti-Communist and threatened the Soviet Union, but they also took actions that could lead them into war with France, England, and perhaps the United States, and an intra-capitalist war was the catalyst that Stalin thought would finally catapult Communist regimes answerable to Moscow in power around the globe. It made no difference if the Germans, Japanese, and Italians were anti-Communist if their first priority was to take down the Western global order, a priority that would inevitably produce a long war of attrition, not unlike World War I, among the capitalist states with the USSR sitting on the sidelines and gaining strength daily and the wherewithal to enter the conflict at an opportune time to dictate a new Communist world order.

To effect his nuanced policy of containing the radical right threat without eliminating it, Stalin changed tactics for the Comintern and for Soviet foreign policy. The new Comintern policy was called the "Popular Front" and it was inaugurated at the Seventh Comintern Congress in July–August 1935.[1] In Europe, the Comintern reversed policy and started to form a "Popular Front" of cooperating with other socialist parties against the radical right. It encouraged Communist parties to join with socialists and to try to build electoral alliances to win power in various states. Its most successful effort at cooperation came in France in 1935 when the communists and socialists formed a "popular front" government. The idea was for the communists in Europe to get involved in political life and convince governments and voters to be on guard against radical right extremism without actually taking any military steps to shut down the radical right regimes prematurely.

In Asia, on the other hand, the Comintern doubled its effort to provoke a war between China and Japan. Once the Anti-Comintern Pact was signed in November 1936, the Comintern increased its pressure on Chiang Kai-shek to join the CCP in an alliance against Japan by promising to supply a KMT-CCP alliance in a war against Japan and by persuading some of Chiang's Manchurian commanders that their interests would be bettered served if the KMT and CCP joined forces. As Chiang Kai-shek pondered the offer and pressure (he was put under house arrest by his Manchurian commanders), the Japanese attacked his forces in 1937 and soon Asia was awash in blood.[2]

Stalin was pleased with the commencement of the Sino–Japanese War in 1937 and thought that it would help curb the Japanese threat. He kept the Red Army on the Manchurian border as a precaution against a Japanese incursion into Siberia, which did happen in the region of the Ussuri River in 1938, but the Japanese pulled back after a series of bruising battles and decided to wait to see what their ally in Berlin did before they made their next move. In the meantime, they found themselves increasingly preoccupied with China and drawn south toward the Philippines and Southeast Asia, regions that pointed them in the direction of clashes with the United States and the European colonial states. As for the KMT and the CCP, they fought against the Japanese and suspended their own civil war, but they did not trust one another and both forces operated as independent units.

Stalin's initiative in Soviet foreign policy was called "Collective Security." It called on capitalist countries to cooperate with the Soviet Union to preserve peace through the League of Nations and various treaties of cooperation. Under this initiative, the Soviet Union signed nonaggression treaties with Poland, Lithuania, and Romania, established diplomatic relations with the United States in 1933, joined in 1934 the League of Nations where in Geneva Maxim Litvinov pitched Collective Security to the world, and set up cooperative agreements in May 1935 with Czechoslovakia and France. There were no military requirements in these treaties, but they were intended to inform Hitler that his aggressive policies were not isolating the Soviet Union and could lead to military agreements.

Stalin's policies of Popular Front and Collective Security, however, did not contain Hitler. He used the Czech–Soviet agreement to isolate Czechoslovakia in Europe. He called Czechoslovakia "Bolshevism's Central European aircraft carrier," implying falsely but effectively for propaganda purposes that Czechoslovakia had become a launching pad for Communist revolution and Stalin's depraved policies of collectivization.[3] In March 1938 he annexed Austria in the so-called *Anschluss.* In September 1938 he took the Sudetenland from Czechoslovakia after the English and French decided to appease him at the Munich Conference in the hope of avoiding war. In March 1939 Hitler dismantled the rest of Czechoslovakia, making Bohemia and Moravia into protectorates of the Reich, turning Slovakia into a satellite of the Reich under a puppet by the name of Monsignor Josef Tiso, and giving Carpatho-Ukraine to Hungary, which then became a Nazi ally. At the end of March England and France issued a joint ultimatum that threatened war if Germany attempted to move against either Poland or Romania, but, in light of the Munich Conference, the ultimatum could be empty rhetoric and, when push came to shove, these powers might make further accommodations to Hitler. After all, he was driving east toward the USSR.

Stalin had not factored in the West's fear of communism and thus its willingness to appease the radical right, if appeasement ended up producing war between

Soviet Russia and Germany and Japan. He now tried desperately to work out an arrangement with Hitler. He sent conciliatory notes to Berlin in 1938 and in May 1939 he replaced Litvinov, his Jewish foreign minister, with his right hand man, V. Molotov, implying both an end of Collective Security and a concession to Hitler's anti-Semitism, but nothing worked.

Fortuitously for Stalin, the English and French decided to put teeth into their ultimatum by sending a diplomatic delegation to Moscow at the end of May 1939 to persuade the Soviet Union to join them in a military arrangement that would confront Germany with the prospect of a two-front war. Stalin now had the leverage he needed to make an opening to Hitler. He dragged out negotiations with the English and French in Moscow, patiently waiting for Hitler to act.[4] On August 21, Hitler sent Stalin a note, indicating that he wanted Joachim Von Ribbentrop, his foreign minister, to be received in Moscow by August 23 at the latest and to sign a nonaggression pact that would allow Germany to deal with Poland without the threat of an eastern front.

Stalin was receptive to receiving Ribbentrop, but he wanted a secret protocol attached to the agreement that carved up parts of Eastern Europe into German and Soviet spheres. The Germans would take western Poland and Lithuania, while the USSR would take Estonia, Latvia, Finland, and eastern Poland. Hitler agreed. It was a stiff price and ensured war between Germany, Britain, and France, and put space between Stalin and Hitler through the re-annexation of the borderlands, but Hitler thought it was worth it because it removed the threat of a two-front war.[5] Hitler believed his armed forces would quickly roll over Poland and then he could persuade the French and English to abandon the western front, which would allow him to cancel the agreement and turn his army against Soviet Russia. On 23 August, the Nazi–Soviet Non-aggression Pact was signed.

In making this move Stalin was hoping for a long period of collaboration with Hitler and for a long and exhausting war between Germany and the Western Allies. When both were worn down and when their peoples were prepared for a revolutionary means of exit out of the bloodbath, the Soviet Union would come in fresh and sweep the field, ensuring the triumph of the world revolution in the West as in the East. Stalin believed Nazi Germany would be his means of destroying the stabilized conditions that eventually followed the First World War and return everything to the flux where the intervention of a fresh, strong Soviet Union could put across the world revolution in the West as in the East. He informed the Politburo on 19 August 1939 that an agreement with Germany would lead to war in the West and would permit "us to stay out of the conflict, and we may hope [later] to be able to find our way advantageously into the war. [Our] experience of twenty years shows that, in time of peace, it is not possible to have a Communist movement in Europe [in any one nation] for the Bolshevik Party to take power."[6]

On 1 September 1939, the Nazis attacked Poland and the Soviet Union invaded Poland from the east on 17 September 1939. The cataclysm of World War II soon engulfed the world. Pius XI died in February 1939 and was succeeded by Cardinal Pacelli, who took the name of Pope Pius XII. He had witnessed the Communist government's crusade to destroy Western values from 1917 through the 1920s and

1930s. His papacy was consumed with an effort to destroy communism, to preserve Western civilization, and to reassert Western values as the basis for global order.

Soviet government and the Catholic Church, 1935–1939

In the period from 1935 to 1939, reports in the Vatican archives on the condition of the Catholic Church in the Soviet Union came from Bishop Neveu until his departure from Moscow in the summer of 1936 and then from Fr. Braun. They both described a story of continuing and intensifying persecution.

On 7 April 1935, Bishop Neveu outlined in a letter to Mons. Giobbe that he had been ill from 21 March to 2 April because he had eaten spoiled pieces of rye bread, but that he was now fully recovered and could persist with his reports on the Catholic Church in the Soviet Union. He started by stating that his heart was gladdened when he heard on Radio Paris the Holy Father's address to a recent Consistory and news about the appointment of Cardinal Pacelli as the papal legate in Lourdes. He then went on to thank Mons. Giobbe for sending a package of food, especially the flour used to bake "the bread of the altar" and the raisins, both of which were shared with Father Patapy, who was so sick in a distant hospital that he could not say Mass. Neveu also said that he was keeping the "Tanquerey book," a reference apparently to Father Adolphe Tanquerey's *The Spiritual Life*, which was published circa 1930 and was included in the package from Mons. Giobbe. Neveu said that "dear Dr. Titov" wanted to read the book, but that he was "arrested and will undoubtedly be held for many years." He also stated that he had informed "the three Apostolic Administrators" and several priests whom he saw about changes in the liturgical calendar, which he did not describe other than to say that they were prudent changes in light of conditions in Soviet Russia, which implied that the Vatican gave the Church in Soviet Russia canonical flexibility.[7]

Neveu also reported that Exarch Fedorov had died on 7 March in Vyatka and that he thought that Ambassador Attolico of the Italian Embassy had informed the Vatican. Neveu declared that since World War I this holy man "had passed almost all of his life in prison or in exile" and that "the tsar did not go any easier on him than the Bolsheviks." Neveu reported that many Orthodox Christians had prayed at his graveside.[8]

Bishop Neveu then went on to update the Vatican with news of more arrests of Catholic clergy. He wrote that Father [Raphael] Deitrich was arrested and sentenced to ten years in prison, Father George Baier was arrested and then placed in a prison hospital because he had fallen ill, Father [Adam] Gareis was arrested again in Voronezh, Father [Alexander] Staub was arrested and deported to Tambov, Father [Anton] Dobrovolsky from the village of Mannheim was arrested in January, Father Johannes Albert from Kandel [part of Odessa district] was arrested in February, and Father Florian Schultz was arrested and sentenced to hard labor in Volkhovstroy. In addition, the following priests were arrested: Fathers [Johannes] Beilmann, Joseph Wolf of Selz, [Philipp] Haufmann of Ponetovka, and three German priests, Fathers [Michael] Köhler, [Johannes] Tauberger, and [Alexander] Hoffman. He wrote further, "In the entire Volga region, there are only four priests." He also reported that the cathedral in Saratov, where Fr. Hermann was the pastor, had not yet been closed and that the local *soviet* was demanding that useless repairs be made and paid for before the church was converted into a "bakery."[9]

In the same letter of 7 April 1935, Neveu expressed anguish over the fact that both the Nazis and the Communists were now assailing the Catholic Church. He wrote, "Hitler persecutes Germany's Catholics and the Bolsheviks are all too happy to follow his example. . . . It is 'insanity.'"[10] He also revealed, perhaps unwittingly, Stalin's growing fear of Hitler and the possibility that the many non-Russians, including some of whom were Catholic, who lived in the borderlands, might be a liability to Moscow because of its policies of collectivization and religious persecution and, thus, an asset to Hitler. He reported that the Soviet government starting in January 1935 had been and was continuing to sweep the border regions of people it felt were unreliable. "All along the western Soviet border, from Leningrad to Odessa, a mass deportation of the German and Polish populations is under way. Hundreds of thousands of people are secretly being taken from their homes and sent to the north or to Siberia, without quarter. In one night, the vast majority, or perhaps the entire village, is hastily evacuated and it often happens that parents are sent one way and children the other."[11]

This evacuation, Neveu went on, had severely damaged the Catholic Church and population. He said that the GPU revoked "the passports of priests from Volynia and Podolia" and demanded that "they move beyond the Dnieper." He also pointed out that the sheer number of the deportees was mindboggling and declared that such a policy was "an abomination" and yet "no one in Europe raises their voice to call out these brutalities." He reported that the German consul in Leningrad had seen a deportation order for just one day, and there were many days with such orders, and that on that one day the order called for removing "over 20,000 persons, including entire families," and that "this number will yet multiply by three times, four times, and still more, and this is only for the city of Leningrad."[12]

As a result of the mass deportations, Neveu continued, "there are no longer any priests" in parts of Belorussia and "only ten priests, three of whom are completely disabled, five are elderly men, and only two are young and fit to work" in all of Mogilev, Vitebsk, and Minsk, a region that had "nearly 700,000 parishioners" in 1906. He noted further, "from 1933 to 1934, in the same region, fifteen Catholic churches were closed and ten priests were arrested." He went on to list some of the priests and nuns arrested, deported, or disappeared as well as churches closed across the USSR. He also asked the Vatican to send 3,000 rubles to pay the taxes for a church in Batum, where Father Raphael Nyebyeridzye was resident.[13]

Neveu also informed Giobbe, "Sister Marietta, as well as Father Hermann, told me that the famine dominates the Volga region and Ukraine. Apparently the station in Kiev is completely filled with the unfortunate people that are fleeing the famine, or were driven out by it. It is the same spectacle as two years ago, I tell myself."[14]

With Moscow refusing to issue Fr. Florent's visa, Neveu decided to consecrate Amoudru a bishop in April 1935 and told the Vatican that Amoudru "will receive whatever he needs on the feast day of St Catherine of Sienna, on 30 April."[15]

A visa was finally issued to Fr. Florent in May following the signing of the French-Soviet Mutual Assistance Treaty on 2 May 1935. Bishop Amoudru then departed in August and went on to the Vatican to brief Pius XI on the religious situation in the USSR, which the pope characterized as "desperate and hopeless."[16]

On 19 May 1935, Neveu disclosed to the Vatican that the French ambassador to the Soviet Union, Charles Alphand (1933–36), stopped by on 18 May to report that French Foreign Minister Pierre Laval (1935–36) during his recent visit to Moscow had met with Stalin and Molotov and had attempted to persuade Stalin to ease up on the Catholic Church and to improve his relationship with the Vatican. Ambassador Alphand, who was in the meeting, stated that Laval brought up the Catholic Church and told Stalin that, in Alphand's words, "it would be advantageous to the whole world if the Soviet state would consider dialogue with the Vatican and would reduce religious tensions."[17]

According to Alphand, Stalin seemed perplexed and replied to Laval, and here Alphand quoted Stalin verbatim: "I would rather get along with powers that have soldiers and rifles." Laval retorted, according to Alphand, that material force was not the only form of power, that there was also spiritual power that was "very influential and imponderable."[18]

Stalin and Molotov, according to Alphand, shot back that the USSR already had a religious détente, and then Stalin, in a joking way, said to Laval, "You say this because the pope has made you a Roman count." Laval answered that that papal honor made him a man of the Church about as much as Stalin's "friendship with Herriot made him [Herriot] a colonel of the Red Army," which, according to Alphand, made everyone laugh.[19] Alphand said that he thought Stalin understood Laval's point and added that he, Alphand, had had lunch recently with the secretary of the Soviet Embassy in Paris, a certain Sokolin, who, Alphand thought, was well connected in Moscow and who suggested that Moscow was open to "an arrangement" with the Vatican and had shown its "good intentions" by allowing Frs. Braun and Florent to come to Russia and that now the Vatican should take the initiative by publishing its appreciation of Soviet actions in *L'Osservatore romano.* Alphand stressed that Neveu should inform the Holy Father of these discussions and declared that as soon as *L'Osservatore romano* did what the Kremlin wanted, then " I will find myself in a better position to ask for new settlements."[20]

On 16 June 1935, Neveu reviewed the ongoing persecution, the concentration camps, and the continuing removal of clergy. He also recorded that Fr. Braun, who listened at length to international radio broadcasts for current news, especially Radio Vatican, believed that no Orthodox Churches would be open by 1937 if the rate of closings proceeded.[21] In the spring and summer of 1935 he recounted that while there were clashes between the Renovationists and the supporters of Metropolitan Sergius, the so-called Tikhonians, the GPU seemed to be angling for an end of the schism and a reunion of the churches.[22]

On 28 July 1935, Neveu wrote to the Vatican that he met again with Ambassador Alphand, who informed him that Litvinov claimed that Neveu was an agent of the Vatican and used the diplomatic pouch to send information abroad. Neveu confirmed that he was indeed "an agent of the Vatican" and that he hoped Litvinov was not attempting to recruit him to be "an agent of the Third International." Neveu also reported that *Terre Nouvelle*, a French journal of so-called Christian revolutionaries who supported Bolshevism, named him as "an enemy" of the Communist government, and he proudly proclaimed that he was indeed "an enemy of the Bolsheviks," and if that meant he would die, he hoped that "having been of little use in life, I may be able to better serve the Kingdom of our Lord with my death."[23]

Neveu also gave news on 28 July 1935 about the Catholic clergy. He said that the USSR had negotiated a prisoner exchange with Lithuania that involved sending, among others, two priests to Lithuania – Father Joseph Josiukas and Mons. Mieczystaw Joudokas, who was the apostolic administrator of Kazan, Samara, and Simbirsk, including Ufa. Apparently, both clergymen were removed from the exchange and sentenced to hard labor, after which their fate was unknown.[24]

Bishop Neveu also reported in July that there was no news on Mons. Bartholemew Remov since his arrest on 21 February 1935. Neveu wrote that Remov had initially been taken to Butryka Prison and then was transferred to Taganskaya Prison, but his sisters and his elderly nurse could find no trace of him and suspected that he had been executed and his body incinerated. Neveu added that the prison authorities made it frustratingly difficult to visit prisoners and cited as one example the experience of Fr. Schubert's niece, who had permission to visit her uncle, who was in prison near Petrozavodsk on Lake Onega, not far from Leningrad. She traveled there with great difficulty from Odessa, only to find out when she arrived that he had been transferred to Solovetsky Prison and that she had to return to Odessa because the GPU had not given her permission to travel to the new location. Neveu bemoaned that this was typical of what he sarcastically called "Soviet humanism" and took a swipe at Maxim Gorky for being an apologist for such a system.[25]

It later turned out that the suspicions of Archbishop Remov's sisters and nurse were well founded. He was executed on 17 June 1935. Bishop Neveu later wrote, "There is no doubt that odium fidei was the cause of Bishop Remov's arrest and that to the end he remained faithful to the Catholic Church and to the Holy Father, whom he loved and whose commands he was ready to fulfill at any cost."[26]

Neveu also announced that the Seventh Comintern Congress was being held in Moscow. He reported that its main thrust was a running attack on fascism and noted that a French communist by the name of Marcel Cachin had the gall to assert that the Catholic Church supported the right-wing "Cross of Fire" movement in France and was the engine behind French fascism. He also informed the Vatican that there were many foreign tourists and visitors in Moscow and that St. Louis des Français Church offered four masses to accommodate the demand. He took pleasure in announcing that the niece of Dr. Alphonse Bertillon, a pioneer in the science of forensic anthropometry, became a "fervent Catholic" after visiting the museum of atheism in Leningrad. He included in his post to the Vatican a copy of *Bezbozhnik*, which featured "horrendous caricatures" of Pope Pius XI.[27]

On 3 November 1935 Bishop Neveu complained to the Pro Russia Commission that there was hardly any publicity about the Soviet government's offensive against religion in the USSR. Instead, he said that Soviet propaganda filled the world with news about religious freedom in the Soviet Union and the large number of Russian Orthodox churches open in Moscow. The Kremlin, he wrote, claimed that Moscow had 273 cathedrals and 431 parish churches, whereas, in fact, only 35 churches were open in greater Moscow that were in union with Metropolitan Sergius. There were a dozen "renovationist churches," but these existed to splinter the Russian Orthodox Church. In addition, Neveu wrote, Abbot Stanislas Raiko, who was in Moscow for a five-day visit, had passed through Podolia and found only one Catholic priest in a region that, according to past reports, had almost 1 million Catholics. Furthermore, Neveu wrote, the Armenian Catholic Church, which had been somewhat spared in the general persecution of the Catholic Church, was now heavily persecuted. Neveu wailed at the Soviet government's "fury of destruction and looting!" He also complained of what he called its "Asiatic arbitrariness." He cited as an example of the latter behavior the fact that the police arrested and sent to a forced labor camp the brother of one of the Dominican sisters because he had held a modest family reunion on the day of Kirov's assassination, even though he was unaware of and knew nothing about Kirov's untimely death. Neveu pleaded with the Holy See to "publish these facts in American journals."[28]

On 17 November 1935, Neveu sent word to the Vatican that Ambassador Alphand had attended mass at Notre Dame Church in Leningrad and met with Fr. Florent. The bishop stressed that Fr. Florent's superiors should encourage the young priest to stay vigilant and guard against GPU tricks because the GPU had "a thousand ways to trap him."[29]

On 17 November 1935, Neveu reported that the GPU had harassed a lady who went to confession to him. The police informed her that Neveu was a "robber," the "center of Catholicism" in the USSR, and the barrier to improved relations between the Vatican and the Kremlin. He also noted that Bishop Frison was arrested, which left him as the only Catholic bishop in the USSR, a situation that he said the GPU wanted to change by removing him.[30]

On 10 January 1936 Bishop Neveu recounted for the Vatican and Pope Pius, who was kept informed of Neveu's reports by the Pro Russia Commission in weekly audiences, the great suffering of the Church in Soviet Russia, the countless interrogations and arrests of nuns and priests and bishops, the imprisonment of clergy, and the fortitude of the nuns and priests, who, in spite of being accused and often found guilty of everything from "money laundering" to being "active agents" in an "espionage operation" run by Neveu, were still faithful and courageous Catholics. Neveu then went on to detail the status of imprisoned or banished priests and nuns about whom he had current information.[31]

On 30 January 1936, Neveu disclosed to the Vatican that he was seriously ill and that the physician from the American Embassy diagnosed him as suffering from hardening of the arteries and aortic sclerosis ("cardiosclerose et de sclerosa de l'aorta"), which meant he was a candidate for a heart attack and needed to seek specialist care abroad. He affirmed that he was quite tired and that Fr. Braun was quite kind, helpful, and energetic – doing the "work of two." Neveu also noted that the Catholic clergy were suffering, that "there is not a single priest in Crimea," that Father Mikhail Tsakul, who was at SS. Peter and Paul Immaculate Conception Churches in Moscow, had disappeared since June 1935, and that the Polish consul in Kiev had distributed alms to the poor the previous Christmas. In January and February 1936, Neveu continued to report on the sorry condition of the Church, the reduced number of priests and nuns, the ruinous exchange rate the Soviets imposed on foreign currency, and the constant persecution of the GPU. He reported that Mother Catherine Abrikosova was "living martyrdom." Pius XI, along with Cardinals Pacelli and Tardini, were informed of Neveu's news.[32]

In March Neveu communicated that a confidential source informed him that the French government had again approached Moscow about "a détente between the Vatican and the Soviet government." Neveu said Laval had made the same proposal the previous May and since then "the persecution has increased, not diminished." He also reported that the Polish consul in Kiev had attempted to guard Catholics, that the Italian ambassador would ask Moscow to send Bishop Frison abroad, and that the GPU claimed that a priest in Kiev had a copy of Hitler's *Mien Kampf* in his possession, which "served as a pretext to arrest him." He also related that his health was slipping and that he could only say Mass at St. Louis des Français on Sundays and that Fr. Braun had picked up the slack. On 2 April, he announced that the International Red Cross had asked that Mother Catherine be permitted to depart, but he thought that the request would be rejected because she "inspires fear in the Bolsheviks," who thought that she would take up the pen and write "against them (How could we write FOR [them]?)" in the same vein as Julia Dansas. He also informed the Vatican in April and May that he was too exhausted to perform Holy Week duties, that the Russian Orthodox Church had only forty churches open in Moscow, and that he had to turn down a plea from some 30,000 Catholics in Kiev to come to Ukraine to administer the sacraments because of "onerous" Soviet rules on travel in USSR by foreigners. Again, the pope was briefed on all of Neveu's reports.[33]

In April 1936, the Comintern had a number of the European Communist parties extend a semblance of the "Popular Front" and "Collective Security" policies to the Catholic Church. The initiative started on 17 April when Maurice Thorez, the head of the French Communist Party, the largest one in Europe, declared that communists in France were willing to coexist with the Church, a policy dubbed "la polittque de la main." Eventually, the German and Belgian Communist Parties followed suit, but there was no change toward the Catholic Church in the Soviet Union or in the Comintern's global policy, and the European effort proved more rhetoric than substance.[34]

On 17 May, Bishop Neveu reported that he had dinner recently with William C. Bullitt, the American ambassador in Moscow. Neveu said that Bullitt, who was "very well informed" about Soviet foreign policy, stressed that the Comintern was pushing international revolution, that the Communist Party in France was following a policy of moderation and working with the socialists, that Moscow was pleased the Communists had joined a "syndicalist-anarchist" government in Spain that they planned to turn into a "revolutionary government," and that the

Kremlin was overjoyed that the Japanese had pulled "two regiments" off the far eastern border because of their deepening involvement in China. Neveu found the analysis fascinating and thought that the Vatican would find Bullitt's insights relevant. He also wrote that Ambassador Alphand was gravely ill, that Fr. Dilurgian in Krasnadar was under house arrest, and that Mother Catherine's husband was attempting to arrange passage for her out of the USSR.[35]

In June and July Neveu reported that persecution of religion was intense, that two priests were killed in Ukraine, that he could not undertake hard work because of his illness, and that Fr. Braun and he distributed about 250 to 300 communions per week at St. Louis des Français and that Fr. Florent indicated in a visit to Bishop Neveu in July that he distributed 27,000 communions since the beginning of the year at the church in Leningrad. Neveu also reflected on the curious willingness in Europe and elsewhere to praise fulsomely the new Soviet constitution and its assertion of rights, including religious liberty, and to overlook the existence of the GPU that was subject to no law and prevented anyone from exercising those rights. It seemed to him that "the world wants to be deceived." He also indicated on 23 July that he would be leaving the USSR with Ambassador Alphand to seek medical treatment in Paris and that he was naming Fr. Braun as the apostolic administer with full powers until he returned. The pope was briefed throughout the summer on Neveu's reports.[36]

With Neveu's departure on 31 July, Fr. Braun assumed the duty of informing the Vatican about the Catholic mission in the USSR. In late 1936 and early 1937 he wrote that there was a shortage of money to carry on activities, that persecution of the Church persisted, that antireligious propaganda intensified, and that the Soviet newspapers and periodicals included many attacks on the pope and the Holy See. He also reported that the Soviet population seemed largely "indifferent" to the massive antireligious push and remained below the surface a religious people.[37] Neveu, who was in Paris, added information on the declining status of the clergy, including news that Fr. Deubner was killed, Father Vladimir Klöpfer had died in prison, and Frs. Nikolay Aleksandrov and Józef Żmigrodzki from Kiev had expired in Solovetsky Prison. He also declared that Fr. Braun was doing a superb job.[38]

In March 1937 Pope Pius XI reached a critical decision. He decided that it was time to abandon his long-held belief that the Soviet Union was open to conversion. He and the Catholic leaders at the Vatican, including Cardinal Pacelli, the secretary of state, had tried to work with the Communist government for decades. Their effort found neither reception nor reciprocity in Moscow. Instead, the Communist regime pursued a policy of unrelenting persecution that severely wounded the Catholic Church. In addition, it undercut human dignity, assailed reason, rejected Western values, and leveled a berserk and genocidal attack on Ukrainians and a bloody rampage against Polish, German, Belorussian, and Russian Catholics who resided in the USSR. It also fomented international revolution and provoked extreme radical right movements that equaled the Communists in their determination to destroy Judeo-Christian civilization in order to make way for a world of blood, violence, and totalitarianism. The pope was ready to issue a broad condemnation of communism.

However, there was a problem. Nazism, which communism had helped precipitate, was becoming as menacing as communism and thus any censuring of communism might appear or be interpreted as an implicit endorsement of Nazism. The Catholic leaders decided that the only solution was to warn the world about both of these virulent ideologies – to decry Nazism and then denounce communism.

On 14 March 1937, Pope Pius issued an encyclical entitled *Mit Brennender Sorge*, which was coauthored by Eugenio Cardinal Pacelli, soon to be Pope Pius XII (r. 1939–58), and three German bishops and was written in German, which was unusual but was a sharp message to the Germans. It recounted how the Church had signed a concordat with the Reich and had believed that the government would allow the Church to function. However, it continued, the Nazi government had pursued policies that "blacken the German skies," undercut "confessional schools," destroyed "free elections," leveled "systematic hostility" against the Church, and violated "every Christian conscience." The encyclical went on to condemn anyone who "identifies, by pantheistic confusion, God and the universe," who "follows that so-called pre-Christian Germanic conception of substituting a dark and impersonal destiny for the personal God," or who "exalts race, or the people, or the State, or a particular form of State, or the depositories of power" above "an order of the world planned and created by God."[39]

Five days later, on 19 March 1937, Pope Pius XI issued the encyclical *Divini Redemptoris*, which condemned communism. It was coauthored by Cardinal Pacelli and informed Catholics that they should not align or cooperate with communists because "Communism is intrinsically wrong, and no one who would save Christian Civilization may collaborate with it in any undertaking whatsoever."[40] It was a pointed and cogent analysis of what communism had come to in the USSR and what Russian civilization under the Leninist-Stalinists had unloosed on the world. By 1937 the Church saw two enemies, and only danger for Western civilization.[41]

After *Mit Brennender Sorge* was proclaimed, a few Soviet publications praised the Catholic Church's opposition to Hitler in Germany and attacked Hitler's persecution of the Church. They took note of Hitler's campaign against Catholic schools, publications, teachers, priests, bishops, and youth groups, and they denounced the replacement of the crucifix with Hitler's portrait in Catholic classrooms. They also published news about the pope's Christmas address in 1937 that criticized German treatment of the Church. *Antireligioznik* praised "the millions of believing Catholics in Germany, Italy, Austria, France, Spain, and all countries of the world" for joining the "Communist struggle against Fascism and war, for bread, peace, and freedom." As late as 1939, the journal *Mirovoe khoziaistvo i mirovaia politika* reported, "the Nazis set fire to the Reichstag, then the synagogues, and now it was the turn of the Church."[42] However, the politically motivated outrage over Nazi attacks on the Catholic Church did not alter Soviet persecution of the Catholic Church. As far as *Divini Redemptoris* was concerned, the Soviet Union published no news of this scathing condemnation of communism and carried on with its policy of persecution.[43]

In April 1937 Bishop Neveu was ready to return to the Soviet Union, but Moscow refused to issue him a visa. The French government protested, but to no avail.

On 7 April 1937 Fr. Braun reported that the French ambassador had intervened in Moscow to help with Neveu's visa, but nothing had happened. However, he reported that Bishop Neveu was managing to advise him on issues from Paris.[44]

In other letters Fr. Braun communicated to Giobbe and Neveu that persecution of the Church in the USSR intensified in 1937. In July he reported that the Moscow commissar for cults demanded that Braun turn over to his office the baptismal registry of St. Louis des Français Church, but backed off when both the American ambassador, Joseph Davies, who replaced Bullitt in 1936 and served until 1938, and the French ambassador, Robert Coulondre, who paralleled Davies' time in Moscow, supported Braun's refusal to make church records available to civil authorities.[45] In September 1937 he declared that St. Louis des Français Church was under constant surveillance by the GPU and in December he reported that the antireligious drive had heightened, that the level of violence against religion, particularly the Russian Orthodox Church, was appalling, and that he had news that Father Michel Promgart in the German Volga region and Fathers Rosenback and Lubiensky from Kursk had been arrested. His one piece of good news was that St. Louis des Français Church was filled at Christmas midnight mass and that many foreign diplomats were in attendance.[46]

On 20 January 1938, Braun reported to Cardinal Tardini that he had heard that more priests were arrested and that some priests surfaced only to say Mass and administer sacraments and then went underground to avoid GPU surveillance.[47] On 21 February, he reported to Mons. Giobbe that the antireligious literature was prominent and that word had reached him that the Catholic Church in Saratov was closed and that Fr. Hermann had been arrested in June 1937.[48] In March he reported that xenophobia was rampant in the Soviet Union, the Catholic Church in Rostov was closed, Father Kwasniewski was arrested and executed, and Father Joseph Tetoyan of Batum was arrested.[49] In May he wrote that Father Nicolas Mikhalov of Taganrog was arrested and that two more Catholic churches were closed in Zhitomir.[50] In March 1938 Fr. Florent in Leningrad was expelled, and Fr. Braun thought that he might be next.[51]

On 13 June 1938, Braun divulged that the American chargé d'affaires, Alexander Kirk, who was in charge of the U.S. Embassy during the hiatus between Ambassador Davies' departure on 10 June 1938 and Ambassador Laurence Steinhardt's arrival on 11 August 1939, had informed him that the Soviet government's treatment of him was a violation of the Roosevelt-Litvinov Agreement.[52] On 11 July 1938, he reported to Giobbe that the Soviets had intimidated members of the St. Louis des Français Church's council.[53] On 23 August, he wrote that more churches were closed, including those of the Georgian and Armenian rites, but that most of the closings were Orthodox churches.[54] In September he reported that Fr. Joseph Tatoyan in Batum was arrested and that he had been informed that Father Dirlughian had been arrested in June 1936.[55] On 3 October 1938, he wrote that the diplomatic community was abuzz with news that the Soviet government was making overtures to Germany.[56] On 18 October, he announced that two Catholic churches in Vitebsk and St. Alexander and St. Nicholas Catholic Churches in Kiev were shut, that dozen of Orthodox churches and one Lutheran church were closed, and that three synagogues were demolished.[57] On 2 December 1938, Braun told Mons. Giobbe that the government had taken over all churches in Leningrad except for Fr. Florent's French church and that the historic St. Catherine's Church was scheduled to be demolished. He also said that the Soviet Union's survey in 1937 on religious beliefs was flawed and biased and actually revealed that religious belief was still strong. He also noted that a Soviet journal touted the fact that "papists" in the USSR had significantly declined by 1926 and that deportations to Siberia continued.[58]

On 23 January 1939, Braun divulged that the Polish ambassador had made an attempt to organize and strengthen the Polish Catholics in Moscow and that Deputy People's Commissar for Foreign Affairs Potemkin rebuffed him and declared, "The church is not a concern of the Polish ambassador, but of *the Polish Catholic community of Moscow*." Braun also decried the inhumanity of the Stakhanovite system that constantly raised work quotas and particularly hurt women with children and the hypocrisy of the Soviet press that claimed that "liberty of conscience" existed in the USSR but not in Spain.[59] For the remainder of 1939 and throughout the war years until his departure from Moscow in December 1945, Braun was harassed and pressured, but he stood as a witness of the Soviet government's determination to wipe out the Catholic Church in the Soviet Union and of the Church's steadfastness in the face of persecution.[60]

In February 1939 Pius XI died. The struggle for souls in Soviet Russia and in the world beyond had been going on for more than twenty-two years. It took the leaders of the Catholic Church in the Vatican almost twenty years to realize that there was no chance of changing the Soviet government and that that incubus had to be removed before there could be any opportunity to reengage the beautiful souls of the Russian, Ukrainian, Belorussian, and other diverse national groups on the Eurasian plain. In fact, the reason for the slowness in absorbing the lesson was that below and beyond the Soviet government was patent evidence of deep and profound yearning for and evolution toward spiritual fulfillment and truth and thus hope for unity and communion.

Notes

1 The foreign Communist parties, particularly the French Communists, and the head of the Comintern, Georgi Dimitrov, encouraged Stalin to adopt the Popular Front policy and he reluctantly endorsed it. See the coded cables in Frisov, Klehr, and Haynes 2014, pp. 51–67; and Dallin and Firsov 2000, pp. 7–43.

2 For details on Japan's brutal and bloody advance in China, see Chang 1998.

3 Rothschild and Wingfield 2000, p. 3.

4 The Vatican was well aware of the fact that both the Germans and the English and French were interested in an accord with the Soviet Union. See Blet, Martini, and Schneider 1965, nrs. 47, 52, 55, 56; and Blet, Martini, and Schneider 1968.

5 Dunn 1998, pp. 98–99. The best book on the Nazi–Soviet alliance is Read and Fisher 1989.

6 Quote is from the copy of Stalin's speech that T. S. Bushuevaia found in the "Secret Booty Funds of the Special USSR Archive," first published in *Novy mir* in 1995 and cited in Raack 1996, p. 51. Comintern records contain no evidence that Stalin viewed

the alliance as an expedient move to build up Soviet forces to attack Hitler. See Firsov, Klehr, and Haynes 2014, p. 248.

7 L'Archivio della Sacra Congregazione degli Affari Ecclesiastici Straordinari, Pontificia Commissione, Pro Russia, scatola (box) 43, fascicolo (file) 251, Neveu to Giobbe, Moscow, 7 April 1934, fogli (sheet(s) 52, prot. 166/28 (henceforth cited as AES, Pro Russia, s., fasc., f.). The three apostolic administrators were apparently Frison, Remov, and Joudokas or, possibly, Demurov. Dr. Leonid Titov was a friend of Fr. Sergey Soloviev and Archbishop Bartholemew Remov and was studying for the priesthood with Bishop Neveu. He was arrested on 22 February 1935, sent to Solovetsky Prison, and executed in 1938. For details, see Czaplicki and Osipova 2014, "Biography of Dr. Leonid Titov," at https://biographies.library.nd.edu/catalog/biography-1473 (accessed 4 April 2016). Fr. Piotr Potary was an Orthodox priest who converted to Catholicism, was arrested continuously in the 1920s and 1930s, sent to camps on the Kirov Railroad, and finally banished to Podvoitsy Station on the Murmansk Railroad where he died 14 August 1936. See Czaplicki and Osipova 2014, "Biography of Holy Servant of God, Father Piotr (Patory) Emilianov," at https://biographies.library.nd.edu/catalog/biography (accessed 4 April 2016).

8 AES, *Pro Russia*, s. 43, fasc. 251, Neveu to Giobbe, Moscow, 7 April 1934, f. 52–53, prot. 166/28.

9 AES, *Pro Russia*, s. 43, fasc. 251, Neveu to Giobbe, Moscow, 7 April 1934, f. 53, prot. 166/28. Fr. Deitrich of Saratov was arrested in 1930 and his fate was unknown. Fr. Baier was arrested in 1930, released, and rearrested and shot in Novosibirsk Prison on 13 January 1938. Fr. Gareis was in and out of prison since 1930 and died apparently on 23 April 1935. Fr. Staub was arrested and banished and sentenced to hard labor; he died in 1961. Fr. Dobrovolsky died on 14 August 1936. Fr. Albert was arrested in 1935 and charged with illegal receipt of money from abroad for famine victims. His fate was unknown. Fr. Schultz was arrested in 1930 and exiled to the Northern Territory in 1933 and his fate was unknown. Fr. Beilmann was arrested in 1930, released, and rearrested in 1935 and died in 1940. Fr. Wolf was arrested in 1935, sentenced to hard labor for ten years, and died in exile. Fr. Haufmann was arrested in 1935 and shot in 1938. Fr. Köhler was arrested in 1934, banished to Central Asia, where he survived, and died in 1983. Fr. Tauberger was arrested in 1934 and charged with organizing aid from foreigners for Soviet Germans and transmitting "provocative information about the severe famine and material adversities in the USSR." His fate was unknown. Fr. Hoffman was arrested in 1930 and his fate was unknown. All information related to the clergy is from the biographical sketches found in Czaplicki and Osipova 2014, at https://biographies.library.nd.edu/catalog/biography (accessed 4 April 2016).

10 AES, *Pro Russia*, s. 43, fasc. 251, Neveu to Giobbe, Moscow, 7 April 1934, f. 53, prot. 166/28.

11 AES, *Pro Russia*, s. 43, fasc. 251, Neveu to Giobbe, Moscow, 7 April 1934, f. 53, prot. 166/28.

12 AES, *Pro Russia*, s. 43, fasc. 251, Neveu to Giobbe, Moscow, 7 April 1934, f. 53, prot. 166/28.

13 AES, *Pro Russia*, s. 43, fasc. 251, Neveu to Giobbe, Moscow, 7 April 1934, f. 53–54, prot. 166/28.

14 AES, *Pro Russia*, s. 43, fasc. 251, Neveu to Giobbe, Moscow, 7 April 1934, f. 54, prot. 166/28.

15 AES, *Pro Russia*, s. 43, fasc. 251, Neveu to Pro Russia Commission, Moscow, 7 April 1935, f. 54.

16 AES, *Pro Russia*, s. 43, fasc. 250, Neveu to Giobbe, Moscow, 8 October 1934, f.40, 42, prot. 166/28. Zadvornyi and Yudin 1995, p. 27; *Istina i zhizn'*, No. 2 (1996), 33–39.

17 AES, *Pro Russia*, s. 43, fasc. 251, Neveu to Giobbe, Moscow, 19 May 1935, f. 31.

18 AES, *Pro Russia*, s. 43, fasc. 251, Neveu to Giobbe, Moscow, 19 May 1935, f. 31.

19 AES, *Pro Russia*, s. 43, fasc. 251, Neveu to Giobbe, Moscow, 19 May 1935, f. 31–32. Édouard Herriot had been the French foreign minister and was known to be pro-Soviet. He toured Ukraine in 1933 and denied that there was a famine. See Courtois 1999, pp. 159–60.
20 AES, *Pro Russia*, s. 43, fasc. 251, Neveu to Giobbe, Moscow, 19 May 1935, f. 32.
21 AES, *Pro Russia*, s. 43, fasc. 252, Neveu to Pro Russia Commission, Moscow, 16 June 1935, f. 7–8; 1 July 1935, f. 11; AES, *Pro Russia*, s. 43, fasc. 251, Neveu to Giobbe, Moscow, 7 April 1935, f. 34.
22 AES, *Pro Russia*, s. 43, fasc. 251, Neveu to Giobbe, Moscow, 7 April 1935, f. 54, prot. 166/28; AES, *Pro Russia*, s. 43, fasc. 252, Neveu to Giobbe, Moscow, 28 July 1935, f. 31, prot. 166/28.
23 AES, *Pro Russia*, s. 43, fasc. 252, Neveu to Giobbe, Moscow, 28 July 1935, f.31, prot. 166/28.
24 Czaplicki and Osipova 2014, "Biography of Father Joseph Josiukas," at https://biographies.library.nd.edu/catalog/biography-0362, and "Biography of Monsignor Mieczys-taw [Mikhail] Joudakas," at https://biographies.library.nd.edu/catalog/biography-0363 (accessed 4 April 2016).
25 AES, *Pro Russia*, s. 43, fasc. 252, Neveu to Giobbe, 28 July 1935, f. 31, prot. 166/28.
26 Czaplicki and Osipova 2014, "Biography of Archbishop (Nikolay) Remov," at https://biographies.library.nd.edu/catalog/biography-0559 (accessed 4 April 2016).
27 AES, *Pro Russia*, s. 43, fasc. 252, Neveu to Giobbe, 28 July 1935, f. 32, prot. 166/28.
28 AES, *Pro Russia*, s. 43, fasc. 253, Neveu to Pro Russia Commission, Moscow, 3 November 1935, f. 3.
29 AES, *Pro Russia*, s. 43, fasc. 253, Neveu to Pro Russia Commission, Moscow, 17 November 1935, f. 8.
30 AES, *Pro Russia*, s. 43, fasc. 253, Neveu to Pro Russia Commission, Moscow, 17 November 1935, f. 7–8.
31 AES, *Pro Russia*, s. 43, fasc. 253, Neveu to Pro Russia Commission, Moscow, 10 January 1936, f. 27–29. For examples of the Pro Russia Commission briefing Pius XI on Neveu's reports, see AES, *Pro Russia*, s. 43, fasc. 253, Pro Russia Commission to Pius XI, audience note, 3 November 1935, f. 5v; 24 November 1935, f. 9; 5 January 1936, f. 18.
32 AES, *Pro Russia*, s. 43, fasc. 253, Neveu to Pro Russia Commission, Moscow, 30 January 1936, f. 32r; 13 February 1936, f. 37r, 38r; 25 February 1936, f. 41r; Pro Russia Commission to Pius XI, audience note, 8 February 1936, f. 31r, 32r, 34r; 16 February 1936, f. 39rv; 27 February 1936, f. 44r. Fr. Tsakul had been arrested many times, "broke down" in interrogation in 1931, was sentenced to banishment, but was eventually allowed to return to Moscow and resume his ministry at Sts. Peter and Paul in 1933–34, and was again arrested, according to the *Book of Remembrance*, in 1937 and shot sometime thereafter. Neveu reported that he had not seen him since June 1935. See Czaplicki and Osipova 2014, "Biography of Father Mikhail Tsakul," at https://biographies.library.nd.edu/catalog/biography-0658 (accessed 4 April 2016).
33 AES, *Pro Russia*, s. 48, fasc. 284, Neveu to Pro Russia Commission, Moscow, 8 March 1936, f. 45; 23 March 1936, f. 62r, 63v, f.64r; 15 April 1936, f. 72; 19 April 1936, f. 74r; 17 May 1936, f. 88; Pro Russia Commission to Pius XI, audience note, 8 March 1936, f. 47rv; 15 March 1936, 59rv; 26 April 1936, f. 75; 3 may 1936, f. 73; 17 May 1936, f. 78, f.88; 7 June 1936, f. 85.
34 Kolarz 1961, pp. 190–91.
35 AES, *Pro Russia*, s. 43, fasc. 253, Neveu to Pro Russia Commission, Moscow, 17 May 1936, f. 77, f. 85, and f. 88.
36 AES, *Pro Russia*, s. 43, fasc. 254, Neveu to Pro Russia Commission, Moscow, 14 June 1936, f. 3–4; 23 July 1936, f. 14; Pro Russia Commission to Pius XI, audience note, 14 July 1936, f. 5rv.
37 AES, *Pro Russia*, s. 42, fasc. 252, Braun to Pro Russia Commission, 21 April 1937, f. 36. Braun noted, too, that he collected the antireligious literature. See Archivio du

Padri Assuzionisti, Roma, 2DZ, No. 70, Letter from Léopold Braun to Father Ernest Baudony, dated feast of St. Thomas de Villeneuve [22 September] 1936.

38 AES, *Pro Russia*, s. 43, fasc. 254, Neveu Pro Russia Commission, Paris, 23 December 1936, f. 23; Braun to Pro Russia Commission, Moscow, 17 December 1936, f. 28; 25 February 1937, f. 32, 15 April 1937, f. 35.

39 Pius XI 1937b, *Mit Brennender Sorge* (14 March 1937) at http://w2.vatican.va/content/pius-xi/en/encyclicals/documents/hf_p-xi_enc_14031937_mit-brennender-sorge.html, (accessed 4 April 2016). P. P. Pius XI, *Acta Apostolicae Sedis*, Vatican City, 1917–1939 (Acts of the Holy See), 29 (1937): 145–67.

40 Pius XI 1937a, *Divini Redemptoris* at http://w2.vatican.va/content/pius-xi/en/encyclicals/documents/hf_p-xi_enc_19031937_divini-redemptoris.html (accessed 4 April 2016). P. P. Pius XI, *Acta Apostolicae Sedis*, Vatican City, 1917–1939 (Acts of the Holy See), 29 (1937): 65–106. Pius XI 1937a, *Divini Redemptoris* at http://w2.vatican.va/content/pius-xi/en/encyclicals/documents/hf_p-xi_enc_19031937_divini-redemptoris.html (accessed 4 April 2016).

41 In any comparison between the extreme right and the extreme left, both come off as abominations. Stalin was easily Hitler's superior in terms of body count, and the ability of the extreme left to stay in and expand power after World War II meant that class-based killing surged throughout the remainder of the twentieth century. For details on the legacy of communism, see Courtois 1999. At the end of World War II and throughout the Cold War, Soviet propaganda denounced the Vatican as a supporter of Nazi Germany and maintained that anti-Communists were tools of the Nazis and their allies. See, for example, GARF, f. R4459, op. 27, d. 4225 (1945), l. 95; and f. 6991, op. 6, d. 318 (1969), l. 3.

42 For a collection of such articles, see GARF, f. R4459, op. 25, d. 23 (1937–39), l. 1–6. Also see *Antireligiznik*, no. 7 (1937).

43 During World War II, however, after the USSR joined the Western-led alliance and after the Red Army was moving into Eastern Europe, the Soviet news agency TASS often reported that Vatican-Kremlin rapprochement was possible and countered *Divini Redemptoris* by quoting prominent Catholics who declared, for example, that no "Catholic doctrine . . . would be contrary to the policy of cooperation with the Soviet Union in order to preserve world peace." See GARF, f. R4459, op. 27, d. 1775 (1943), l. 48. The Kremlin also had the real threat of its occupation of Eastern Europe to pressure the Vatican to modify its anti-Communism and cooperate or face "separation" from the 50 million Catholics in Eastern Europe. See GARF, f. R4459, op. 27, d. 3071 (1944), l. 45, 228.

44 AES, *Pro Russia*, s. 42, fasc. 252, Braun to Pro Russia Commission, 7 April 1937, f. 33; 2 September 1937, f. 66.

45 Both Davies and Coulondre were favorably disposed toward the Kremlin and thus presumably had some influence with the Soviet government. See Coulondre 1950; Davies 1941.

46 AES, *Pro Russia*, s. 42, fasc. 252, Braun to Pro Russia Commission, 2 September 1937, Moscow, f. 66; 9 December 1937, f. 7–9; 16 December 1937, f. 11; Braun to Tardini, 20 January 1938, Moscow, f. 21; Hamburg, pp. 11–12 (accessed 11 March 2016); on Braun's experience, see Braun 2006.

47 AES, *Pro Russia*, s. 42, fasc. 252, Braun to Tardini, Moscow, 20 January 1938, f. 21. On the arrests, see Oleshchuk 1939, p. 55.

48 AES, *Pro Russia*, s. 42, fasc. 252, Braun to Pro Russia Commission, Moscow, 21 February 1938, f. 33, 36.

49 AES, *Pro Russia*, s. 42, fasc. 252, Braun to Pro Russia Commission, Moscow, 9 March 1938, f. 36.

50 AES, *Pro Russia*, s. 42, fasc. 252, Braun to Pro Russia Commission, Moscow, 17 May 1938, f. 52.

51 Archivio du Padri Assuzionisti, Roma, no registration number, Letter from Braun to Pie Neveu, 22 March 1938, in Hamburg, pp. 13, 19 (accessed 11 March 2016).

52 AES, *Pro Russia*, s. 42, fasc. 252, Braun to Pro Russia Commission, Moscow, 13 June 1938, f. 60 also see Dunn 1998, p. 93.
53 AES, *Pro Russia*, s. 42, fasc. 252, Braun to Pro Russia Commission, Moscow, 11 July 1938, f. 7, 9–10.
54 AES, *Pro Russia*, s. 42, fasc. 252, Braun to Pro Russia Commission, Moscow, 23 August 1938, f. 13.
55 AES, *Pro Russia*, s. 42, fasc. 252, Braun to Pro Russia Commission, Moscow, 19 September 1938, f. 19.
56 AES, *Pro Russia*, s. 42, fasc. 252, Braun to Pro Russia Commission, Moscow, 3 October 1938, f. 22.
57 AES, *Pro Russia*, s. 42, fasc. 252, Braun to Pro Russia Commission, Moscow, 18 October 1938, f. 24–25.
58 AES, *Pro Russia*, s. 43, fasc. 254, Braun to Pro Russia Commission, Moscow, 15 April 1937, f. 35; s. 49, fasc. 292, Braun to Pro Russia Commission, Moscow, 12 December 1938, f. 40, 42–43.
59 AES, *Pro Russia*, s. 49, fasc. 292, Braun to Pro Russia Commission, Moscow, 23 January 1939, f. 50, 52, 54. (Italics in original).
60 On the continuing harassment of Braun, see Léopold Braun to Fr. Gervais Quenard, AA, 4 March 1946, *Documents divers 1946–1949*, Archivio du Padri Assunzionisti, Roma, 2ET, No. 74; Léopold Braun to Doyle, Moscow, 8 July 1945, 2ET, Nos. 51 and 59; Cresent, AA, to Father General, 2ET, No. 41, *Documents divers 1940–1945*, Archivio du Padri Assunzionisti, Roma. On his forced departure, see U.S. Department of State 1945, pp. 1125, 1126, 1126 n.94, 1129–31. TASS reported on 3 April 1945 that the so-called Flynn Mission, which helped remove Braun from Moscow, could open the way to improved Kremlin–Vatican relations that, in turn, could neutralize hostility "against Russian Bolshevism" among South American Catholics. See GARF, f. R4459, op. 27, d. 4225 (1945), l. 118.

References

Acta Apostolicae Sedis, Vatican City, 1917–39 (Acts of the Holy See).
Antireligiznik, 1937, no. 7.
Archivio du Padri Assunzionisti, Roma, Correspondence 1935–36, 2DZ, Ns. 1–76.
Archivio du Padri Assunzionisti, Roma, Correspondence 1937–41, 2DZ, Ns. 77–159.
Archivio du Padri Assunzionisti, Roma, Documents divers 1940–45, 2ET, Ns. 1–70.
Archivio du Padri Assunzionisti, Roma, Documents divers 1946–49, 2ET, Ns. 71–121.
Blet, Pierre, Martini, Angelo and Schneider, Burkhart (eds.) 1965, *Actes et documents du Saint Siège relatifs à la seconde guerre mondiale*, vol. I: *Saint Siège et la guerre en Europe (mars 1939-aout 1940)*, Citta del Vaticano: Libreria Editrice Vatican.
Blet, Pierre, Martini, Angelo and Schneider, Burkhart (eds.) 1968, *Records and Documents of the Holy See Relating to the Second World War*, Vol. I, *The Holy See and the War in Europe, March 1939–August 1940*, Washington, DC: Corpus Books.
Braun, Léopold A. A. 2006, *In Lubianka's Shadow: The Memoirs of an American Priest in Stalin's Moscow, 1934–1945*, G. M. Hamburg (ed.), Notre Dame, IN: University of Notre Dame Press.
Chang, Iris 1998, *The Rape of Nanking: The Forgotten Holocaust of World War II*, New York: Basic Books.
Coulondre, Robert 1950, *De Staline à Hitler. Souvenirs de deux ambassades, 1936–1939*, Paris: Hatchette.
Courtois, Stéphane, Werth, Nicolas, Pannél Jean-Louis, Paczkowski Andrzej, Bartošek, Karel, Margolin, Jean-Louis, 1999, *The Black Book of Communism: Crimes, Terror,*

Repression, Martin Malia (foreword), Mark Kramer (ed.), Jonathan Murphy (trans.), Cambridge, MA: Harvard University Press.

Czaplicki, Bronisław and Osipova, Irina 2014, *Book of Remembrance: Biography of Catholic Clergy and Laity in the Soviet Union (USSR) from 1918 to 1953*, Geraldine Kelly (trans.), and made available by University of Notre Dame at https://biographies.library.nd.edu/catalog/biography-0004 (accessed 2 April 2016).

Dallin, A. and Firsov, F. I. (eds.) 2000, *Dimitrov and Stalin, 1934–43: Letters from the Soviet Archives*, New Haven, CT: Yale University Press.

Davies, Joseph E. 1941, *Mission to Moscow*, New York: Simon and Schuster.

Dunn, Dennis J. 1998, *Caught Between Roosevelt and Stalin: America's Ambassadors in Moscow*, Lexington: University of Kentucky Press.

Frisov, Fridrikh I., Klehr, Harvey and Haynes, John Earl 2014, *Secret Cables of the Comintern, 1933–1943*, Lynn Visson (trans.), New Haven, CT: Yale University Press.

GARF: Gosudarstennyi arkiv Rossiiskoi Federatsii, fund R4459, Moscow.

Hamburg, G. M. no date, "In Lubianka's Shadow: An Assumptionist Priest in Stalin's Russia" at http://assumption.us/moscow/Lecture.pdf (accessed 11 March 2016).

Istina i zhizn', 1996, no. 2 (1996), 33–39.

L'Archivio della Sacra Congregazione degli Affari Ecclesiastici Straordinari, Pontificia Commissione, *Pro Russia*, scatola (box), fascicolo (file), fogli (sheet(s), Archivio Segreto Vaticano (cited as AES, *Pro Russia*, s., fasc., f.).

Oleshchuk,F. 1939, *Bor'ba tserkvi protiv naroda*, Moscow: Gos. izd-vo. polit. lit-ry.

Pius XI 1937a, *Divini Redemptoris* at http://w2.vatican.va/content/pius-xi/en/encyclicals/documents/hf_p-xi_enc_19031937_divini-redemptoris.html (accessed 4 April 2016).

Pius XI 1937b, *Mit Brennender Sorge* (14 March 1937), at http://w2.vatican.va/content/pius-xi/en/encyclicals/documents/hf_p-xi_enc_14031937_mit-brennender-sorge.html, (accessed 4 April 2016).

Raack, R.C. 1996, "Stalin's Role in the Coming of World War II: The International Debate Goes On," *World Affairs* 159 (Fall): 47–54.

Read, Anthony and Fisher, David 1989, *Deadly Embrace: Hitler, Stalin, and the Nazi-Soviet Pact, 1939–1941*, New York: W. W. Norton.

Rothschild, Joseph and Wingfield, Nancy M. 2000, *Return to Diversity: A Political History of East Central Europe Since World War II*, New York: Oxford University Press.

U.S. Department of State 1945, *Foreign Relations of the United States*, vol. 5: *Europe*, Washington, DC: U.S. Government Printing Office.

Zadvornyi, V. and Yudin, A. 1995, *Istoriya katolicheskoy tserkvi v Rossii. Kratkii ocherk* Moscow: Izd-vo. kolledzha katolicheskoi teologii in cv. fomy akvinskogo.

9   Conclusion

The Catholic and Orthodox Churches were two world religions that shared the same religious beliefs and were unified until the eleventh century and since then have occasionally worked toward reunion. They each played a major role in generating and supporting different value systems that produced vibrant and diverse civilizations – the Catholic Church serving as a catalyst of Western civilization and the Orthodox Church providing inspiration for the Byzantine and Muscovite-Russian civilizations.

These civilizations were interdependent, borrowed from one another, and often cooperated, but their different values and proselytizing world religions made them global rivals as each civilization for the past millennium or so struggled to make its value system the basis for global unity, interaction, and interdependency. In the course of the centuries that spanned the period from roughly the twelfth to the twentieth centuries, that struggle tilted increasingly in favor of Western civilization. From at least the fifteenth century Muscovy and eventually the Russian Empire, particularly from the reign of Peter the Great onward, moved tentatively toward an embrace of Western values and institutions, which stirred great tension in Russian society.

In the first three decades of the twentieth century, Russia was convulsed in four revolutions or four parts of one revolution that related to that tension. The First Revolution, the 1905 Revolution, turned Russia firmly on to a Westernizing path. As a result of that pivotal event, Tsar Nicholas II was transformed into a constitutional monarch who grudgingly promised civil rights, parliamentary government, open and free elections, peasant landownership, and freedom of religion. If Nicholas had kept on that path and not pursued reckless policies in the Balkans and Central Europe, World War I as we know it would not have happened and perhaps Russia would have developed into a modern democratic state. However, he did interfere in the Balkans and did become entangled with the French and their policy of challenging Germany and led Russia into war and helped make that war a world war. In February 1917 Nicholas abdicated, starting a Second Revolution that brought the Provisional Government to power. It promised an era of parliamentary government and basic civil rights, including new opportunities for religious groups, including the Catholic Church. Most important, the peasants, who had been denied private landownership, achieved de facto control of the land in the chaotic conditions of 1917–18. However, the Provisional Government failed to pull Russia out of the war and soon opened the door to anarchy.

In desperation, the bulk of the population of Russian Orthodox civilization, particularly the peasant soldiers and sailors, turned to a radical left minority group called the Communist Party to end the war. The Third or Communist Revolution of October 1917 did end the war, but it also was intent on beating back the advance of Western values in Russia and around the world, including peasant ownership of land in Russia. Ironically, the ideology of the Communists had partial Western roots, but the West rejected it because it was the antithesis of Western values, particularly its determination to wipe out private property and religion. The Communists embraced it in 1917 to kill not only Western civilization, including the Catholic Church, but also Orthodox civilization, including the Orthodox Church.

The story told in these pages recounts the experience of the Catholic Church in Soviet Russia from 1917 to 1939. It is a story of persecution and of optimism. The optimism radiated from the Catholic Church because it was carrying what it proclaimed to be the good news of Christianity and held that Christianity was expanding and changing the world. Furthermore, it was an apostle for Western values, which were also being embraced by diverse cultures across the globe.

In the late nineteenth and through most of the first four decades of the twentieth century, the Catholic Church under Popes Benedict XV and Pius XI were confident about cooperating with and ultimately converting the Russians. They knew it would be a major challenge, but they were hopeful because the Russians already shared Christian doctrine and the Vatican had seen growth of Catholicism and Western values among Ukrainians, Belorussians, and even Russians by showing flexibility in canonical matters and setting up different Eastern rites in Eastern Europe and Russia that allowed Orthodox Christians to keep their Orthodox liturgy and traditions while simultaneously acknowledging the pope as the leader of Christianity. In addition, the Fatima revelations, the sudden emergence of an independent Catholic Poland on Russia's border, and the collapse of the Tsarist state excited the Vatican about the possibility of growing Catholicism among the Russians. Even the onset of the Communist government, which opened a massive persecution of religion in the reconstituted Russian Empire called eventually the Soviet Union or USSR, gave encouragement to Catholic optimism because Catholic leaders in Rome thought that the persecution might erode Russian Orthodoxy's centuries-old animosity toward the Catholic Church and that, alas, these two great Christian Churches would come together, unify, and produce a new order in Russia that would include changing or eliminating the Communist regime.

The Communist government that came to power in 1917 was also optimistic. It believed that communism, which was essentially the elimination of private property and religion, was the wave of the future and that it was privileged to be the first Communist government in what would soon be a string of Communist regimes across the globe as the Communist revolution spread. The day of Western domination of the world was over and communism, which in its Russian form stressed authoritarianism, abject obedience, and a penchant for violence to move people along the desired path, was the new model for modernization.

The Communists hated the Catholic Church because it was a religion, a Western religion, a universal religion that was a rival to both the Russian Orthodox tradition and now Russian Communism, a religion of non-Russians living in the sensitive and insecure western borderlands, and, finally, a religion that supported and expanded Western values. They detested it because it opened the eyes of Ukrainian and Belorussian and some Russians to new ways of looking at and organizing life and society. The Communists attacked the Catholic Church directly in the Soviet Union. They closed its churches, arrested and murdered its clergy, and intimidated its believers. They also went after the Catholic Church internationally through the Comintern and various Communist parties that answered to Moscow. However, they were not focused on wiping out the Catholic Church outside of the USSR, but instead on taking down the Western state system, capitalism, and Western values that guided and produced international law, believing that the implosion of the capitalist world order would automatically eliminate the Catholic Church and all religion, which they believed derived life from capitalism's exploitation of labor.

The Catholic Church was not cowed by the malignant anti-Catholicism of the Soviet government. In Soviet Russia, it objected to the persecution, but it also tried to find ways of working with the Kremlin and of maintaining and even expanding Catholicism. In 1922–24 it sent a Papal Famine Relief Mission to the USSR to help alleviate hunger. In 1924 it tried to stimulate the growth of a new Byzantine-Slavic rite on the border between Poland and the USSR and through the efforts of Bishop d'Herbigny attempted to rebuild the hierarchy of the Catholic Church in the Soviet Union, which the Kremlin had destroyed through arrests, imprisonments, executions, or forced deportations. The new rite did not take hold and the Soviet police eventually removed all of the d'Herbigny appointments except for Bishop Eugene Neveu, who was a French citizen, a member of the Assumptionist religious order, the apostolic administrator in Moscow, and pastor of the French-owned St. Louis des Français Church. He became the chief reporter on the persevering Soviet persecution of the Catholic Church from the mid-1920s until he had to depart the USSR for medical treatment in France in July 1936 and was refused a reentry visa. His replacement turned out to be Fr. Léopold Braun, an American Assumptionist who came to Moscow in 1934 as a result of the Roosevelt-Litvinov Agreement. Braun carried on with the reports that Neveu pioneered until he left the USSR at the end of World War II.

Internationally, the Catholic Church tried and succeeded in many countries in checking the advance of the Comintern and its push for international revolution. The Church encouraged the growth of Catholic-affiliated political parties, Catholic politicians, and Catholic Action groups to counter international communism's propaganda and to work in politics to bolster Western values and belief in God. It also signed agreements and concordats with various governments to facilitate its ability to administer its ecclesiastical structures and spiritual mission and to improve stability, peace, and legitimacy, which helped checked the attraction of such extremists as the Communist parties.

On 1 October 1928, the Soviet Union launched its policy of collectivization, what amounted to a Fourth Revolution. It was part of the First Five-Year Plan that aimed to destroy private property, wipe out religion, and industrialize the economy. The Muscovite Communists committed a form of genocide in Ukraine, the Volga, and North Caucasus regions during collectivization that resulted in a massive loss of life among Ukrainians, Germans, and Poles who were living in the USSR, destroyed the best farmers in Soviet Russia and many dynamic religious leaders and clergy of the Catholic, Orthodox, and Protestant Churches, and weakened Ukrainian nationalism, which the Muscovite Communists viewed as a Western-Catholic product that had splintered the unity of the East Slavic peoples whom the Russians believed had to be under Russian or Russified leaders. The result was a fractured Ukraine, a thinning of the population of the western and southern borderlands in the USSR west of the Volga River, a reduced standard of living, a constant underproduction in agriculture, a regime of force and terror, and today in Putin's Russia the peddling of a myth that the genocidal purge of some citizens was necessary to grow a great country and that everyone suffered, so Ukrainians should stop complaining about the injustice Stalin did to them.

Between 1928 and 1932 the Vatican did not know of the Kremlin's policy of genocide. Of course, it was aware of the intensification of the antireligious operation and it responded to this persecution by condemning it and calling for world prayers for the tormented of the Soviet Union. The uncertainty and lack of information on the consequences of forced collectivization were due to a paucity of reports on what was transpiring in the USSR because of Soviet secrecy and isolation, a propaganda blitz by the Soviet government that denied famine or starvation existed in the USSR and offered evidence of its case by exporting food abroad, and, finally, to some Western news reporters such as Walter Duranty, Moscow bureau chief of the *New York Times* from 1922 to 1936, who claimed there was no famine in the Soviet Union.[1]

By 1933 the Vatican received news of the crime and called attention to the famine and the Soviet government's brazen denial of starving masses. *L'Osservatore romano* publicized news of the tragedy and crime, select Catholic leaders publicly denounced the Soviet government's claim, and the Vatican briefed diplomats accredited to the Holy See on the mass murders. Catholic agencies, with the full approval of the Vatican, also scrambled to provide aid to the victims, but their work was hampered by Soviet denials of a famine existing and a lack of certainty of how to get the aid to the victims in light of the Soviet government's denials and unwillingness to facilitate aid distribution.

The nonchalant, sangfroid enthusiasm of the Soviet government to murder deliberately millions of its own citizens in the name of an untried ideology and Russian nationalism masquerading as Soviet patriotism was shocking, dispiriting, draining, shattering, mind-blowing, and life-robbing for Pope Pius XI and other Catholic leaders. It was clear that in Soviet Russia human life was cheap and expendable and individual human beings were meaningless.

By the mid-1930s, when Stalin sensed resistance among some of the Party elite to his policy of forced collectivization and when radical right Nazis took power in Germany partially in response to Communist policies, the Soviet government launched a purge of the Soviet establishment, a partial depopulation of the borderlands and some interior regions that stretched in a broad arc from Leningrad to the North Caucasus and Volga German regions, and the policies of the Popular Front and Collective Security to contain, not eviscerate, the radical right opposition and hopefully turn it against the Western powers. It also persisted in its collectivization drive and campaign against religion. The Catholic Church was attacked in both the USSR and abroad, although some Communist parties and some Soviet publications cynically criticized the simultaneous anti-Catholic policies of Hitler.

By 1937 Pope Pius XI had had enough. He finally abandoned his optimism about Soviet Russia. He now concluded that there was no way to work with the Soviet government and that there was no chance that the Russians would be open to conversion as long as the Communist regime was in power. In fact, the Soviet government seemed to be gaining strength through its industrialization drive despite the fact that it had outright murdered by starvation and occasionally by execution between 5 and 7.5 million of its own citizens, purged the Soviet elite, and depopulated the borderlands. The pope was ready to condemn communism and to prohibit any Catholic from supporting or working with the Communist movement. However, there was a problem. Any condemnation of communism would or could be misconstrued as support for Hitler's raging anti-Communism. The pope approved of anti-Communism, but he disapproved of Nazism. Nazism was not only an anti-Communist ideology, but it was also anti-Christian and anti-Western. Like communism, it aimed to destroy Judeo-Christian civilization. To solve the dilemma, the pope decided first to proscribe what the German Nazis were doing so as to put it on the record that the Church opposed the Nazis and were not supporting them by damming communism and then to admonish the Communists. On 14 March 1937, Pius XI issued the encyclical *Mit Brennender Sorge* that excoriated Nazi policies on race and religion. On 19 March, he published *Divini Redemptoris*, which condemned communism and prohibited any Catholic from cooperating with the Communist movement.

After trying to work with the Kremlin for nearly two decades, the Catholic Church came to the conclusion that communism was a dire threat and had to be destroyed. As the clouds of World War II formed, the Vatican tried to convey the lesson of its experience to Western leaders, but discovered that the Western governments, in its opinion, were naïve about Soviet Russia.[2] The Vatican appreciated the fact that they were focused on destroying the Nazi and Axis threats, but it wanted to make the Western leaders aware that the communists were as bad and perhaps worse than the Nazis and policies had to be developed to extirpate both ideological regimes if peace were to prevail and Western values were to resume their global march.

In the end the Western powers had to defeat the Nazis and their Axis allies because of the latter's immediate danger to Western civilization and global order and they could do so only by allying with the Communist extremists, which allowed the Soviet Communists to expand in both Europe and Asia. However, after the defeat of the radical right, the West, led by the United States, turned to the task of vanquishing the Communists in a protracted conflict called the Cold War.

The Catholic Church had a major role in bringing down the Communist movement in the second half of the twentieth century and, in that sense, its optimism in the expansion of Western values around the globe and in Russia was justified, but in the period between 1917 and 1939, the future did not look very rosy.

A final word must be said about the many martyrs who died because of their faith, not just Catholics, but Orthodox, Protestant, Jewish, and Muslim believers. The courage, steadfastness, and example of souls willing to profess faith in the face of flagitious and wicked persecution helped turn the battle for souls against the Communists and in favor of human life, dignity, and belief in God.

Notes

1 Taylor 1990.
2 Pope Pius XII and the Vatican leaders in 1939 and throughout World War II discovered that the Western leaders, particularly Roosevelt and Churchill, would take no steps to prevent a huge accretion of Soviet power in Central and Eastern Europe. See Dunn 1998, p. 177; Dunn 2004, pp. 116–19; and Dunn 1977, pp. 102–03, 120–21, 134–35. Pius XI thought the Western democracies were naïve. See Kertzer 2015, p. 14.

References

Dunn, Dennis J. 1977, *The Catholic Church and the Soviet Government, 1939–1949*, New York: *East European Quarterly* Series, distributed by Columbia University Press.

Dunn, Dennis J. 1998, *Caught Between Roosevelt and Stalin: America's Ambassadors in Moscow*, Lexington: University of Kentucky Press.

Dunn, Dennis 2004, *The Catholic Church and Russia: Popes, Patriarchs, Tsars and Commissars*, Aldershot, UK: Ashgate.

Kertzer, David I. 2015, *The Pope and Mussolini: The Secret History of Fascism in Europe*, New York: Random House.

Taylor, S. J. 1990, *Stalin's Apologist: The New York Time's Man in Moscow*, New York: Oxford University Press.

Index